T0306593

Log Jam on the Upper Hudson   Stoddard Photo

The Heydays
of the Adirondacks

Maitland C. DeSormo

North Country Books
Utica, New York

THE HEYDAYS OF THE ADIRONDACKS

SECOND PRINTING 1975
THIRD PRINTING 2001

ISBN 978-0-932052-70-4

Library of Congress   74-84746

Manufactured by Canterbury Press
Rome, NY

NORTH COUNTRY BOOKS
311 Turner Street
Utica, New York 13501

Dedication

To Sue — nimble typist, proof reader par excellence, business manager sans compare and much-enduring spouse. Thanks for everything.

photo by Lustyik

Malone, N.Y. "Auto Club" — Courtesy of Robideau Studios

Table of Contents

List of Illustrations

10

Preface

This volume, which was a long while in the making, represents a wide variety of topics that have occupied my interest and attention during the major part of my lifetime. While some of it clearly contains many personal references and reminiscences, there are still a dwindling number of people left in the land of the living whose memories will hopefully be triggered by the persons and places featured in this modestly comprehensive coverage of the so-called olden, golden days in Adirondack annals. By doing so they will not only share my particular remembrances of days long-gone - but also be given a chance to indulge to their hearts' content their own sentimental journeys backward into nostalgia land.

Understandably, some readers will be too young or too new to the area to recognize few if any names and places mentioned in some of the chapters, so for them this book should serve as a doorway to the past, a sort of Who Was Who and composite introduction to regional history.

Of course County Fairs are still an annual event in the North Country but they are no longer the big deal that they were way back when people had much less time and money and far fewer sources of mass entertainment. Granted that some people were more gullible, unsophisticated and easier to amuse then than now, but they nevertheless managed to squeeze more pleasure out of their leisure hours simply because there were so few of them and therefore more likely to be savored. Nowadays, the universal profit motive so completely dominates the total scene that there is little opportunity offered for either pleasure or visual instruction. Then too the circuses of today are of course only puny reminders of what used to be when Ringling Bros. and Barnum & Bailey toured the hinterlands.

The two chapters on the hop industry - Schroeder's tragic fiasco and the heyday of the hops - are fairly adequate but superficial reminders of an age of agricultural speculators who make present-day's risk-taking farmers seem like timid, conservative pikers, by contrast.

The era of the huge hotels such as the Loon Lake House, Paul Smith's and Saranac Inn obviously demanded more than a modicum of gambling blood too - not only on the side of the owners but for the insurance companies who issued the policies on the rambling firetraps as well. [N. B.: If you are ever in the area and if the fast-deteriorating structure is still up when you get there, take a good look at what is left of Saranac Inn, one of the fabulously fashionable vacation meccas of bygone summers. It's the only one left of its size and kind: all the other better-known hostelries have long since been devoured by flames. Or, as was true of the massive Prospect House at Blue Mountain Lake, the Sagamore at Long Lake and the first Wawbeek on Upper Saranac Lake - white elephants demolished for tax-saving purposes when the Auto Age arrived.]

Three of the chapters are based on the notebooks of Fred A. Hodges, my late father-in-law and Adirondack photographer of considerable skill and reputation, especially in the Blue Mountain Lake, Raquette, Fulton Chain and Piseco sections. His recollections of those areas and their noteworthy past have enabled me to widen the scope

Malone Fire-Fighters on Parade, Memorial Square c. 1885 — Courtesy of Robideau Studios

Main Street, Malone about 1910 — Courtesy of Robideau Studios

of this volume and give a measure of attention to at least some of the lore of those picturesque regions. Not many are left around who knew Ed. Arnold and very few habitués of the Central Adirondacks have lived long enough to remember its early steamboats, so such chapters should be of reasonable interest.

Paul Smith's scrapbooks, left to the Adirondack Collection of the Saranac Lake Free Library, proved to be a motherlode of fascinating ephemeral items. Culled from newspapers and magazines from all parts of the country, some dating back to the 1880's and '90's, these clippings furnish an almost kaleidoscopic coverage of national and local events which would otherwise be very difficult if not virtually impossible to locate. Naturally, there are many references to Paul Smith and his woodland empire so the four volumes are invaluable sources of material on the remarkable hotel, the legendary owner and his family.

Moreover, the scrapbooks yielded many of the yarns and tall stories, hitherto unfamiliar, which made Oom Paul one of the greatest of the Adirondack raconteurs. Joyce Meagher and Helen Gregory of the Saranac Lake Library were very helpful with this research project.

Back issues - way back to the 1870's in some instances - of the famous old *Forest and Stream* magazine were also a genuinely intriguing mine of well-written stories on many sections of the mountains. Now extremely hard to locate and increasingly expensive to acquire, this eminently readable periodical was in a class by itself as a purveyor of Adirondackana.

Much of the material of Early Saranac Lake and the river-driving days came from the scrapbooks and *Forest and Stream.* The same sources, plus the books by Todd, Headley and Street - and the Stoddard photos-supplied the best portions of the chapters on the roads, hotels and guides - especially the matchless Moodys.

Dr. LeRoy Wardner's excellent account of the history of Adirondack medicine gives well-deserved honor to a very important phase of area history and to its particular heroes.

The longest chapter in this book, the one on Prohibition and the bootlegging era, is undeniably over-ambitious and over-long but, since it is still a topic of never-ending fascination and relived recollections, I tried to provide my rendition of the "noble experiment" with national as well as local significance.

Since the North Country and the near-by Canadian Border was the dramatic theater of operations for the oft-recurring confrontations and battles of wits between the Laws and the Outlaws, this was and is a subject of great regional interest. A single chapter on what could conceivably be made into several volumes is, admittedly, only token treatment, but it nevertheless represents a cross-section of exciting experiences which will undoubtedly generate a flow of anecdotes featuring similar encounters, high speed pursuits and daring deeds by participants on both sides of the notorious 18th Amendment.

Much valuable help and information in the preparation of this lengthy account were furnished by Franklin County Judge Ellsworth N. Lawrence; Bill Herron; ex-Sergeant Schermerhorn of the State Police; the Troop B staff in Malone; Douglas S. Dales, Public Relations, New York State Police, Albany Headquarters. Also Mike D'Ambrisi, Charlie Green, Doug Willette, Jim LaPan and Bob Herron - all of Saranac Lake.

Still others whose help I gratefully acknowledge are Harold Brown and Ray Russell of the Malone *Evening Telegram*; Dave Minnick, Una Stewart, librarians and Bob Hanna, president of the Board of Trustees of Wead Library; Mitch Tackley, Don Paye and Mary Lou of Station WICY.

Bill Verner, Curator, Adirondack Museum at Blue Mountain Lake, made available a print of a Stoddard painting.

Also thanks to the following: Norb Robideau of Robideau Studios, Malone for providing several of the prints which enhance the text of Chapter 1; Mrs. Alys Cox for the loan of two excellent pictures for use in same; Carol Dening, of the Goff-Nelson Library, Tupper

Excursion Train to County Fair c. 1895 — Courtesy of Mrs. Alys Cox

Lake and Alberta Moody, who supplied the interesting photo of Mart and Minerva Moody.

Lou Simmons, editor of the Tupper Lake *Free Press*, in his "Old Times" column furnished much grist for the literary mill - especially the reprint of the privately printed book by Ferris Meigs on the *History of the Santa Clara Lumber Co.* [1888-1920].

Since I have already done what I could to revive interest in Stoddard, van Hoevenbergh, Noey Rondeau and French Louie (the latter by aiding and abetting the reprint of Harvey Dunham's classic), I felt that there were lesser known but almost equally interesting people who also deserved a better fate than virtual oblivion. People like Fred Hodges, Ed Arnold, Lon Fuller, Earl MacArthur, Schroeder, Lute Trimm, Harvey and Cort Moody - and many others. In my opinion they were anything but nonentities, so I'm indeed happy to introduce you to them in memory if not in person.

Another motivating factor was my desire to make a substantial literary contribution to the up-coming Bi-Centennial Celebration. Most locales covered being Franklin County areas, this should aid that effort in this fascinating neck of the woods.

Years ago I came across a passage in the preface to G. B. Shaw's *Man and Superman* which sums up aptly and eloquently my attitude toward writing regional history: "This is the true joy in life: the being used for a purpose recognized by yourself as a mighty one; the being thoroughly worn out before you're thrown on the scrap-pile. The being a force of Nature instead of a feverish, selfish little clod of ailments and grievances complaining because the world will not devote itself to making you happy."

All in all this collection, which can hardly be considered more than a minor-scale anthology, is the result of many years of intense personal interest and persistent acquisition of relevant information on the North Country. Many of the articles have already been published by my friend Glyndon Cole in such periodicals as *North Country Life* and its successor, *York State Tradition*; and pal Bob Hall in *Adirondack Life* when it was the supple-

14

ment of the Warrensburg-Lake George *News.* By rounding them up and presenting them in hard cover form and by adding other related material, they are now more readily available to readers who have already given my previous efforts a much-appreciated wide acceptance.

Incidentally and finally: if any reader discovers discrepancies or goofs in this major opus I hereby get off the critical hook by quoting Dorothy Kilgallen's classic retort to a burst of verbal abuse - "I'd like to be right all the time - but sometimes I just can't make it!"

Maitland C. DeSormo
Adirondack Yesteryears, Inc.

Franklin County Fair c. 1905

Getting Ready for the Fair c. 1890 — Courtesy of Robideau Studios

Chapter 1

Recollections of County Fairs, Circuses and Other Pastimes

My boyhood days began in Canton and Hermon but most of my early childhood memories focus on the Malone area (Adirondack foothill country). At that time even more so than today, it was a thriving farming community surrounded by hopfields and dairy farms. In those days - from 1912 on - the village fostered many types of businesses - the J. O. Ballard (all wool and a yard wide!) and Lawrence-Webster woolen mills, several sawmills, lumberyards and feed stores, milk processing plant, foundries, tanneries, pulpmills, livery stables, saloons, hotels large and small, three banks, department stores, an ice cream plant (Kirk Maher, later Sealtest), automobile agencies and other prosperous business firms. Also two railroads - the New York Central and the Rutland and their satellite yards and buildings.

The county seat, it had the courthouse, jail and other government buildings. And it also had the Fairgrounds, rated the biggest in the state after Syracuse. There, in September was held annually what had to be the biggest red letter week in the calendar for everyone in the Northern Tier. Fair Week generated literally thousands of visitors from both sides of the Border and things were very lively all during that period. The various exhibit buildings always housed a colorful, eye-catching collection of prize-winning products ranging from premium-winning vegetables to home-made materials of all sorts - rugs, quilts, aprons, fruit displays, etc. The stock barns were full of blooded cattle, horses, cows, pigs and sheep with their panoply of ribbons tacked to their stalls and stanchions.

The Midway concessions exploited the usual carnival sights and sounds - the Ferris wheel, roller coaster, motorcycle silo (Velodrome), freak exhibits, grossly-fat people, midgets, tattoo artists, snake-medicine pitchmen with their de-fanged rattlers, gaudy girlie shows and con games of all types. Local civic groups manned booths where meals were served and saltwater taffy, gooey popcorn balls, candy canes, flashy souvenirs and Kewpie dolls were sold. There were rifle ranges, guessing games and many other so-called attractions to beguile the more gullible visitors into parting with their proverbially hard-earned cash.

The main attractions were the harness races and livestock shows, which always packed the Grandstand. Highly-touted trotters and pacers showed their mettle and much moola changed hands over the outcome of the races. Another thriller — barnstorming airplanes put on a dazzling display of aerial acrobatics plus wing-walking, parachute jumping, power diving etc. Adventurous folks were taken aloft for a five-dollar, ten-minute circle over the countryside. Annette Kellerman and other dare-devil performers staged high-diving acts from 75 - 100 foot towers into ten-foot canvas tanks. Tightrope and trapeze artists, multicolored clowns, unicycle riders, trick riders, jugglers, gymnasts and other entertainers - including musical groups and soloists - all did their stuff.

The Saturday night finale featured the most spectacular pyrotechnic displays I have ever seen. A small fortune was spent on the rockets, kaleidoscopic pinwheels, Roman candles, fan-shaped explosive items, northern lights or aurora borealis patterns and - to wind it up - real smasheroos such as the battle between the Monitor and the Merrimac, the eruption of Mt. Vesuvius or the attack on Ft. Moultrie and the Alamo. No people involved of course.

The Fair was a definite economic booster shot in those days as well as now and provided work for nearly everyone - young and old alike - who was willing to hustle. My brother Lee got himself one of the most unusual assignments of them all. All he had to do was crouch under the flooring that housed Dodo, the Dog-faced Boy, an ingeniously contrived horror item if there ever was one. On cue Lee scraped away with a crude bow across thick wires, thus producing a weird screeching sound augmented at intervals by human (Lee's) moans and groans. Very effective to say the least and it drew a goodly number of suckers.

After the Fair was over several of us always converged on the grounds and spent nearly all that Sunday methodically searching for money and empty, returnable booze bottles, which brought two cents apiece at the nearest gin-mill. Most of the coins and an occasional bill or two were generally found under the seats of the Grandstand but it involved long hours of pawing over scraps of paper, ticket stubs and discarded programs. One very productive search netted nearly $5.00 plus the take from the returned bottles, which we hauled away in wagons heaped high with burlap bags.

Malone was host to thousands those days. Hotels and rooming houses were full, lawns near the Fairgrounds became profitable parking lots, restaurants made up for leaner days the rest of the year. Streets were packed with people walking or hiring hacks - horse and motor drawn - ("Hack for the Fair-ground! Going right down!"). Farmers and their families in some cases had worked hard all summer to save up enough money to "take in the Fair" and far too many youngsters and more than a few oldsters were gulled out of their money by gyp artists, pickpockets and other assorted swindlers. But all this added a fillip of appeal and excitement to the annual festivities. The Fair over, things soon fell back into the even tenor of the ways. The harvest season came and houses were banked for the winter.

Another annual highlight was the Chautauqua, which usually was set up on the campus of the old Franklin Academy. Unlike the Fair, which was for the most part low-level entertainment, this had a truly cultural impact on the people and was therefore eagerly anticipated. Lectures by leading speakers on the topics of the times, politics, musical and dramatic programs such as the Ben Greet players gave the area citizenry some of the topflight entertainment available in that era.

The really big deal, however, for the kids in particular, was the yearly summer visit of the circus. The biggest of these were Ringling Brothers and Barnum and Bailey, but Miller's 101 Ranch and Sells Floto were close behind in audience appeal. Always heralded well in advance by huge poster displays which bedizened barns, signboards and vacant buildings, the population of the entire North Country looked forward intently to the arrival of the Big Top and its side shows.

Since I lived within a block or so of the Rutland Railroad yards, where the circuses unloaded, I got into the act very early. Well before daylight in fact, attracted by the clamor of the cars being switched to the sidings to keep the mainline clear, I would hastily dress

18

*The Start of the **Pee**rade — Courtesy of Robideau Studios*

Santa Came Early That Year — Courtesy of Robideau Studios

19

Corner of Main and Elm Streets, Memorial Park c. 1890

Big Day in Town c. 1890 — Courtesy of Robideau Studios

20

and run to join the already large gathering of curious onlookers. There in the shadows the signal lanterns would describe wide red and green arcs in the gloom. Orders would be shouted, gaudy animal cages would be eased down the ramps, the elephants would nudge the carriages along to the street edge and the flatcars would slowly be relieved of their burdens of assorted circus vehicles and their exotic cargoes.

Burly workers, vari-costumed men and women circus folk, a huge steam organ (calliope) would gradually emerge from the darkness until eventually the whole show was lined up and ready for the road. Usually I got into the act by offering to water the insatiable elephants in return for free tickets to the show but sometimes, like other kids of all ages, I had to sneak in under the canvas soon after the circus tent had been erected.

While all this was going on there was simultaneous activity on the big lot between East Main Street and the Rutland Railroad embankment, where the municipal skating rink was located during the winter months. I can also recall seeing at least several circuses out at the Junction and still remember watching with fascination the erection of the huge main tent. Dozens of roustabouts would unroll the great expanse of canvas; that chore completed the workers would split up into four-man cadres of which one held the big stake while the other three in close sequence almost effortlessly hammered home the stakes with 16-pound sledgehammers. Years of practice made short work of this phase; next the men grabbed ropes and following shouted orders, in rhythmic cadence gradually hoisted the heavy canvas to the tops of the mast-like poles. Quite a feat and quite a visual treat as well!

About 11 a.m. everything was all set and the parade down Main Street would begin. Elephants, camels and giraffes usually led, next the calliope and the equestrians on white horses. The troop of clowns cavorted along the flanks, followed by animal cages and the rest of the kaleidoscopic cavalcade. Lions, tigers, monkeys, the wild man from Borneo and the family of dwarfs, the zebras, hippos and rhinos, ostriches and many other examples of God's creatures human and so-called sub-human were put on display. Sword-swallowers, human pin-cushions, magicians, acrobats, freaks of all kinds were usually included.

The night show was always magnificently memorable. The resplendent ringmaster taking charge of the simultaneous acts; the fearless (?) animal trainers, males and females; the shapely, beaded, bangled and bowed lady acrobats with their frozen smiles; the corps of clowns, the thrilling spectacle of horses and equestriennes; the highwire artists; the intricate and clever trained dog acts - and of course the finale. The blare of bugles as the cavalry detachment's advance guard cantered in, the high-stepping horses, the uniformed riders, the guidons and flags streaming out. The stagecoaches filled with handsome men and women, the outriders and then the blood-curdling war whoops as the band of painted Indians trotted in. Then came the chase and the accelerated action as the canters became gallops, shots resounded, clouds of acrid smoke billowed up, both sides got shot up in the general fusillades. Victims were hauled out of the surrounded coaches, soldiers and Indians alike bit the dust after death-defying, trick-riding capers. Whites were scalped and Reds were slaughtered in the resulting fracas and all contributed their quota of noise, color and smell to the overall effect.

One year the fabulous Buffalo Bill (William Cody) and the amazing Annie Oakley herself showed up in Malone. Her marksmanship with rifle and revolver, especially the over-the-shoulder act using mirrors to direct her shots at the small clay targets, is still vivid in my memory. Years later I learned that such incredible marksmanship was due to the use of fine shot loads in the cartridges thus creating a scattergun effect which made it possible to score on even fairly wide misses on the small colored balls.

In contrast to such spectaculars the village life during the rest of the year was understandably low key but not monotonous. Swimming at Ballard's Dam or at Big and Little Sandy just above or at Trout River dump, fishing in all the region's brooks and rivers, occasional bicycle or hiking trips to Lake Titus or the Chateaugay Lakes helped break the routine during the warmer weather. Scouting with the Methodist Troop headed by Maurice Plumb and Leon Colton also played a prominent part in my adolescence. Camping at Mountain View and Meacham were interesting interludes, especially the latter because it brought me for the first time into contact with the wilderness after living in the foothills. Bill Center's beanhole beans, the canoe trips at dusk along Meacham's shoreline when it was considered unusual if we didn't see at least 20 deer, coons and other animals en route.

In those days Malone boasted of two movie houses - the Novelty and the Strand. The former was a small, dingy building located where the Sealtest plant is now. I can't remember how it was lighted but it always seemed dark inside until the projector operator started rolling the films - Keystone cops first and then the feature. Since talkies were still five or six years away, there had to be background, mood music served up by a very busy and necessarily versatile piano player, who occasionally had his rendition of "Hearts and Flowers" interrupted by showers of unpopped popcorn. His fingers fairly flew when he had to keep up with the action of "The Perils of Pauline" and "The Black Box," two of the most fascinating melodramas I've ever seen.

Probably the most memorable matinee of them all was insidiously provided by one of my resourceful pals who released a horde of moths, millers and June bugs just before the climactic necking scene was flashed on the curtain. Obeying their phototropic instincts the insects naturally soared right into the broad beam from the projection booth; the resultant blurred images on the screen evoked cries of protest from young and old alike. Needless to say we were soon spotted and summarily ejected from the premises.

Another highlight of my growing-up days, an occasional event that made an indelible imprint on my impressionable mind was the evangelistic campaign conducted under a commodious tent pitched at the corner of Duane Street at the foot of Academy Hill (now a village parking lot). Among the visiting spellbinders were eminent disciples of Moody and Sanky - and Billy Sunday, himself, probably the most formidable foe of John Barleycorn of them all. All of these men had powerful voices, obvious sincerity and the ability to turn emotions on and off like a faucet. Moreover, in retrospect, each could hit all the notes in the vocal scale. Other persuasive personal assets were a keen sense of timing reinforced by such conviction and histrionic ability that within five minutes they invariably succeeded in squeezing tears and sobs from a generally large and pre-conditioned audience of resident and migratory drunkards, families of same and merely curious but fascinated onlookers.

Admittedly some of the audience were there for the sole purpose of heckling or sadistically enjoying the misfortunes of others less fortunate, but the rowdies were soon silenced by the deadly serious participants and, if necessary, by a few well-chosen remarks by the featured attraction himself. Continued disrespect and misbehavior, usually generated by the more incorrigible village brats, inevitably resulted in the bum's rush or a fast departure by ducking under the nearest tent-wall slightly before the laying-on of unfriendly hands. Since the unwelcome interludes usually occurred early in the service, the desired psychological and emotional tone of the meeting was generally sustained.

Undoubtedly much spiritual spadework had previously been done by the militant members of the local branch of W.C.T.U. and the Salvation Army because their representatives, accompanied by ministers of the more evangelically concerned area churches, were always seated on the platform and took part in the program.

Fourth of July Parade c. 1890 — Courtesy of Mrs. Alys Cox

10-Minute-Ride for $5.00 in this Travelair 1929 — Courtesy of Robideau Studios

After a fairly lengthy warm-up period the principal speaker catalogued the whole spectrum of horrendous details and the inevitable, fiery, sulphurous fate which loomed just ahead for the hapless victims of the Demon Rum. Strange that they never mentioned the other varieties of intoxicants. The stage was now set for the climactic scene. Then he pointed out all was not yet lost provided the besotted ones took full advantage of this opportunity to kick the habit then and there and forever. While hymns such as *Little Brown Church, Onward Christian Soldiers, Old Rugged Cross,, Rock of Ages* and *I Need Thee How I Need Thee* were being sung and emotions reached fever pitch, singly or in clusters those still under the influence and others recently, temporarily sober made their unsteady, often groping way down the sawdust-covered, middle-aisle trail to the front of the tent. There they were implored to publicly confess their weakness, prayed over patiently and then detained for further attention, instruction and encouragement. Very much like but on a much smaller scale than the typical Billy Graham services on T.V.

Since Malone and every other relatively sizeable community in the region had and has far more than its reasonable quota of saloons, the periodic temperance meetings were very much in order. While there were undoubtedly many alcoholics who not only took the pledge and thereafter lived up to it, far more men - and women too - were understandably never salvaged. But at least those who didn't make it were given the chance to dramatize their plight and ask, according to their individual degree of character and conviction, for outside sympathy and assistance.

Interestingly enough it is noteworthy that the basic factor in the successful functioning of present-day Alcoholics Anonymous is the willingness of its members to admit to being slaves of alcohol. Until the afflicted individual faces up to that harsh personal fact, he can never hope to conquer his nemesis. The old-time temperance and camp meetings had just

All Aboard and Ready for the Hill

Community Skating Rink 1920's — Courtesy of Robideau Studios

such a psychological foundation stone but lacked the moral and sustaining strength provided by group therapy and constant concern and supervision provided by the A. A. But, obviously, the temperance organizations and their often spectacular meetings were very much on the right track in their purposeful, often effective service to their fellowmen. Great men and women working for a great cause.

Bobsledding, scooting and skiing were also sources of enjoyment in those days. The bobs, owned by wealthier or more ingenious and resourceful boys, provided thrilling and almost fatal fun. Those early bobsleds, consisting of two small sleds connected by long boards between, would carry up to 10 or 15 passengers and were steered by ropes. The starting point in the halcyon days before many autos hit the roads was usually the top of Franklin Street hill. From there the course was down Webster Street across the open campus now occupied by the High School, across to Jane Street and down Academy Hill past Duane and on out to Main Street.

With its cargo of human freight aboard these heavy sleds gained top momentum rapidly on the steeper slopes and sometimes were deliberately ditched in order to avoid crashing into trees, buildings, horses or autos. Lookouts were usually stationed on the more dangerous stretches and thus prevented accidents, but sometimes the youngsters got impatient and slid without proper precautions; several kids were badly shaken up and at least one became an invalid as the result.

Skiing in those days was uneventful and slow compared with nowadays. The equipment was often home-made and the speed was modest.

Scooting or skittering - riding on a slab of wood, nailed to a small log, then both secured to a barrel stave - was another cheap substitute for kids who couldn't afford bobs, skis or toboggans. An even less expensive and much-used piece of winter sport equipment was a 5 or 6 foot section of corrugated tin. Bent slightly upward in front, with a rope poked through a hole in the center of the curve to hang onto, the contraption was steered by sticking out one's foot on the side the occupant wanted to travel and usually gave the riders all or even more thrills than they wanted - especially on the bumpier, steeper slopes where the makeshift conveyance often became air-borne for seemingly lengthy spans of time. Since the sides of the metal sliding surface were sharp, there were not infrequent cases of torn pants and ugly cuts.

Incidentally, the more cautious, chickenish enthusiasts always had the option of substituting heavy strips of cardboard for the metal but these were much slower, less durable and far less maneuverable and thus hardly worth the bother when then, as well as now, speed was the main motive and desideratum of nearly every red-blooded, thrill-seeking North Country lad.

Way back when I was in what is now called junior high school, things used to get right lively after school started in September. In those days hazing and interclass rivalry were not only condoned but actively encouraged. Letting off some excess student energy was considered to be altogether fitting and healthy. Moreover, it provided a long-awaited annual entertainment enjoyed almost equally by villagers and school kids. Occasionally things got out of hand but generally there was relatively little serious personal or property damage.

As I recall the yearly competition featured several days of traditional contests between the junior and senior classes plus several events slated for the freshmen and sophomores. Much ingenuity and considerable daring was needed in one game - flaunting the class colors from the highest available elevation. On one occasion fearless Maurice Fortune climbed a narrow ladder to the top of the hundred-plus-foot Borden smokestack at the Junction, ripped off the rival colors and replaced them with those of his own class - and on a small ledge three feet higher up!

Probably the bloodiest and most turbulent act of them all took place on the narrow, steep lawn of the old Courthouse. Since the seniors had already tied their colors to the top of the flagpole, it was up to the juniors to yank them down. A very formidable and messy job indeed because the pole had also been previously coated with axle grease. Furthermore, anyone attempting to do so had to break through the cordon of protectors stationed around the base. This necessitated the launching of a series of assaults to wear down the defenders and then drag enough of them away to enable someone to scramble up the slippery mast. Nor was it possible to make it in one attempt because the gooey stuff had to be rubbed off at successive levels by the clothes of the climber and whatever towels or absorbents could be rustled up. Understandably, a real Donnybrook often ensued but the police and older men usually broke up the brawls before they got too gory.

Still another but more amusing contest was the annual tug-of-war between the upper classes. One year in particular they held the event behind Duffin's lumberyard on Elbow Street just above the Pearl Street bridge. At least 25 of the biggest bruisers in each class took hold of opposite ends of a long rope stretched across the 40-50 yard width of the Salmon River. Although the water was only five or six feet deep at that point, the muddy bottom and the fairly steep banks made the going a bit rough. A half hour or so of sashaying back and forth, first one side then the other gaining a little ground, feet flying to keep traction in a last ditch effort - then a great splashing, grunting and cursing as the losers hit the water and were keel-hauled across to the opposite shore....

In retrospect those long-gone days and ways have provided a deep reservoir of memories which have given me many pleasurable moments over the fast-drifting, intervening years.

Chapter 2

Schroeder, Lord of De Bar

The history of the Adirondacks has been neon-lighted by a considerable number of dynamic and obsessed men whose grandiose schemes invariably fell short of becoming great successes. These colorful people whom we less imaginative individuals call crackpots and "characters" seem to have been driven by an overwhelming desire to build for themselves small-scale empires in various parts of the unaccommodating wilderness. Without exception, their visions were based on reasonably sound plans and their projects could quite conceivably have become financially profitable in other less formidable localities. Usually their tragic failures were traceable not only to their lack of judgment and/or business sense but also to the obstacles inherent in the region itself - the short and unpredictable growing season, the destructive power of the spring floods, the distances from population centers and, in many instances, to the very topography of the country itself. That too, was the case of William Gilliland, who carved out a small empire on Essex County's lower Boquet before politics and pillage during the early days of the Revolutionary War brought him to ruin and painless death from freezing and exposure in his own woodlands. A further and even more credible explanation would be that in this great expanse of forest and mountains apparently only giant-sized enterprises would do. Whatever the reason or combination of reasons each vision and each visionary seemed to flourish for a brief time and then, in the vernacular of the section, hit the skids toward ultimate disaster for the central figure, his family and his creation.

Some of these legend-evoking men were Herreshoff of Brown's Tract, Henderson of Tahawus, the Duanes in Franklin County, the French émigrés in St. Lawrence and Lewis Counties and Gilliland on Lake Champlain. Whether they sought to make a fortune in iron, as was the case of Henderson, Herreshoff and Duane; or to found settlements which would eventually pay off by sale of lands - all such dreams never came to fruition. Other obsessed but ill-fated giants were John Hurd, a successful timber-slasher but whose New York and Ottawa Railroad took him down the one-way road to ruin. And Col. Christopher Norton of Plattsburgh, the lumber king of the Saranacs, who also died bankrupt. Such too was the fate of Pierre Chassanis, whose splendid scheme to develop a half-million-acre tract, mostly in Lewis County, for the French-owned Company of New York and himself, ended in a series of financial disasters. Still another was Alexander Macomb, who in 1792 paid a piddling eight pence an acre for a domain containing 3,934,899 of them. Although he soon became bankrupt he did put his name on the land, a minor consolation indeed considering the cost.

Charles F. Herreshoff, William Gilliland

Ruins of Herreshoff Manor, near Old Forge

A further example is found in the story of Brown's Tract (John Brown of Providence not the John Brown of Ossawatomie and Harper's Ferry), which has all the elements of classic tragedy with melodramatic overtones. Brown, a man of magnificent projects and extraordinary energy despite his ponderous bulk, bought an immense tract of land - 210,000 acres - in the Moose River country, and invested huge sums of money only to see all his roads, mills and improvements revert to wilderness. Charles F. Herreshoff, his Prussian son-in-law, vowed to "settle the tract or settle himself!" - which he did by suicide after spending his entire fortune plus funds advanced by friends.

Still another such dream of carving a 60,000 acre baronial domain, this time out of the uncooperative Independence River wilderness of Lewis and Herkimer Counties, collapsed and James Watson, the congenial, luxury-loving protagonist in this drama sought his solution by slashing his own throat.

Robert Schroeder

Schroeder Castle about 1915 [Torn down in 1939]

Not a single big-scale attempt by prosperous individuals or well-funded corporations to conquer the Adirondack wilderness has ever been truly successful. The woods and riverbanks still hide the tell-tale ruined foundations of massive buildings, abandoned forges and smelters, lumber and grist mills - silent but eloquent reminders of bygone misfortunes. Those who succeeded were those who wisely kept their ambitions under reasonable control, and who made minimal effort to alter the environment became prosperous in the process. The exceptions were such shrewd hotel-keepers as Paul Smith, who amassed a 2½ million fortune by parlaying various deals; Ferd and Mary Chase, Virge Bartlett, the Stevens and Bennett brothers

But the failures listed did not have a monopoly on misfortune. Right up there in the foreground should be placed another man whose failure was just as costly and king-sized. Robert Schroeder was the red-bearded, pleasure-loving son of a wealthy German brewer. In the early 1880's he arrived in the northern Adirondacks on a hop-buying mission for his father, who preferred that his spendthrift, eccentric, venturous son live in America and on a princely annuity, a typical "remittance man" as the British would say. He was attracted to that region by the quality of its hops, which consistently sold at the highest market prices.

Business brought him often to the area and on one of these trips Patrick Clark of Malone, one of Schroeder's local associates, suggested that the two of them go to De Bar Pond for a day's trout fishing. At that time Jim Bean, who ran a small hotel at Duane, owned a shanty and some fifty acres of land bordering that beautiful little sheet of water in the shadows of De Bar, Baldface and Loon Lake mountains. Bean had acquired the property from the family of guides named De Bar. John De Bar, a French-Canadian trapper, had discovered the picturesque, remote pond, a mile long and a half-mile wide, on a hunting expedition in 1817. His son, Lyman, and his grandson George were rated as two of the best guides in Franklin County.

Undoubtedly he must have visualized the holdings as a bit of the Rhineland transplanted to the Adirondack wilderness, a place of primeval grandeur which his wealth could transform into a scene of opulence and pleasure and where he could entertain royally. Instead of vistas of unbroken forests, he probably conjured up visions of a feudal castle and numerous out-buildings with happy, busy people everywhere and sleek thoroughbreds grazing in emerald-green pastures. Before nightfall he became the new owner.

Schroeder was the type that always attracts attention. A robust, thick-set man of medium height, 5'8" or 9", with an affable, ruddy face fringed with well-groomed reddish whiskers, he always dressed like the dude he was, seldom walked, usually rode in a two-seater surrey pulled by a pair of matched chestnut horses with a uniformed driver. His passion for horses was equalled only by his yen for vintage wine and high living. Nothing seemed to give him keener enjoyment than driving at reckless speed over the quiet country roads. The regional farmers would look up from their fieldwork to watch a fast-approaching cloud of dust roll up the turnpike. Then, as they wagged their heads in awe, they would say to each other, "Well, there goes Schroeder, the hop buyer."

At friendly gatherings, when the wine and food suited his gastronomic standards, he could exude charm as a gardenia imparts fragrance. His love of companionship, which characterized much of his life, gained him a wide acquaintanceship if not friendship in Malone.

According to people who knew him Schroeder always walked with his hands behind his back, chin thrust forward and peered over his pince-nez glasses which seemed to be habitually at half-mast. However, those closer to him classified him as eccentric and that would be putting it mildly. His moods were mercurial and unstable. He was in fact predictably unpredictable. But on one thing there was complete agreement: the mansion which he constructed on De Bar Pond was the talk of the North Country.

At the top of a knoll some forty or fifty yards from the shore of the pond, the man who thought that money was made to be spent as fast and freely as possible built his first palatial home. Although he deprecatingly called it a cottage, it was anything but that. Under his close and erratic supervision the pleasure dome project proceeded with customary haste. Not satisfied with the quality of local labor he brought expert workmen - particularly carpenters and masons, from New York and Brooklyn. Everywhere there was great hustling and bustling as teams strained and tugged to haul materials over the rough dirt roads leading to the building site. Finally the pretentious manorhouse was completed and elaborately equipped but at great expense to its owner.

Invitations went out by the dozens and Schroeder's bibulous downstate bachelor buddies - and their well-endowed female companions - arrived en masse for the housewarming ceremonies. What a Bacchanalian wingding that must have been! And you can bet your last pfennig that the bill of fare for this Lucullan occasion wasn't limited to such culinary items as pfannkuchen, haasenpfeffer, kartoffelklase, sauerbraten and

Stained Glass Window, one of two

Ruins of Conservatory

31

apfelstrudel -- sluiced down with bumpers of Pilsener or Muenchen beer and ale.

But, unfortunately for the lord of the manor the big, mostly wood structure went up in flames less than two years later. Before the ashes hardly had time to cool, the owner gave orders for an even bigger mansion to replace it. This time, however, Schroeder decided to take every possible precaution to prevent a recurrence of the previous disaster. Fire of course has always been the constant nemesis of wooden buildings.

The next structure consisted of two sections - one of frame construction to house his numerous guests, the other of stone which was to be his own quarters. Separating the two there was a huge firewall of masonry 30 feet high, 10 feet thick at the base and 3 feet through at the top. A corridor with an iron door at the end provided a passageway from the kitchen and servants' quarters. This castle contained more than sixty spacious, high-ceilinged rooms, brown frescoed; solid mahogany staircases, hardwood floors, a paneled dining room, ballroom, library, palm room, billiard room and conservatory. The entrance hall alone cost nearly $4,000 and featured four large stained-glass windows with the old Teutonic coat of arms and foot-high initials. These were imported from Germany while most of the furniture was shipped over from Holland.

Not taking any chances the second time around, Schroeder installed double doors on nearly every room - the inner of thick oak or birch and the outer made of heavy-gauge steel with large hasps and bolts.

When his second baronial residence was ready for occupancy, the lord of De Bar brought his bride, the daughter of the owner of the Hoffman breweries, to this feudal domain in the mountains. Anna was, according to a cook who worked there, a solid, stolid typically Teutonic but very pleasant woman who was not particularly fastidious about her appearance - a habit that her husband intensely disliked. As with most corpulent people her feet bothered her a great deal so she slopped around in sandals.

From that time on their life was a series of expensive parties although the guests were invariably of her husband's selection. Her fortune, as well as his, was spent recklessly to indulge his insatiable mania for luxurious living. His stable of thoroughbreds seemed to occupy much of his attention and interest, and he would while away the hours watching them from his seat in a surrey-type carriage located in the center of his private half-mile racetrack. A supply of Mumm's champagne was always kept properly chilled in a tub of ice at his feet. When his style of living finally resulted in gout, he had a captain's chair anchored to a stoneboat constructed and daily toured his property in that manner.

Besides his feudal mansion and other essential satellite buildings Schroeder had put up a huge dormitory structure at the crest of Studley Hill to house his hopyard help. From there in the early daylight the small army would travel by wagons to the fields, the women to tie the vines and the men to do the clumping and hoeing. By this time he had carved out a small empire which eventually covered 2100 acres, over 300 of which were planted in hops. At the time this qualified him as the owner of the biggest hop plantation in the world, a green pole and vine jungle where one could easily get lost. Much of this land was sold to him by the shrewd local owners, many of them former Vermonters, at greatly inflated prices and was anything but productive.

Schroeder was a very impulsive and impatient man who was always in a hurry. When his two homes were being built he made frequent last-minute spot decisions and ordered the workmen to make numerous changes in the building plans. Everything had to be done on the double. It is said that he often became annoyed when the mail coach was late and would send a messenger galloping down the road in order to get it sooner. His payrolls were delivered in Pony Express manner from a Malone bank. On one occasion he bought a pair of horses in Utica and drove them over the rough roads to Duane in a record-setting two days' journey. On another trip from Lake Placid to De Bar he and a companion got into an argument over which one of two horses had more endurance. By the time they reached the castle they had found out- and the weaker horse was of little use thereafter.

The often-affable landlord was a very inconsistent host. Ordinarily he liked company and was at his best when properly mellowed and surrounded by his Old Country companions doing justice to his expensive wines and sumptuous food. His ruddy face would glow benignly and his laughter would resound throughout the castle walls. But this mood, however, was always of short duration.

Although he hunted and fished ocassionally and liked wildlife he apparently had very little knowledge of their habits. One day someone gave him a tame hawk. Schroeder watched the captive for awhile and concluding that the creature was lonesome, had another one caught for company. Within the hour he found that one of the fascinating raptors had killed its companion.

The Mr. Hyde side of his mercurial nature showed itself one day when he entertained a group of prominent Malone merchants on a fishing trip and on their departure urged them to return soon. They did and when from the verandah he saw them coming down the long driveway toward the Castle, he dispatched a stableboy to find out "Vat de Dunder" those intruders wanted. When informed that they were his recent guests, he roared out for their benefit as well as his: "You tell dem dot ven I vant dem I'll send for dem!"

A barber summoned from Malone would often be kept loitering around the place for days, waiting until Schroeder would allow him to trim his bristling red beard.

Schroeder's attitude toward his servants was not much more humane and considerate than his treatment of his horses. There were about 30 or 40 German families, recent arrivals in America, in his employ as household servants and farmhands. Quartered in dingy, poorly-heated and over-ventilated shacks these people often became sick during the bad weather periods. In a typical feudal manner he treated these miserable serfs as though they were cattle. Dr. Watson Harwood and Charles Beyerl, his manager, never could convince him that he had a legal responsibility and obligation to provide proper medical attention. This often led to angry arguments which the doctor tried to settle without calling in the sheriff.

One day he was called in to see a woman who was far gone with penumonia but the stubborn Prussian refused to let Harwood take her to the Malone hospital. Teed off the doctor declared, "Whether you like it or not I'm taking this woman with me! - Or else I'm leaving here and will come back with an officer."

"Vat can you do to make me?" blustered Schroeder.

"Well, since I'm the county health officer I can force you to obey!"

Schroeder was finally out-talked and gave his grumpy consent to the sick woman's removal.

On his way to the hospital Doc Harwood growled to Beyerl, "What in hell does that damned old Dutchman think he's doing up there?"

Beyerl, himself a German as well as Schroeder's business manager and closest friend, merely shrugged his shoulders and shook his head slowly but expressively.

Another instance of his insistence that everything be done speedily as well as when and how he wanted them done took the following form. In an effort to make his woodland estate more self-supporting, one Spring he bought 24 young pigs. By early September they had grown to be sizeable porkers, so Schroeder summoned men from Malone to do the butchering. They advised him to wait until colder weather and pointed out that the meat

De Bar Pond

Echo Lodge built for Tubercular son

34

would spoil if they carried out his orders. But, acting against their better judgment and experience, Schroeder ordered some of his farmhands to do the job. They did - and several weeks later consigned several tons of putrefying pork to a large hole hurriedly dug in a field nearby.

Here's another example of Schroeder's arrogance and unwillingness to take advice: Jerry Marlowe, a highly respected Whippleville hop-grower, strongly urged him to sell his crop at an especially favorable price - $2.00 a pound, almost a record amount. But Schroeder pig-headedly knew better of course and held out for still higher prices and a real killing. Others argued that he was wrong but with no results. Schroeder wouldn't change his mind. With typical bad judgment he hung on. The market became glutted, the prices broke wide open and Schroeder found himself holding the bag - forced to sell his harvest for $2.00 a wagonload - not even enough to make it worth the bother of hauling them to the freighthouse in Malone.

Besides such costly, obstinate and unnecessary errors in judgment which exacted an increasingly greater financial toll, there were other personal tragedies. Their only son became tubercular and died a lingering death in Echo Lodge, a large cottage built especially for him. Their daughter, Elsa, was a pleasant but not-too-bright girl. During her girlhood days at De Bar, Elsa had her own team of Shetland ponies hitched to a two-wheeled rubber-tired wicker dogcart. She loved to take her small visitors on rides along the estate's roads and to give parties and dances on the huge front porch of the Castle.

When she was only 15 or 16 she became infatuated with a self-styled "Baron" Von Arkony, a clerk in a New York cigar store who entranced her with stories about his titles and estates in Hungary. She married him and found out later that he was an impostor and the son of a Budapest dentist.

Her father, who vehemently opposed the marriage, got rid of the fortune hunter by means of a generous allowance provided he leave the country. He did but the addled child-bride followed him across, where they lived luxuriously in Paris. After the death of her mother and desertion by her impostor-husband, Elsa returned to New York and reconciliation with her father. But her experience had cost the Schroeders at least $200,000.

There are two contradictory stories about what finally happened to the daughter. One account maintains that the heart-broken girl killed herself by poison in the Carlton Hotel, London on April 15, 1913.

The other, more credible version is that she was confined briefly in a mental institution and, upon her discharge, went to live with a Tucker family in Watertown. As former employees at De Bar they took a sincere interest in her and she lived with them the rest of her days. But she never did become exactly rational. For example, on one occasion she went to visit friends in New York City and, while changing from the Rutland to the New York Central Railroad at Malone Junction, she mistakenly boarded the Montreal car instead of the southbound passenger train.

The family's finances were being stretched to the limit by then. The enormous cost of maintaining such an ornate establishment, plus meeting the staggering entertainment costs, put a deep dent in their dwindling funds. His hops, which usually brought at least a dollar a pound during peak years, were now bringing 18¢ or 20¢ per pound. Then, to compound his problems, his father died and his two far more practical brothers saw to it that the spendthrift never again had a chance to tap the family till. His wife's fortune had by then also been depleted to the point where she determined to salvage as much as possible. At her insistence Schroeder gave her a $50,000 mortgage as partial compensation for large loans from her own father.

Shortly afterward, Schroeder went back to Germany in an effort to recoup both his health and his fortune. While he was away she sold or, rather, exchanged the mortgage for some building lots in Brooklyn - a deal which also went sour. The horses and costly furniture were sold at auction in New York City. Soon afterward the De Bar property was liquidated at a colossal loss and the end of the skidway career rapidly approached.

When Schroeder returned from Europe, broke and owing hundreds of thousands of dollars which he could never repay, he and his despondent wife lived for a time in very modest quarters in Brooklyn.

Mrs. Schroeder's mental health was by then - 1910 - badly shaken and she solved her personal problem by asphyxiation. Three years later - on July 25, 1913 - Schroeder used the same method to destroy himself. On that fatal Friday morning, Charles Beyerl, his constant companion for 30 years, found him on the floor of the bathroom, pillows under his head and a rug over him, with gas pouring from the open valves of a radiator.

According to the obit in the Brooklyn *Daily Eagle* and confirmed by the North Country people who knew him best, Schroeder, although erratic and eccentric, was generous and kind to those he liked and respected. Very likely the little Methodist Church at Duane Center would never have been built except for him....

The Castle remained deserted for about five years before it was purchased by Berton and Herbert Reynolds and Clarence Briggs of Malone with the idea of converting the mansion into a clubhouse or sanitarium. Within a very few days a couple hundred acres of the tract were sold for a sum less than Schroeder's wine bill for a single year.

Then in the early 1920's the Reynolds-Briggs Associates and Howard Taylor, cousin of the Reynolds' decided to branch out into what seemed to be the hottest and most profitable business of that era - raising silver foxes. As part of the construction project they hired most of the 1924 Franklin Academy football squad, whose captain was Horace (Horty) Reynolds - Herbert's son - to dig the deep ditches for the close-meshed heavy wire fences designed to separate the cantankerous, costly and vicious pelt-bearers from chewing each other to ribbons. We peons wielded picks and shovels from early morning until mid-afternoon, when we knocked off work and practiced football until supper-time. Occasionally, when we weren't too bushed, some of us toured the northern Adirondacks in Coach Miller's car.

Our headquarters was the abandoned Castle, which we explored from attic to cellar - especially the latter - immediately after arrival. The several wine cellars, still stocked with rank upon rank of long-necked wine bottles - all emptied by prior occupants and itinerant guides and tramps - were nevertheless a source of intense curiosity. By then the foundation, walls, ceilings and staircases showed unmistakable signs of galloping dilapidation. The fountain statuary was green with corrosion and the huge, impressive, brightly-colored stained glass windows were broken and leaking. Altogether it was a spooky but fascinating relic of the so-called olden, golden days of magnificently ostentatious opulence.

The place deteriorated rapidly from that time on as vandals looted everything of value - fireplace tiles, stained glass, brass fixtures and chandeliers, mahogany staircase railings, farm equipment, etc. Then in 1939 came another change of owners: this time to Arthur A. Wheeler of New York and Palm Beach, who promptly ordered the demolition of the eyesore Castle. A gang of workmen under the direction of Henry Wood, local contractor, soon razed the big building and work started on the construction of a $100,000 seventeen-room, peeled-log cabin twenty yards or so from the site of the old Castle.

Lodge Built by William A. Wheeler

Twenty years later, in August of 1959, the 1000 acre scenic property changed hands still once more when Farwell T. Perry of Greenwich, Conn., a World War II Navy pilot, took over. The sonorous sound of his powerful twin-motor seaplane symbolized the advent of yet another era in the transportation history of the mountains....

Although Schroeder and his castle have now become just another regional legend, there are still area people like myself around who have never quite forgotten the story of the visionary German who imparted more than a modicum of grandeur, fascination and medium-high tragedy not only to that particular area but also to the ever-growing literary legacy of the whole Adirondack region as well.

Admiring the Trophy at the Windsor Hotel, Elizabethtown in 1890's

38

Chapter 3

The Heyday of the Hops

Within their lifetimes many older members of the present generation of Northern New Yorkers have seen several once-flourishing industries eventually show unmistakable signs of dying on the vine. Some of these businesses have already passed out of existence and others show obvious symptoms of sliding down the skidways toward economic oblivion. Among these casualties can be listed iron mining, big-scale lumbering, the large summer hotel trade and the extremely speculative hop-growing gamble.

Several years ago there were brief flurries of seasonal activity at the Lyon Mountain and Port Henry branches of the Republic Steel Company, but today, probably because of the competitive pressure applied by the vast Labrador iron discoveries, both operations have been closed down. At its Tahawus plant the National Lead Company is just as much interested in titanium, a by-product, as it is in iron. Except for closely-controlled, well-managed and diversified firms such as Finch-Pruyn, the St. Regis and the International Paper Companies, the Draper holdings in St. Lawrence County, and the smaller Diamond Match Company concern, large-scale lumbering of both hard and soft woods has become practically a thing of the past.

These victims of a declining economy have of course had their unfortunate impact on the incomes of many people who depended on such businesses for their livelihood. Understandably, at the same time, such personal financial disasters have made a very deep dent in the profits of the merchants with whom the workers traded.

While most people are acutely aware of decreasing activities and the resulting lack or lag in local employment opportunities in mining, lumbering and summer hotel businesses, the chances are that the same people know very little about hop-growing, a risky sideline which provided many Franklin County farmers with all the heady gambling thrills they ever wanted during the changeful period which stretched from the 1870's to the late 1950's. Each of those years susceptible men succumbed to the compulsive urge to stake their skill and luck against the whims of weather, insect pests, increasing competition, rising costs and uncertain profits.

Some years, when poor harvests elsewhere in this country or in the world caused hop prices to skyrocket to an all-time high of $2.00 a pound, some major plungers found themselves up to $50 or $60,000 richer. Other years, however, when frosts came early to the Adirondack foothills, almost equally heavy losses were recorded. The most spectacular failure of them all was Frederick Schroeder.

Nor is it common knowledge that in 1879 five counties - Otsego, Oneida, Madison,

Schoharie and Franklin - produced more than 2/3 of all the hops grown in the State and half the entire United States crop for that year. Just twenty years previously the Empire State had accounted for 7/8 of the nation's crop. Although the average world yield per acre at that time was about 800 pounds, the usual production cost about 10¢ per pound and the normal selling price about 20¢. these figures were subject to drastic fluctuations which could either enrich or impoverish those individuals who took a flyer at raising the "yellowish strobiles or collections of imbricated scales."

Perhaps it was also no mere coincidence or happenstance that this scaly, cone-like fruit, so closely related to hemp, the source of marijuana, seemed to exert a powerful influence over those who speculated in this beer-flavoring agent. Incidentally, this special flavor is imparted by a yellow, resin-like substance called lupulin, which is found at the base of the bracts or scales.

There were a lot of other things about hops and hop-growing which I did not know when I was growing up in Malone during the First World War and shortly thereafter. At that time the town was surrounded in summer by green jungles of vine-encircling poles. From the front porch of my home on Fort Covington Street the view westward was one vast expanse of the tepee-like structures of stacked poles, and the numerous curing barns were common sights then and still to be seen even in the 1950's in the Whippleville - Chasm Falls area and north to the Canadian Border.

By then Franklin County was noted for the special flavor of its hops, an added something engendered by the higher altitude and faster growing season. Therefore the crop commanded premium prices among the buyers and thus gave the growers an advantage over down-state farmers.

Besides gazing at hopyards from a comparative distance I have a vivid, still-evergreen recollections of a close-hand, personal encounter with those vines which always twist from left to right around the tall supporting poles. In fact on that unforgettable, unforgotten occasion I found out exactly what it feels like to be *hopping* mad.

My brother and I and our wives had gone up to Malone for a late August - early September vacation. As usual we husbands found ourselves needing additional money to meet expenses and, rather than borrow from a bank, decided to work in the hop-yards. We had often heard our mother tell how she and her sisters had always earned their spending money picking hops. Whole families in those days would go into the fields and earn enough to take in the Franklin County Fair in style besides netting considerable additional income. She cautioned us that it was very tiring, exacting work and also warned us to be *very* careful not to jiggle the box. She did not go into any great detail about just what would happen if we did. The results of such clumsiness were made very clear to us soon enough.

By checking the Help Wanted ads in the local paper we learned that several hop-growers needed hands. The likeliest place, one we had seen often as we passed by, was a yard owned by a man named Marlowe, who lived in Whippleville. There we reported for work early one morning. Other people, including whole families of Indians from the St. Regis Reservation, were there also. The owner was somewhat skeptical of our ability as hop-pickers, but he was working against time and Nature so he told us how to go about it. He also cautioned us about bumping the box and made it clear that we had "to pick clean. No leaves, no stems!" The logic behind both warnings soon became clear....

We also soon found out about the boxes themselves. The exact dimensions of a standard hop box are given in a most interesting thin volume entitled *Hop Culture in the United States*, by one E. Meeker of Puyallup, Washington Territory and copyrighted in 1883. He was the biggest hop-grower in the nation at the time. On page 19 of this fascinating book is the following description: "The standard box is five feet ten inches in length by one foot four inches wide at the bottom. All inside measure. On each side of the box is a fir strip eight feet long and one and a quarter by four inches wide. These sidepieces serve as handles with which to carry the box."

Some mathematician can have the curious honor of figuring out exactly how many of those Christmas-tree shaped fruits of the hops it takes to fill the box, but I assure all and sundry that it takes plenty. Having been told that we would be paid $5.00 per box, Lee and I had sudden visions of $40.00 or so apiece for a couple days' work. Little did we wot what we would really have to show for a day and a half of drudgery, because if we had known we would have plucked nary a clump.

However, since we were full of high hopes for enough loot to give our spouses and us a memorable evening in Montreal, we started work. We pulled our own poles in order to make 50¢ more pay, leaned them against the box - and immediately found out why we had been warned twice about jouncing the container. The reason was very evident: when placed carefully in the receptacle there is enough air space between each cone to give the illusion of its (the box) being far fuller than it actually is. The "joker" is that whenever the seemingly insatiable box is even the least bit jostled, the contents suddenly settle down by inches before one's very eyes. After several such minor accidents punctuated by unbrotherly curses, we finally learned to be more careful.

The day grew hotter and even though we worked as fast as we could, we made surprisingly slow progress. We sweated profusely and the chemical in the spray used on the hops stung like bees each time we touched the cones - and that had to be often. Gloves were too clumsy because the fingers had to be free in order to pick fast: in short it was rapidly becoming plainly evident to both of us that this was anything but the world's easiest way to earn a few fast bucks. However, since we were both stubborn cusses, we kept our fingers flying as fast as possible.

Every so often the owner or his assistant would come over to us, look at the inside of the box, pick out some debris in the form of unsalable leaves and stems and caution us again "to pick clean." Before the day was over we had begun to think that we had heard that command more than a few times too often.

The only comic relief which the day provided was the often-repeated shout - "Gil-be-r-rtt, (Gilbert) get the hell out of that poison ivory!" Working in the row beside us were Gilbert's mother and three sisters of varying sizes. The boy, aged about seven or eight, was a typical heller, a dead ringer for Dennis the Menace, constantly roaming around on exploring trips. Several times they managed to get him close-by, but each time he banged against the box; so he was shooed away. The brat, like an iron filing drawn to a magnet, generally found his way back to the ivy patch, and we would wait expectantly and never disappointedly for his mother to cut loose again with her hog-calling voice. Occasionally Gilbert would call back - "Aw, go soak your head!" Several spankings finally straightened him out and temporarily subdued him.

Another interlude that helped make the long day more bearable came when some people drove to the edge of the field and near to where we were working. They thought we must be old hands so we expounded expertly (we thought) on the hop business. Before long, however, the woman realized she had seen my brother before - which she had - and our phony act was over, but not before they had taken our pictures while we posed like real hop-pickers.

Finally, about the middle of the long afternoon, we filled our first box. Other pickers by that time were well along with their third or fourth boxes. That annoyed the devil out of us because even though our fingers seemed ready to fall off, we just couldn't seem to make appreciable headway.

At 5 o'clock we knocked off for the day; our second box had only a few inches of hops on the bottom....The next day with help from the wives we managed to chalk up another victory, a second box.

The third day, my mother and our wives (out of pity for a couple of stubborn lunks) went back out with us. All five of us worked feverishly to fill the third box by noon. Gilbert and his mother put on their diverting act several times to liven up the proceedings. With the conquest of the third box complete, we all decided that a trip to Montreal was not worth the labor involved. Total take for twenty-four hours of very hard, intensive work --- $15.00. We very nearly didn't get that because Mr. Marlowe protested loudly about the foreign matter - leaves and stems - in the boxes. However, when my brother - 210 pounds and 6 feet 2 inches and I (202 at the time and 6 feet even) made menacing noises, he reconsidered and grudgingly paid us the hardest-earned money we had ever made.

Such is the saga of the hopyards. Even today the expression "hoppin' mad" is always good for a reminiscent chuckle from other members of my family. Moreover, whenever I drive through that section of the Salmon River country, I always feel that I know just a little more than the average person does about hops and hop culture, now just another part of Franklin County's past.

Nowadays, even though the U.S. is still the world's leading producer of hops followed by England, Germany, Czechoslovakia, France and Austria in that order, few if any are grown in New York state - and to the best of my knowledge none in the Adirondack region. The Pacific Coast states of California, Oregon and Washington are now the nation's sole producers.

But while the period lasted that precarious, fascinating but highly speculative industry highlighted the history of Franklin County.

The Mrs. and Drexie

Chapter 4

Mrs. Chase and the Loon Lake House

During the final decades of the last century and even until the stock market crash of October 1929, the Adirondack region featured many noted hotels. Except for the ill-fated Prospect House (1881-1915) at Blue Mountain Lake, all the largest, most fashionable and most flourishing of these resorts were located in Franklin County.

In the order of their origin these three were Paul Smith's (1859); Saranac Inn, earlier known as Hough's and later as the Prospect House, (1864) and the subject of this article - the Loon Lake House (1879).

Although the inexperienced Mr. Hough failed in his venture, Saranac Inn, during the ownership of the Ward-Riddle interests and under subsequent management, became renowned. Paul (Apollos) Smith was a millionaire twice over plus when he died in Montreal's Royal Victoria Hospital in 1912, following a kidney operation. That same year the Statler Hotel Company offered Ferd and Mary Chase, a million dollars for their Loon Lake properties. They refused. In all likelihood this decision, undoubtedly a difficult one, was made by the resolute, strong-minded Mary Howe Chase respectfully called "The Mrs."

Twenty years later, when the advent of the automobile had radically changed the vacation habits of the summer guests, (who no longer spent the entire season in the same place), and after the Wall Street disaster had sealed the fate of even the smaller hotels, the indomitable Mrs. Chase found herself land-poor, over-extended and virtually bankrupt - a

Ferd Chase

Mrs. Chase

Ferd and Buckboard

situation which no doubt hastened her death in 1933.

Obviously the rise and fall in the fortunes of such a person and her creation contain all the elements needed for an intensely interesting life story - and hers is no exception.

As had many other notable Adirondack hotel-keepers such as Paul Smith and the Stevens Brothers of Lake Placid, the Chases also migrated from Vermont: Mary Howe having been born in Jericho in 1843 and Ferd in Wheelock Hollow, a hamlet up in the northeastern corner, in 1840. Considered to be an accomplished musician as a young girl, she taught piano and voice; she rode her horse sidesaddle while making the rounds to the homes of her students.

Ferd Chase served throughout the Civil War. After his return home he worked for several years as expressman on Central Vermont Railroad before becoming clerk at the Central House in Essex Junction. After their marriage in 1874 the young couple managed that hotel for four years. During that period they, like many other restless Vermont people, listened intently to fascinating reports about the nearly unspoiled wilderness region whose alluring, serrated peaks beckoned irresistibly from beyond the western shore of Lake Champlain.

After several vacation trips to the Loon Lake vicinity they found exactly the spot they wanted: ten virtually untouched acres on a high knoll overlooking the upper lake. The decision having been reached the Chases went back to Vermont and made the necessary arrangements for the long-anticipated trip. They arrived at Loon Lake in October, 1878 and Ferd lost no time starting work on his own place. They spent that first winter in the nearby tavern owned by Prentiss (Print) Lovering. This was a log building located on the old Port Kent to Hopkinton turnpike. Later on the Chases bought and improved it and renamed it the President's Cottage after President Harrison, who occupied it in 1892-93. Presidents Cleveland and McKinley also vacationed there.

House in 1879

House in 1883

First Annex in 1893

Loon Lake Stage c. 1890's — Stoddard Photo

Ziegler's, Later Seven Keys Lodge [burned Nov. 1972]

46

On May 19, 1879 the three-story, 31-room log structure was ready for guests, whose first five names appearing in the register were a Mr. Bixby of Plattsburgh, C. Turner of Schuyler Falls, Henry Wetherby of Burlington, Vermont, E. Hubert Allen of New York and Jasper Kane of St. Albans. These men were there for the early trout fishing because the hotel did not officially open until July 6th. A total of 455 guests signed the register during that first season.

Besides catering to hunters and fishermen during the early 1880's, people suffering from tuberculosis were also accommodated, and Mrs. Chase helped many of them to regain their health. She apparently had instinctive nursing skill and a genuine desire and ability to inspire courage and confidence. One of her patient-guests was the wife of President Benjamin Harrison, who made two trips from Washington to visit her.

Those first years were not easy. Mrs. Chase did all the housework and there were times when the going was very rough indeed. On one occasion the supply of provisions was practically depleted - as was their pocketbook. Without available cash to stock up for the season, they had to scrape along on a week to week basis. When they found that they were running short of food and money at the same time, their guests and they still had to be fed somehow. So Ferd hitched up the team to the buckboard and the Chases headed for the nearest store, which was in Ausable Forks, a round trip that took all day and half the night. There an obliging storekeeper, J. Rogers, trusted them for a barrel of flour and other staples.

But the Chases were not people who became easily discouraged. Within thirty years they had extended their original ten acres and one small hotel into an enterprise that eventually comprised 4,000 acres of forestlands, a hotel and two annexes, a golf course and numerous other service buildings and improvements - all of which were valued at well over a million dollars. The reputation of the Loon Lake House eventually reached a point where it accommodated nearly 800 guests in 1929, the last big season.

This compulsive urge to expand and then keep on expanding became a virtual obsession with "The Mrs." She used to the utmost her exceptional administrative ability and never ceased planning for an even bigger establishment. The profits from one season would be spent to add more annexes, cottages, barns, service buildings and other improvements which, besides the golf course, bowling alleys and tennis courts, also included a private acetylene lighting plant and a mile-long sewerage system that cost $5.00 for each foot dug through earth and $10.00 for the rocky sections, where the twin 12-inch tile lines had to be installed in a tunnel 92 feet deep at one point. A two-main water supply system was also a costly undertaking.

Development plans for the Loon Lake House also included the construction of many cottages; these finally totaled 53. They ranged from small buildings which would accommodate only one family to far more elaborate log structures of the hunting lodge type. Since the hotel was operated under the American plan, the cottages were not equipped with kitchen facilities; therefore the guests were required to use the Main House dining room. This system of course proved very profitable for the management.

Another example of Mrs. Chase's business acumen was the arrangement for short-term leases which she made with several of her regular guests who were willing to pay a high price for the privacy of their own camps. Families such as the Mulfords, Jacksons, Demorests and Macdonalds were permitted to build their cottages on choice locations on her property. At the expiration of the lease, which sometimes ran for as short a time as ten years, the occupants could either renew or, after a fair appraisal had been made, sell the buildings to "The Mrs." In this way she acquired many additions to her holdings.

The most impressive "cottage" of them all was built by William Ziegler of Philadelphia. About 1890 the main camp was constructed of logs with a huge fireplace at one end and six more elsewhere. This building served as the living room. Other small structures were used as bedrooms, servants' quarters, etc. The huge boathouse had a ballroom above it. Gardens, tennis courts, trellised walks, summer houses and other features completed the establishment, the total cost of which was estimated to be $300,000.

After the Zieglers stopped spending their summers there, it became a fashionable girls' summer camp and was renamed Greylock. Mrs. Chase considered the young ladies to be a source of distraction and somewhat of a nuisance so she bought the place in 1915. Although it rented for $10,000 for several seasons, it was generally used for big parties and for overflow accommodations. Later called Seven Keys Lodge and owned by Sam Garland it became a fairly successful small hotel. After it again changed ownership, it burned to the ground in late November, 1972.

"The Mrs." was a very astute business woman. She had no use for the blatant type of advertising used by many hotels. Convinced that third person or word of mouth testimonials and recommendations were enough in the early years, she usually just sent out a card each spring to former guests announcing the opening dates for the coming season. Later on, however, she made good use of well-illustrated brochures.

Although Ferd Chase was very active in the early management stages of the enterprise, his wife made all the major management decisions after the turn of the century. He then devoted most of his time to running the hotel farm and the outside operations. He had always felt more at ease with the guides and farm help than with the guests.

Like so many former guides and outdoorsmen Ferd loved his liquor and the newly-found means to splurge. Judging by the hotel register, 1884 must have been a profitable year because at its close the congenial boniface threw what had and has to be one of the longest and liveliest parties the old mountains have ever seen. The 168 guests represented the "Who's Who of the Northland" because just about everybody who was anybody signed their names. The list is much too long to print in its entirety but here's a sampling: From *Bloomingdale* - R. H. McIntyre and wife, Miss S. H. Morrison, E. L. Patterson and wife, W. L. Hough and wife, Isaac Rice and wife, Isaac Chesley and wife, Alonzo P. Smith, E. A. Bruce, C. J. Stickney and lady, H. E. Gillespie and Norman Flanders. From *Saranac Lake* - A. J. Morehouse, Miss Fanny Wilkins, Charles H. Smith and wife, Anson Parsons, W. Avery, C. H. Kendall, A. F. Merrill, George Berkley, J. W. Slater, Rob Moody, Justin Farrington, Alonzo Dudley, P. A. Robbins - most of them accompanied by wives or ladies.

From *Lake Placid* - S. H. Hardin, F. X. Major, E. L. Hays, Charles Martin, R. C. Rice, George A. Stevens, F. B. Stickney, Martin W. Brewster, Ben Wood, Henry Allen, Thomas Peacock - with wives or ladies. From *Malone:* Walker Moody, Frank Eldridge, W. H. Gray and R. M. Miller.

From *Duane:* George Selkirk, William Ayers and companions; from *Ray Brook:* Daniel and Byron Cameron and wives; *Paul Smith's* and *Brighton:* - C. A. McArthur, Phil and Ambrose King, H. B. L. Smith and George Lyon - all with wives or ladies.

The musical entertainment was supplied by a six-piece orchestra from Malone, which consisted of Charles A. Esterbrook, Will C. Kaine, Will Meitzke, E. N. Johnson, Bert Coburn and Anson Moses.

This must have been *the* social event of the era and probably lasted for several days before the revelers were in a fit condition to make their homeward trip by cutters and sleighs.

Interestingly enough a close inspection of the Loon Lake House registers indicates that

Waitresses at Loon Lake House 1890's

Outside Help at Loon Lake House 1890's

49

there was never another such gala affair put on as an encore. But knowing Mrs. Chases's strong aversion to both alcohol and the squandering of money, it is easy to assume that Ferd Chase got a tongue-lashing that left deep scars in his ego and planted the seeds of vindictiveness that twenty years later resulted in open alienation.

Among Ferd's other interests were breeding deer for sale to parks and zoos, heavy philandering and membership in a swank Canadian hunting and fishing club. During the period seemingly irreconcilable personality clashes reached the point the Chases scarcely spoke to each other for the last 15 years of his life. There was, however, a partial reconciliation during the period of illness preceding his death from pneumonia on November 27, 1916.

Throughout the long estrangement Charles Stevens, a Tufts engineer in their employ, acted as an intermediary. Both the Chases liked and trusted him. In fact Ferd thought so highly of him that he took him along on several European voyages and a world cruise. Moreover, according to the terms of Ferd's will, the liaison officer was left $50,000 and a half-interest in his estate. "The Mrs." had to buy back the Stevens's share in order to regain full control of the company.

For some reason Mrs. Chase seemed to have no desire to travel. She lived the year round at Loon Lake and left there only infequently and then but for brief emergency trips to Plattsburgh or Burlington. Apparently, she was content to remain close to the place which her administrative skill and downright persistence had brought into being. Indeed the Loon Lake House was always her main interest in life and became a virtual obsession.

"The Mrs." never allowed herself to show outward indications of anger except for a reddening of her face. She never raised her voice when provoked. Sarcasm was her main resource against the relatively few people whom she instinctively and intensely disliked.

Typical of the way she handled objectionable guests is the encounter with the wealthy individual who arrived with a large party one Sunday. Since the Hotel had built up an enviable reputation for its delicious food, as many as a thousand people were often served in shifts in the huge dining room overlooking the lake. The regular guests were of course accommodated first, so the influential stranger started to get impatient and protested loudly and often that he was not accustomed to such treatment. The head waiter sent one of his assistants to report the incident to "The Mrs.", who took charge immediately. She explained the situation and assured him that he and his guests would be taken care of as soon as possible. They were finally served an excellent dinner which they enjoyed very much, so he stopped at the main desk on his way out to express his approval.

"Mrs. Chase," he said, in his most expansive manner, "that's the best dinner I've ever eaten! I shall come back often. How much do I owe you?"

"You owe me nothing," replied Mrs. Chase.

"Nothing! But I can't accept that. Why I . . I . . just couldn't possibly come here again if I didn't pay you now!"

"That's just exactly the way I had it figured out, mister," Mrs. Chase retorted. "Good day, sir!"

Another example: A Mrs. Vanderhoff, a very domineering dowager, one rainy day felt the full force of the formidable vocal weapon. The imperious lady had neglected to remove her rubbers before going into the dining room so, when she had been seated, she ordered Laura Hart, her waitress, to take them off. Her tone of voice was so hostile that Laura retorted, "I won't do it! I'm here to wait on your table - but I'm not a maid servant!!!"

"Very well," replied Mrs. V., "we'll just see about that. I'm going to report you to Mrs. Chase!"

Sure enough: after she had finished dinner she flounced herself directly out to the front office and demanded to see "The Mrs.", who came out of her own office to hear the complaint. After sounding off vehemently for several long minutes, the irate lady finally delivered her ultimatum: "There is only one way to settle this: either the girl goes or *I* go."

"All right," said Mrs. Chase, who had listened quietly to the tirade. "if that's the way you want it, one of you certainly will have to go. But Laura is the one who *stays. You* go!" And she meant it too.

Although she usually was seen in black silk dresses and sweaters, Mrs. Chase sometimes wore light green, her favorite color. This provided a strong contrast for her sand-colored wigs, of which she had four. Scarlet fever had left her nearly bald.

She wore a black veil, disliked hats and seldom wore one. One day, however, she donned one as a disguise. Word had reached her through the grapevine that several of the help were goldbricking. Preferring to verify this in person, Mrs. Chase put on a large hat with veil attached and ordered one of the hotel Packards to be sent around. A trip to the scene of the alleged inactivity confirmed the report and soon thereafter the unscheduled rest break was cut short by a messenger who told the loafers that "The Mrs." wanted to see them. It took the "culprits" a long time to figure out how she had found out about them.

She also had a well-developed espionage system which enabled her to keep thoroughly informed about every phase of the hotel's operation. She slept only four or five hours per night (said that no one needed any more rest than that) and was up by five each morning to make her daily rounds of the kitchen and grounds. Although she was well up in her 70's at the time, she still had a keen mind and keener eyes. Nothing sloppy or half-heartedly done ever got by her sharp glance and sharper tongue. In fact about all anyone with any degree of management responsibility had to say to get prompt cooperation was - "I'll tell The Mrs.'!"

She invariably read two New York papers each day not only to keep posted on world happenings but also to keep tabs on regular and prospective guests. If any of her summer people got involved in scandals, those individuals found it extremely difficult or even impossible to get reservations at Loon Lake the following season.

Apparently she had no strong religious convictions or, if she did, she never discussed them. As a girl she was a member of the Baptist Church but evidently something happened that soured her against ministers and religion. One soliciting clergyman was rocked back on his heels when Mrs. Chase told him that she would indeed make a donation to his worthy cause - but only after he had earned it at the woodpile out back. She declared that she wanted to know exactly where her money went, so her practical Christianity found expression in gifts of money to countless deserving or needy people. She often paid the funeral expenses of indigent former employees and several times paid the expenses for rebuilding homes of burned-out neighbors. Moreover, she sent several hundred young people - mostly boys but also some girls - through medical and law courses.

Mrs. Chase was generous but not gullible, as one St. Lawrence University student found out. Since he came from a poor family and also had one of the less remunerative jobs at the famous summer resort, she told him that she would underwrite his college education at S.L.U. During the following years his written requests for money came frequently and his expense account showed indications of obvious padding. His benefactor became suspicious and finally insisted that the lad send itemized statements. This he did but he also senselessly included bills from his mother for doing her son's laundry. That did it! Mrs. Chase was understandably indignant to learn that the mother wasn't even willing to do that little bit to help out. So no more checks from Loon Lake for him.

Not long before she died Mrs. Chase told June Jarvis, her maid, to get all her cancelled checks together and then burn them. She said that she didn't want anyone to know what she had done for people. This request was promptly carried out in spite of the repeated protests of the outraged Mr. Stevens, who was apparently concerned about the legality of the act, but quite likely equally curious to know how she had spent her money.

Although she was usually nearly psychic in her ability to judge character, she was nevertheless victimized by two employees who lost nearly $200,000 of her money in deals involving a laundry and an airport. Incidentally, that small fortune could have warded off bankruptcy three years later.

Mrs. Chase believed firmly in the transmigration of souls and that conviction probably helped explain her love for animals - particularly dogs and cats. She was especially solicitous of a donkey which had nearly lost its sight hauling cartloads of dirt and rocks when the sewerage system was being installed. "The Mrs." once declared to her secretary that dogs and cats came first in her affections, men came next, and women and children were welcome to whatever love she had left over.

One day in the kitchen she and Steve Leonard, one of her cooks, got into a conversation about her favorite topic - the souls of people inhabiting the bodies of animals.

"Stevie," she said, "when you die you're going to turn into a dog."

"If that's true," replied Steve, "I certainly hope that I don't turn into a pug dog!"

"Why not?" asked the Mrs.

"Because those dogs always have crooked tails," Steve complained. Both of them chuckled heartily over that bit of repartee.

Besides numerous dogs and cats "The Mrs." also had a parrot named Drexie, an ill-tempered, finger-biting creature that hated the narrow confines of a regular enclosure and was kept in a monkey cage instead. For several months after its acquisition the cooped-up carnivore was on display behind the main desk, near the bellhops' bench. Its location was changed shortly afterward when the bright-feathered bird was heard screaming raucously - "Tip the bell-boys! Tip the bell-boys!" A resourceful lad from Malone named Walter Mullarney was credited with that cadging endeavor.

The parrot's disposition did not mellow with age. She got even more ornery instead. Not wanting to see it cooped up all the time Mrs. Chase often let Drexie out of her big cage. The gaudy bird showed her perverted sense of gratitude by digging deep divots into the furniture and upholstery, shredding magazines and catalogs and not infrequently attempting - sometimes successfully - to take sizable chunks from the fingers of anyone who touched her, as I found out for myself.

She was certainly no prize as a pet but nevertheless her owner tolerated and even liked her. Therefore when Mrs. Chase was critically ill with pneumonia, she asked June if she would take care of Drexie. Although Miss Jarvis did not want to hurt her beloved employer's feelings she gently refused. Somewhat disappointed Mrs. Chase then added, "You are the only one I would give her to. But if you honestly don't want her, June, why that's all right. I want her to be with me." So after the death of "The Mrs.", the parrot was chloroformed and placed in the coffin beside her.

Another amusing incident involving Steve illustrated Mrs. Chase's pronounced sense of humor. All the kitchen help were furnished white uniforms. One rainy day as he came up from the laundry with a fresh supply, two bell-hops met him. One of them jokingly said, "Steve, how would you like to make four dollars?"

A little cautiously the jovial chef said, "Sure, how?"

"That's easy," was the answer. "All you have to do is roll over twice in that big puddle over there."

Steve agreed and got himself drenched and four dollars richer. Then he went over to his room and changed clothes.

What he didn't know was that Mrs. Chase had watched the whole performance from the pastry room window. When he walked into the kitchen, she was there to meet him.

"Well, Stevie," she remarked, "it's a darned good thing for you that you don't have to pay your own laundry bills!"

Realizing that she must have seen him, Steve agreed and tactfully offered her the money.

"Keep it," she said as a twinkle appeared in her eyes. "You certainly earned it by making a jackass of yourself in that filthy water!"

Mrs. Chase ate all her meals in the kitchen. She also was her own head chef and saw to it that the food was prepared exactly the way she wanted it - the finest ingredients flavored to suit her taste. She firmly believed that the reputation of a hotel was based mainly on the excellence of its meals - and the Loon Lake House was noted for the quality of its victuals.

Of the countless compliments which Mrs. Chase received, one in particular stood out because it also reflected her ready wit. A party from the Lake Placid Club drove over for dinner and were duly impressed by the meal. One of them stopped at the desk on the way out and expressed his approval.

"Mrs. Chase, that was a marvelous meal," he said, "just marvelous! Particularly the chicken."

"Very glad you liked it," replied "The Mrs."

"But tell me," he continued, "we were served nothing but white meat. How can you do it?"

"Oh well," she quipped, "that's easily explained: We send the legs and wings over to Dewey's." (Lake Placid Club)

The seasons of 1930-31 were critical for the Loon Lake Hotel Corporation and Mrs. Chase. By then the depression was well underway and business was going from bad to worse. A receivership representing the creditors took over and finally, on one grim afternoon in late 1931, Mrs. Chase was called into a meeting and summarily told that while she would of course be welcome to remain at Loon Lake House as long as she wished, from that day on she would have nothing to do or say about its management. According to Henrietta Earle, her secretary, when "The Mrs." came out of the room, she burst into tears - the first such display of emotion the former had ever seen during the more than 20 years of her employment.

The bitter experience seemed to break her spirit because she never showed much interest in life or living thereafter, according to her maid, June Jarvis. Had she lived until the following October 7th she would have been 90, but "The Mrs." died of pneumonia on Thursday, January 18, 1933. As she lay there four kittens played around and even on the deathbed. Her secretary watched but did not disturb them because she felt that their antics would have amused Mrs. Chase.

In accordance with her wishes that no fuss be made, no church service was held. She had also requested that burial take place as soon as possible so the committal services were held the next afternoon in Jericho, Vermont, her birthplace. The pallbearers were all former employees - clerks and bell-boys.

For hours after her death became known the hotel phones rang constantly.

People called from all over the country asking that the funeral be delayed so that they might attend, but her wishes were honored and there was no postponement....

After her death and for the remainder of the Great Depression the hotel operated on a small scale. About 1946 the Loon Lake House was sold to a syndicate which also owned another place in Florida. This firm continued to run it for a number of years.

In the early 1950's it was operated as a summer camp for girls and boys.

About midnight on September 19, 1956, fire broke out in the kitchen of the Main House. The flames quickly spread and in a short time the great oblong structure was ablaze. Since the place had been closed for the season several weeks previously, there were only a few men available to fight the fire. The water pressure also proved to be inadequate, so by the time that help could get there from neighboring villages, it was already too late. Fortunately, a change in the wind direction saved the large annexes and nearby cottages. The conflagration marked the end of another era for this famous old summer resort, for it could never again operate on the same large scale.

In recent years the place has changed hands several times and rumors have been spread that it will get a new lease on life, but except for a cottage colony, nothing outstanding has developed.

Although the old Loon Lake has now become just another fascinating phase of Adirondack history, there are still a dwindling few of us who worked there and "knew it when." For us the very mention of the place evokes pleasant memories of it and the person who made it memorable - the unforgettable, unforgotten Mrs. Chase.

Chapter 5

Meacham — Then and Now

Very little is known about the early history of Meacham Lake and that little still leaves a great deal to conjecture. As was all too often the case with other pioneer Adirondack localities, the white man whose name is now on the land was usually only a seasonal occupant of a bark shanty (or shantee) on the shore of the lake. The water and the dense surrounding forest provided a seemingly unlimited supply of trout, fur and venison so early visitors acted accordingly. Those who followed certainly made the most of this wilderness paradise — and also made no attempt to conceal or control their killer instincts, not only for their own food but for the commercial market as well.

But even before Thomas Meacham, who called Hopkinton in neighboring St. Lawrence County his home, discovered this beautiful body of water and gave it his name, the far-ranging Mohawk Indians had already been there ahead of him. On either side of their reservation at Hogansburg two fairly large rivers — the Salmon and the St. Regis — flow into the majestic St. Lawrence. With such convenient waterways at their doorstep, it is safe to surmise that these wilderness rovers had followed both streams to their sources.

Either waterway would provide a readily accessible point of entry, the harder by the Hatch Brook tributary and the easier via either the East Branch of the St. Regis River or the Deer River. The river passages to Meacham would require comparatively few difficult carries.

Probably it is also unnecessary to point out that the Indian canoes and dugouts drew only a few inches of water. Moreover, these rivers which are sizable even today, then had a far greater and more constant flow of water. This held true until extensive and intensive lumbering operations practically denuded the country of its mature evergreen cover.

Along the northern and western approaches to Meacham the first trees to succumb were the salable stands of lofty white pines, many 60 inches in diameter and 165 feet high. Many specimens nearer the great river had diameters of 84 inches and heights of nearly 250 feet. Some of these were used for local lumber but most of them were rafted down the St. Lawrence to Montreal, where they were sold as masts for vessels of the British Navy. According to Seaver the best of these timbers commanded prices as high as $3,000 to $4,000 each in the coin of the realm.

Next to topple were the hemlocks. In this case, during the early 1800's only the bark was taken for its tannin content used in curing leather; the skinned logs were left to rot where they had been felled. Finally, during the last of the 19th century and well into this one, the spruces and balsams were leveled to feed the hungry blades of sawmills and paper-mills which sprang up on nearly every good-sized stream. Only the most remote and steeply mountainous areas survived the onslaught of "progress." The Meacham region was somewhat spared until the 1930's.

Thomas Meacham undoubtedly made his way up the St. Regis to this game-filled solitude, where, for a while at least, he seems to have had a natural monopoly. His nearest neighbor must have been John De Bar, a Canadian hunter and trapper who in 1817 had discovered his own promised land on the lovely little pond some six miles away over the shoulder of the mountain that also bears his name. Although there is no existing report of the game that fell before his or his son Lyman's gun, it is likely that he could boast about the same sort of gory glory which appeared in Meacham's obituary when he died at Hopkinton in May, 1849. The impressively repulsive (by conservationist standards) total consisted of the following: 77 panthers, 214 wolves, 210 bears and 2,550 deer. How many tons of trout he caught was not considered worthy of mention. Is it any wonder then that within 25 years sportsmen were complaining bitterly that the more accessible Adirondack areas had been practically fished out and hunted out?

Apparently, during the decade before he died and possibly even before, Meacham did not continue to have undisputed sole claim to his lake. Guides from the Shattagee (Chateaugay) Woods had included this area in their wanderings and knew enough about it to convoy their sportsmen-employers there. The first of the latter to write of his experiences in that section was S.H. Hammond, an Albany journalist who was in quest of both health and sport. Tucker, his guide, who haled from the Chazy Lake section of the Great North Woods, was thoroughly familiar with the entire Saranac watershed. Hammond wrote two books about this trip, which was probably made in 1852, entitled *Hills, Lakes and Forest Streams* and *Hunting Adventures in the Northern Wilds*. They are except for small details only one book, published first in 1854 and again in 1856, but with a fresh title. The three startling illustrations in the latter book all feature Tucker's spine-chilling encounters with the Mohawk and are of course in suitably gaudy colors.

However misrepresentative the duplication may be, this book can still generate a great deal of unalloyed interest. Not so rhapsodic as Hoffman, Headley, or Street in particular, it is nevertheless very satisfying reading. Tucker's tall stories and Hammond's enthusiastic and genuine love of the woods make it an Adirondack classic. The same guide bragged about the way he had run a half-breed family out of the Meacham Woods some years before for crusting deer, a reprehensible habit which he himself occasionally indulged in, and an early example of minority persecution.

Unusual about this tramp through the Chateaugay Woods, as Hammond subtitled his book, is the fact that they came overland most of the way from the Chateaugay Lakes. They followed the township lines which James Frost, a surveyor for the James Duane iron interests, had run during an eighty-day period in 1822. So the area was being gradually opened up. Interestingly enough, Hammond and Tucker found a pole and bark shantee — probably Meacham's and after making needed repairs, occupied it during their stay.

Not long after the death of Meacham and Hammond's stay at the lake, a woman named "Aunt Mary" Wine, as Seaver called her in his *Historical Sketches of Franklin County*, lived in a cabin on the shore. She and her son "put up" visitors in a rather homespun way. Crude quarters but warm hospitality. After the Civil War John B. Titus built a bigger structure; he sold it to Henry Woodford, who in turn was bought out in 1872 by Isaac Chesley and Alonzo R. Fuller, both of Malone. They also added other buildings and made many needed improvements. The first hotel consisted of several separate buildings connected by porches, an arrangement necessary for both convenience and fire

Alonzo [Lon] Fuller, Manager of Meacham Hotel

protection.

Mr. Chesley remained a partner for only a short time — just a season or two to get the place on a going basis. Mrs. Chesley also helped out by doing the cooking and the house-work. After the dissolution of the partnership Mr. Fuller managed the hotel alone for about twenty-five years.

Mabel Chesley, daughter of Isaac Chesley, recalled with vividness and pleasure some of those early years at Meacham and particularly her recollections of her father's partner. Lon Fuller was a born naturalist, a correspondent of both Louis Agassiz and the great periodical *Forest and Stream,* and a respected consultant on the artificial breeding of fish. In fact he was one of the first men in the state — if not the first — to stock the streams and Lake. He also knew exactly where the rarest wild flowers grew and would take privileged guest to those spots — nearby Clear Lake, the Osgood River and the Stillwater of the East Branch of the St. Regis below the bridge over the Outlet.

Mr. Fuller loved all forms of wildlife and intensely disliked seeing or even hearing about any animal being killed. Miss Chesley had a coal-black kitten named Weety, who was a very slinky and successful stalker of immature or not-too agile quadrupeds — usually baby rabbits, squirrels or chipmunks. The ebony-hued feline seldom ate her prey but, pleased as punch, she would usually bring home her bloody trophies for Miss Chesley's approval. Understandably Mr. Fuller, who was well aware of Weety's hunting ability, allowed some of his revulsion toward the kitten to involve the owner also. As a consequence Mabel was sometimes excluded from the nature trips.

The hotel owner was also very careful to protect such rare plants and flowers from extermination and in every respect was an enlightened conservationist. A woman artist named Ellis, who was a frequent guest there, often accompanied Mr. Fuller on the jaunts to see arbutus or unusual swamp flowers. People who have seen her paintings say that they showed exceptional talent.

Lon (Mr. Fuller) also owned a fine set of Audubon's works — but not the so-called Elephant folio — which was a great source of pleasure to him. These he kept under lock and key and displayed them only when he was certain that the other person was sincerely interested. When the first hotel burned to the ground about 1900, the prized prints were destroyed. It was such a blow to him that he never wanted to even talk about them again.

This gifted gentleman seemed to be more concerned with nature than with business and therefore did not prosper as did other Adirondack resort owners such as Paul Smith, the Stevens brothers of Lake Placid or the Chases of the Loon Lake House. Many of his business deals turned slightly sour, and as a result he eventually was forced to sell the place. Later he removed to Malone where he had formerly owned a jewelry store in partnership with Oscar Ballard, his brother-in-law. A.R. Fuller, unquestionably the best known of the Meacham hotel owners, died in 1912.

A double tragedy occurred at Meacham during the season of 1883 or '84. One bright day in early summer the same Oscar Ballard already mentioned and a relative named Wainwright left the hotel on a fishing trip down the lake. When they did not return in time for dinner that night, nobody was worried because the weather was perfect and besides when the fishing is exceptionally good, food seems rather unimportant. The hours went by and finally the people at the hotel became somewhat anxious. When morning came and they still had not returned, a group of men set out to find out what had happened.

The searching party located the boat, which had somehow overturned. The bodies were later recovered and buried in Malone, where a high degree of sympathetic excitement prevailed for several days.

Sharing with Mr. Fuller the honor of being the most unforgettable character in Mabel Chesley's childhood recollections was Chief Justice Frank Hiscock of the New York State Court of Appeals. This gentleman, who with his family spent many years at Meacham, was the epitome of charm. According to his young admirer he arrived there late one evening. The next morning when he entered the dining room he greeted everyone as though he had known him for years and placed a high value on that friendship. His gallantry, wit and good nature were so pronounced that she never forgot her first impression of a remarkable man.

About five years earlier, on Oct. 29, 1877 to be exact, another prominent New York State official spent the night at Meacham. Characteristically enough he does not mention the warmth of the hospitality shown by host or guests. Instead, on page 184 of his *Third to Seventh Report on the Topo-Survey of the Adirondack Region,* Verplanck Colvin merely mentioned staying overnight and getting an early start for De Bar Mountain on the morning of the 30th. Anyone who has read the reports of this single-minded man knows that his preoccupation, which bordered on obsession, was to get on with his great mission in life — surveying the Adirondack wilderness. Creature comforts such as soft beds and gourmet foods were trivialities to him, and the men who worked with him. Mills Blake for one, and those who worked under his supervision, seldom got the opportunity to feel pampered.

If Colvin did not seem to appreciate the relative luxury of Meacham's hostelry, he certainly became almost poetically enthusiastic over the view from De Bar Mountain. Here are his exact words: "But telescope was needless to show the grand features of the scene below. Glittering lakes, set in a forest of emerald evergreen, or margined with tamaracks still clad in the golden foliage of fall, shone far and near. Wild mountain masses rose in dark tumultuous billows eastward, where Whiteface, capped with snow, gleamed in Alpine grandeur. Still further northward the flattened crest and clustering lower peaks of Lyon Mountain (densely forest-covered from foot to crown) stretched across the horizon, an obstacle to vision; then the rocky front of Owl's Head, in Bellmont showed itself, and the

First Meacham Lake Hotel [Burned about 1900]

brows of the hills above Malone. Northwestward stretched the vast plain of Canada, and clearly defined between a breadth of dark blue water, like a great band from west to east showed the St. Lawrence, the father of the northern waters." This is a far more eloquent tribute than that of Haviland which was frequently quoted.

In 1894 or '95 when A.R. Fuller was forced to relinquish his ownership of the Meacham Hotel, a firm of Malone men headed by M.E. McClary assumed control. S.M. Howard was the new manager and he proved to be very efficient and pleasant. He held that position until 1907 when the management changed hands once again, with William G. Rockefeller the next owner. George W. Cushman was appointed manager and presumably remained in charge until the season of 1918, when Arthur H. Mould took over.

At the start of the 1921 season Robert Stevens, who had previously managed the McCollom's Hotel, became the next one in charge. Mr. Stevens had been on the job only a short time when fire, that dreaded scourge of the forest, broke out. Thirteen years previously, in Oct. 1908, a disastrous fire had burned over part of De Bar Mountain and devoured 6,000 acres before it was brought under control. That conflagration was traced to sparks from a locomotive on the New York Central. Then too the first hotel had been destroyed by flames less than ten years before that.

The fire that leveled the second hotel at Meacham took place on May 9, 1921. There had been very little rain that Spring and everything was tinder dry. The day started uneventfully with Mr. Stevens working in his office. The fires in the kitchen stove were being shaken down in preparation for the day's cooking. Suddenly from the garden where he was ploughing George DeBar shouted, "Roof's afire!" He had just happened to glance toward the roof and saw a small patch of smoldering cedar shingles. As he later told L. Harris Hiscock, who retold it in his article entitled *"Fire in the North,"* which appeared in the September-October issue of *The Ad-i-ron-dac* for 1955, he (DeBar) declared that he could have put it out in a minute or so if there had been a ladder and a bucket of water handy.

59

Second Meacham Hotel [Burned May, 1921]

As the photograph shows, even though the building was only four stories high, there would have been only a few very crucial minutes during which to get the jump on the flames. Unfortunately, since there was neither ladder nor bucket of water available, the fire got a head start — and in a short half hour's time the second hotel was reduced to charred timbers and smoking ashes. Two Meacham Lake hotels — and both reduced to rubble within a period of only twenty-one years.

So many other of the older wooden hotels shared the same fate — Ayer's Hotel on Lake Duane (in 1918), McCollom's (1924), Paul Smith's (1930) and the Main House of Loon Lake Hotel (1956). Within the relatively small radius of sixteen miles, fires also have wiped out the railroad station at Gabriels, part of the sanitarium there and the original St. John's in the Wilderness at Paul Smith's. Even closer at hand, just before World War I, flames also razed the palatial (20-25 rooms) log mansion built by the Babbitt soap family and later known as the Hyde Cottage on Meacham. Then, too, Schroeder's first mansion at nearby DeBar Pond had also fallen easy prey to fire nearly forty years before — about 1882.

The above disasters are limited to only a comparatively small area of the Adirondacks. Just how many other resort hotels have also shared the same fiery fate is unknown, but an appalling number it must be. Moreover, the regrettable aspect is that many of these structures might have been spared had more precaution been taken. Although in many instances, as at Meacham, indications of alertness were present, the same awareness of the consequences of carelessness was not prevalent.

Numerous instances of incredible carelessness can be cited, just one of which can be considered typical. A not-very-bright kitchen-maid shook down a cooking stove and then dumped the hot ashes into a pile of refuse near kerosene drums, causing one hotel — McCollom's — to become just a flaming memory.

Utter heedlessness on the part of supposedly practical people — natives in fact — caused the great fire of 1903 which burned Van Hoevenbergh's huge Adirondack Lodge. Those men simply did not take the trouble to put out a big stump fire which they had set in the South Meadows in order to clear more land for farming! Even more recently a convivial hunting party, either too lazy or too befuddled to build a fire in the fireplace provided, deliberately started one on the floor of the Conservation Department leanto at Scott's Clearing. The fire produced far more heat than the occupants needed — and the State had a small rebuilding project on its hands.

Sparks from railroad locomotives; fires left unextinguished by picnickers, campers and "sportsmen"; fires set by farmers to clear their land the easy way — all these and many other causes have devastated great tracts of forest land. Viewed at first hand, as the writer has done on several occasions when he has assisted in the infernoish aftermath, such holocausts produce indelible impressions. When one has seen nearly 2,000 acres of the Goldsmith range luridly light up the night sky, the memory of that spectacle remains evergreen and explains why said writer has strong opinions on the subject. Furthermore, it has often forced him to ponder the fascination engendered by the uses, misuses and abuses — especially the last — of Prometheus' great gift to man. Small wonder then that rangers and fire-wardens don't exactly look forward with delight to each new Summer and hunting season.

With all due apologies for the above pertinent detours, let us get back to Meacham. Fortunately, as was the case at both Paul Smith's and the Loon Lake House, the annexes and adjoining cottages at Meacham were all far enough away so that they were untouched. The large laundry building and the big boathouse were still there, so the former became the dining room. The cottagers — families such as the Dennys, Austins, Skinners, Hiscocks and Warnicks — were not discouraged. William G. Rockefeller, the owner, arrived and accompanied by his manager, sized up the situation. After a brief inspection Mr. Rockefeller turned to Mr. Stevens and remarked, "Well, sir, in another year we'll build again and then you'll see : we'll soon have a fine little hotel!"

Ironically enough the owner never saw the place again. The next Spring he went to a baseball game in New York, got a cold, pneumonia set in and he died shortly after.

Sometime previously the wealthy owner had bought the property for the reported sum of $35,000. The holding, besides the hotel and buildings, had included more than 6,000 acres of timberland. The hotel management had also leased hunting and fishing rights on an additional 134,000 acres but this of course was not included in the sale.

After the death of the millionaire owner the choice property was once again on the market. Roy Kellas of Malone, who was Rockefeller's lawyer and local representative, tried to persuade Mr. Stevens to buy it with financial assistance from the International Paper Co. However, when officials of that company gave the matter more serious consideration, they decided against the investment and the deal fell through. Incidentally, the Kellas mentioned is the same lawyer who defended Rockefeller in the famous Lemora case, which by the way was tried before Zeke Perkins, well-known guide and local justice of the peace, in Zeke's home at Duane Center.

Another prospective buyer, this time the West Virginia Paper Co., sent a team of six timber cruisers to Meacham. Their report showed that they did not think that there was quite enough stumpage there to make it a good buy. Moreover, at that time the price of pulp had dropped appreciably.

Robert Stevens, who had managed the Hotel from 1921-28, left there at this time to accept a position as outdoor superintendent at Saranac Inn, where he stayed for eighteen years. His departure marked the end of an era and the end of Meacham as a resort hotel because it was never rebuilt. Afterward Chauncey Davis was in charge during the next two years while the tract was being lumbered. Mr. Davis later managed Elk Lake Lodge for many years.

Early in the 1930's the property was sold by the Rockefeller interests to the Johnson Lumber Co., of Little Rapids, New York. According to the local guides who knew the timber cruisers, the pulp harvest was worth $1,000,000. By this time also the State had stepped into the picture and restricted the purchaser from logging on the east or lake side of Route 10, the main highway. At that time our Conservation Department was just starting to develop what has since become one of the largest campsites in the mountains. This action saved from the pulpmill's maw many of the impressive stands of evergreens which nearly encircled the Lake.

The Johnson Company started its operations soon thereafter and used Meacham as a storage basin for the pulp logs. The writer can recall seeing thousands of them covering the entire water area of the big roadside Carpenter's Bay. At that time also the remaining cottages and buildings were torn down.

By now some readers have probably begun to wonder just when the vital statistics of this attractive nook of the north would be given and just what was and still is the source of its allure. The lake itself is three miles long and two miles wide. The inlet is the winding Osgood river, which flows into the lake on the south side; the outlet is the East Branch of the St. Regis river. Although none of the high peaks of the Adirondacks are visible from the lake level, Loon Lake, DeBar and St. Regis mountains, all topped by fire towers, are there to gaze at.

Other geographic details established the following facts: Meacham is 16 miles from Gabriels, which was the station on the Adirondack Division of the New York Central which served as the usual arrival and departure point. It is also 12 miles from Paul Smith's and 25 miles from Malone, the Star of the North. The elevation is 1650 feet. Furthermore, there are three beaches, the most popular and largest of these, which is right in front of the main camping and picnicking area, has a smooth, sandy bottom which very gradually slopes downward. A person can wade out nearly 100 yards before getting into deep water. The other two beaches, which are across the lake and down toward the outlet, while not quite so convenient, smooth and extensive, are nevertheless never crowded. And that certainly is a big factor in their favor.

The people who like bass, pickerel, perch and some lake-trout trolling, the latter usually in the Spring, can get plenty of action. The fabulous speckled trout fishing has long since become just a memory. Concerning those halcyonic days the late Clarence Briggs of Malone, in a reminiscent mood, told me that even in the late 1890's he could wade out into the lake at the mouth of Winnebago Brook and catch his limit in a few short evening hours — and by his limit he meant a small washtub full. Brook trout of course have no chance of survival in a lake teeming with voracious pickerel and perch whose choicest tidbits are trout eggs or fingerlings.

Therefore, the fisherman who prefers native trout, as I do, heads for the remoter streams and ponds. There are, however, easily reached streams nearby — such as the unposted stretches of Hayes Brook and Duane stream, the East Branch of the Hatch Brook and the East Branch of the St. Regis River well below the bridge over the outlet. There are numerous other productive streams and ponds which can be located by merely consulting a topographical map of the Loon Lake and Santa Clara quadrangles.

I feel reasonably well qualified to extol Meacham's praises because of my frequent trips there over a period of forty years. As a Boy Scout from nearby Malone I spent two fleeting weeks there in 1920. Maurice Plumb and Leon Colton were the leaders of our troop, and Bill Center of Duane was the guide-cook. Our tent site was the clearing across Route 10 from the old boat landing. Still vivid in my recollection are some of those evenings we saw as many as twenty deer feeding on lily-pads, drinking or else seeking watery relief from the persistent flies by wading out until their backs were covered. Great days those for youngsters on their first real forest outing!

Understandably, most stress has been given to the Meacham of the old days. Some details relating to the present — particularly the constant development of the area by our State Conservation Department — have been included. Except for the swampy section around the Osgood Inlet the lake is now ringed by campsites.

The Meacham of today, like any sizeable scenically-endowed body of water, has become a very accessible Shangri-la for thousands of campers and picnickers. On weekends the lake is alive with outboards, some operated with water-cowboy recklessness; the parking lot is jammed, the picnic tables are crowded and all the available campsites have long since been occupied and several hundred people will have been turned away.

On a typical holiday weekend, if the weather forecast has been favorable, many bus loads of our neighbors from across the Border will have arrived to swell the crowd. On such a weekend the population count will frequently approximate over 2,000. This means that there are probably more visitors there on that one day than there were different guests registered at the two successive hotels during the fifty-five year period of their existence, taking into consideration the fact that many of the guests returned year after year.

Therefore it would seem that the word Meacham has come to connote vacation pleasure to many thousands of nature-minded people. And it certainly has every ingredient required of a summertime mecca — a beautiful lake; the Osgood and St. Regis rivers; three beaches, the largest of which is unrivalled in the Adirondacks; mountains on the horizon and stands of evergreens everywhere. In short, Meacham most emphatically has everything that it takes to produce memorable vacations.

This is Meacham then and now but, before closing, one more reference to the *then* should wind this up in a properly reminiscent manner. The following statement or ad appeared in the little brochure put out by the Lake Meacham Hotel Company for the season of 1907:

"Consider the Following Rates and Apply Early."

Our hotel accommodates over 100 guests and the rates are as follows:

Per day . . . .$ 3.00 and upward
Per week . . . .$17.50 and upward
Children same rates as adults.

When two persons occupy the same room, reasonable concessions are obtained.
Special reduction for June."

It seems that we have spent hundreds of years getting out of the woods. Now, in response to an almost atavistic craving for more primitive exercise and adventure, we are trying to get back there again. A person would have to do a lot of looking around before he found a more convenient vacation spot than Meacham.

The Meacham Guides

Chapter 6

The Meacham Guides

The heyday of the Meacham Lake guides covered the era from 1870 to the outbreak of World War I and probably reached its peak during the double decade just prior to 1900. In that golden age the Lake Meacham House, under the management of the much-loved and greatly-respected Lon (Alonzo) Fuller, attracted many wealthy guests and kept them coming back for years. Its obvious natural assets of wide waters, dense forests and modestly magnificent mountain setting were to a considerable degree supplemented by its group of outstanding guides.

These were not of the type satirized so devastatingly by Pieter Fosburgh in his widely-read *"Goyd"* essay. Apparently the Meacham variety was many cuts above the average Minerva product because few if any employers of the former brand ever went on record and thus seemingly never had grounds for serious complaint about either their guides' competence or their character.

This same clever and esteemed author raised a rather interesting question in the more than somewhat acerbic essay in *The Natural Thing*.[1] He maintained the guides ("Goyds" to him) in his particular neck of the woods were/are predisposed to pamper and pad their pork-filled, portly personages with superfluous strata of clothes — both inner and outer. But in some degree of well-concealed wonderment he also asked why they (the goyds) should really overdo things a bit by wearing both belt and suspenders (galluses they called them way up there in far-famed Franklin County).

The explanation for this apparent sartorial redundancy is simple and understandable: the belts make assurance doubly sure when the seemingly slower-witted Essex County character (Goyd) sheds his packbasket. It is quite conceivable that he might clumsily grab said suspenders along with the basketstraps and, in one maladroit movement, divest himself of both pants and his dignity. The belts therefore reinforced his aplomb as well as his paunch.

Nor were there many if any of the Meacham men who would fall into the category labeled by the gifted late W.C. White in his classic *Adirondack Country* as being "courteous scoundrelly guides." Granted that they were uncommonly courteous and unscoundrelly and possibly some of them did, as a caustic observer of 1879 guidehood quoted by White whimsically "fall out of their log cradles into a pair of top boots, discard their bottles for pipes, possess themselves of a boat and a jacknife and become forthwith

---

1. Fosburgh, Pieter. *The Natural Thing: The Land and Its Citizens.* N.Y.C., Macmillan, 1959

full-fledged veteran guides."[2]

Moreover, considerable checking by this writer has so far failed to uncover evidence that any of the many Meacham guides was ever objectionably impudent, lazy, extortionate, cadging, capricious or more careless with the truth than was occasionally necessary. Naturally their story-telling skill sometimes depended for effect upon "those corroborative details which lend artistic verisimilitude to an otherwise bald and uninteresting narrative" (credit W.S. Gilbert, *The Mikado*).

The men of Meacham were colorful enough, capable and forceful enough to have made profound impressions on many of the guests of all ages who returned to that resort for a long series of idyllic summers. Even though no Chittenden, Dawson, Headley, Hoffman, Murray, Stoddard, Street or Warner ever went there and therefore could never immortalize them in prose, several of the guides did receive much more than a local reputation and a name.

The earliest of these guides, as a matter of fact, did not even hail from the Duane area proper. Joe Tucker, S.H. Hammond's guide, made Chazy his home. He and Pete Meigs, an even older Shatagee (Chateaugay) guide, knew well the scenic Meacham-St. Regis area because they had traversed it often prior to 1850.

Then, in the early 1870's, even more recognition — but still far from the fame the greater writers granted Sabattis, Dunning, Cheney, Phelps — came to the Meacham woodsrunners. E.R. Wallace of Syracuse cited two of the region's guides — Al Burr and Chris Crandall — in his *Descriptive Guide to the Adirondacks.* (1875 edition)

Getting his information from Christie Fay of Malone, a well-known artist, photographer and sportsman of that time, and his friend Haviland, Wallace credited Al, father of Bert Burr, a great guide in his own right later on, as being a noted trapper and guide — "A man with a history. Years ago he moved in good society in our town but, on account of some affair of the heart, he retired to the wilderness, where he has remained a recluse ever since." What the informant couldn't know was that the hermit must have relented shortly afterwards because he returned to civilization, married and sired at least one son, Bert.

"Chris Crandall," wrote Haviland for Wallace, "is certainly a noteworthy man — of gigantic frame, long waving hair and beard — a harelip adding considerably to his beauty — and looking altogether the beau ideal of the forest ranger. Years ago, while out still-hunting with a friend miles away from habitation and in the dead of winter, he was accidentally shot in the hip with a rifle ball. He lay in the desolate woods all the long night upon a few branches hastily piled together. His gun had been taken from him by his companion for fear the poor fellow in his agony might destroy himself. There he lay without a fire all that fearful night — tortured, freezing and longing for death — hearing nought but the sighing of the wind through the snow-laden branches or perchance the cry of some wild beast in search of its prey. Assistance came the next day and he was carried out the seven long miles to the settlement. There his leg was amputated and his life saved.

"Indeed it seems incredible that a one-legged man should be able to act as an efficient hunter and guide — in fact be noted for his useful qualifications. Yet, nevertheless, such is the case with Crandall and I know of no better guide in the Chateaugay Woods."

The loss of his leg apparently handicapped this determined man in only one respect: he could not track a guideboat up the St. Regis River because his pegleg would get caught in the stones of the stream-bed and thus cause him to lose both his balance and his sense of humor.

---

1. Cook, Marc. *The Wilderness Cure*: N.Y.C., William Wood & Co., 1881

Two Meacham Guides — left, Lute Trimm; right, Dave Mix

Years later the indomitable Crandall and his wife found that life together was intolerable, so Chris manfully and emphatically solved the problem by building a cabin for himself just across the road. Still later on, unhappy in many respects and finding life itself to be personally unendurable, he ended it with a blast from his Winchester.

The first settlers in the Duane-Meacham region needed no special training to become guides. They either learned how to live with and off their wilderness bailiwick or they left their bones in the woods. Then into their environs came surveyors such as Frost and Colvin and artists-sportsmen such as Tait, Fay and Haviland who were willing to pay the local men well for doing what they did for themselves nearly every day of their lives.

Some of these early residents were so competent, so remarkable that they overshadowed their contemporaries as MacIntyre overtops Mt. Jo. This was especially true of the men who followed Burr and Crandall. In the considered opinion of both their employers and their fellow-guides, only six men really rated being selected as notably outstanding; furthermore, all of these men were "private" guides, the aristocrats of the profession.

Of the half-dozen so tabbed as being the best of their calling two were DeBars — father Lyme and son George. Lyme (Lyman), in the opinion of men well qualified to make such distinctions, was considered to be the best tracker and surest shot in the region. A large, gay-hearted man he was the son of John DeBar, a French-Canadian voyageur who in 1817 had migrated south and settled on the shore of a picturesque pond in what was called Duane. Both the pond and the majestic mountain, now tower-topped, which overshadows it, have been given the family name.

Lyme was also long remembered for his long black hair which he would let grow for as much as two years at a time before cutting it. Such was his pride in his tresses that he and another guide, golden-haired Ike Tucker, would sell their curls to hero-worshipping youngsters and impressionable adults.

George DeBar, while not so flamboyant as his father, inherited his uncanny knack of knowing the ways of the woods animals. So successful was he as a hunter that few indeed were the parties he guided that ever came back empty-handed. He also had an appreciable and appreciated talent for telling stories and his yarns never seemed to lose their savor. His lifetime kill of deer was about 400, the largest a 24-pointer. Fifty bears, two on one memorable day, went down before his rifle. With the passage of the years most of his hunting had to be done in memory only. Then on November 27, 1940, at the end of the deer season, having reached the ripe old age of 86, the venerable hunter died in his cabin in Duane. All three DeBars — John, Lyme and George — were eminently worthy of the title "mighty hunter." The second and third were also great guides.

The biggest man in size, strength and reputation (his photograph had several times been on the cover of a nationally-circulated sporting magazine) was Lute (Lucien) Trimm. Lute was unquestionably the most powerful man in the Meacham Woods. Nearly 6 feet 4 inches tall and weighing around 225 he understandably had little need to assert himself. People just naturally agreed with him and seldom, in their right mind, crossed him. For a period of 38 years he guided Governor Lounsbury of Connecticut, first at Meacham and later on at Raquette Lake. For many years he was supervisor of the Town of Duane and the perennial vice-president of the Malone Fish and Game Club. Lute lived to be 72 and died October 29, 1929 in the little family home near his loved Horseshoe Pond on the Red Tavern Road, Duane.

Just what his contemporaries thought of him is well exemplified by a clipping from the Malone *Evening Telegram* some years after his death. It seems that a group of college boys up for their summer vacation were discussing the outcome of the Poughkeepsie Regatta of that year. An Old-Timer lounging nearby listened in with great interest. "I s'pose," the oldster asked, "that the best oarsman in all them crews you're talkin' about would be quite a feller, eh? D'ye think he could beat one of the old guides — that is a youngun in his prime?"

The collegians smiled indulgently. One of them observed with nice respect for the old man's opinion that the college oarsman of that day was a highly-trained athlete. That such a contest as was suggested would be as unfair as watching John L. Sullivan working on a clumsy lumberjack. Unfair that is for the lumberjack . . .

"Wall now, I dunno," the oldster cut in: "Reminds me of jest sech a race I once saw on Meacham 50-odd years ago." He then told the following story to the little circle of college boys who listened ever more raptly as he went on.

"This race I'm tellin' about," the old man continued, "was back when there was plenty of summer doin's at Meacham. Always had about 25 or 30 guides there. Ev'ry season they was races for the guests and races for the guides.

"They was a young fellow up thar this summer I'm tellin' you about — a strappin' big cuss with a pair of shoulders wider'n the south end of a Percheron hoss. He was a crewman and he'd a contraption that looked like a long toothpick in the water. Boy, he sure could lift it along too!

"Come the day of the races an' he refused to compete with the guests — insisted on entering the event for the guides! When it finally sugared off they was only him and Lute

Trimm left in the race. They was also some heavy bettin' on the side.

"I'member it was a three-sided course an' the college feller left Lute at the start like he was hitched to a post. Looked like they want enathin' to it atall, a-tall!

"Lute he kep' right on rowin' without even botherin' to look aroun' even once. That college shell was skimmin' the water like it was flyin' but Lute's skiff was cuttin' a pow'ful swathe in the water too and leavin' a wake of bubbles and ripples behind! To watch him you'd think he want worried or workin' — jest rowin' in a steady, slow-like motion like a river runnin' strong.

"They rounded the secon' post with the college boy headed down the stretch to the finish line. It still looked like a runaway an' the guides were startin' to mutter that it want 'zactly the fairest test. 'Oughta put 'em in guideboats," someone said.

"Then Lute he rounded the second post an' for the fust time he condescen's t'turn in his seat and squint over his shoulder at the boat up ahead. Then he seemed t'lean over sidewise toward the water like he wus doin' somethin'.

"Lute's spittin' out his chaw! (cud of tobacco) Watch'm come now!' yelled Lyme DeBar. An' just about then the bow of Lute's boat began to lift an' sing across the water. Ev'ry time he'd pull them oars the boat'd lunge ahead like it was bein' goosed. Well, sir, Lute closed up all that gap and won the race with plenty to spare!"

The old-timer then recalled that a little while afterward Lute went over to the college boy, put a hand on his shoulder and said, "Son, you certainly had me scared. You needn't worry about anything, oncet you get back to school!"

The young fellow then shook the guide's hand and said, "I certainly wouldn't worry about anything down there, sir, if you could coach our crew!"

Another of the better Meacham guides was Zeke Perkins who, like Lute had also been born in Duane. He too from boyhood on had familiarized himself with every stream, pond and hill in the region. For 50 years Zeke was employed by Col. William Skinner, president of Colt Arms, first at Meacham, later at Camp Florence, the forest estate near the Deer River, and at the camp on the St. Regis stillwater.

The Colonel was a large man who preferred trout-fishing to hunting so Zeke was his guide on many trips up the Osgood or down the St. Regis (East Branch) and the Deer Rivers.

Congenial, capable, loyal and a crack shot into the bargain Zeke was a fine example of what a first-class guide should be. He also served well his little community as justice of the peace for many years and acquired additional recognition while presiding over the proceedings connected with the much-publicized Rockefeller-Lamora feud preliminary hearing.

As tangible and generous proof of Zeke's popularity and ability Col. Skinner gave him a sizable pension when he got too old to guide. As further evidence of the affection felt for him all three of the Colonel's children — two sons and a daughter — each of whom Zeke had taught to fish, shoot and handle boats, attended the funeral when on January 3, 1941 the high-respected old guide died in North Bangor at the ripe old age of 81. In compliance with Col. Skinner's request Zeke was buried in one of Ballard's (All Wool and a Yard Wide!) best woolen hunting mackinaws and pants.

The fifth of the outstanding Meacham woods-runners was George Selkirk who also like both DeBars, Lute Trimm and Zeke Perkins spent nearly all his life in Duane. As a young man he had been a carpenter before deciding to become a guide. A very pleasant personality and a way with men and guns gave him an enviable rating both as a person and a guide. His long-time employers were the Hiscock, Austin, Coleman and Barlow families.

In 1900 his career in the woods — and very nearly his life — was cut short and almost ended by a hunting accident. Accompanied by another guide, Rob Ladd, George was walking down a trail near Meacham when a shot from a target shooter's rifle hit him in the groin and damaged his pelvis. Dunbar, the "sport" who fired the almost fatal bullet, had carelessly shot at a mark without taking the usual precaution of checking first to see if anyone else was in the area.

The injured man was taken in a wagon to Malone, then transported to a Montreal hospital where he spent the next 45 weeks in a painfully slow recovery. Eventually, however, following further treatment he recuperated well enough to guide many other parties.

When he finally gave up guiding for good, he was appointed a game protector. Still later he became the local justice of the peace, a position he held up to the time of his death. This occurred on October 4, 1937, during his 81st year at his home which he so aptly had named Peaceful Valley.

The last of the cited group of remarkable Meacham guides was Bert Burr, son of the Al Burr mentioned in Wallace's guidebooks. Bert was probably the most respected man of them all as far as personal attributes were concerned. Soft-spoken, friendly, kind he was also one of those rare creatures among guides — a teetotaler. His neighbors maintain even to this day that Bert was without question the finest man they had ever known. The late George Clark of Bronxville, for whom Bert guided over a period of 20 years, loved him "even better than a brother."

Like all the other guides Bert served his apprenticeship by watching the older men in action and absorbing all the advice and information they could give him. Then too of course by carefully studying the habits of the big game animals he was able to learn a great deal by himself. Bert shot his first deer when he was 13 and went on from there to become one of the region's best hunters and guides.

Besides Mr. Clark three other New York area men — a Mr. Green, Mr. Denny and Mr. Austin — kept him busy every fishing and hunting season for many years. He also guided several of these men on moose and caribou hunting trips to Canada. All told his guiding career covered more than 50 years before he became postmaster at Duane. Full of years and wonderful memories he came to the end of his mortal trail at the age of 82 in 1952.

Prompted by a sincere feeling of fairness and respect for the memory of all the other guides — living and dead — who worked at Meacham in bygone days, the writer would like at least to list their names. Lack of space and adequate information makes it impossible to do more than mention them.

Representing the older generation were the following whose names appear on page 262 in the 1875 edition of Wallace's *Descriptive Guide to the Adirondacks* and those Fuller considered the best in Stoddard's *Adirondacks Illustrated* 1880 edition:

Fred Barns, Jim Bean, Joe Clark, Bill Danforth, Charles M. Haskins, Rouse Helms, Elbridge Hyde, Meadore LaFountain, Charlie LeMay, Dan Lathrop, A.C. McCollom, George Pond, L. Rogers, Halsey Sprague, Sherman Stancliff, Charlie Selkirk, Charlie Stickney, Dave Trine and Dick Woodruff.

Other stalwarts of the next generation were Fred and John Garland, Charles H. Haskins, Bonnie Kennedy, Rob Ladd, Dave Mix, Frank Monica, Frank Murphy, Dick Newell, Lawrence Paquin, Mannie Rogers, Bill Sprague, Dave Stickney, Ed and Nate Trimm.

The writer would like to pay special tribute to the memory of Bill Center, rotund guide-cook who made unforgettable his Scouting days at Meacham at the end of World

War I.

The close of the First World War also saw the end of the era for the surviving Meacham area guides. The increase in the number of private parks and fish and game clubs and the destruction by fire of the second Meacham Lake Hotel in 1921 rang down the curtain on the golden age of guides and guiding in that part of the Adirondacks.

Early Days at McCollom's

The Second McCollom's Hotel [Burned June, 1924]

Chapter 7

The Three Macs of McCollom's

Sometime before or very soon after their hotels had been either bought or built, the owners of Adirondack inns had to face an important decision. They had to make up their minds about the type of trade or clientele which they would cater to. Some of these resorts took full advantage of their picturesque locations on lakes and nearness to main highways or railroads and generally concentrated on family business. Such hostelries were of course plushier in their accommodations.

Other hotels which sprang up in the remoter regions of the Great North Woods were much less pretentious and appealed mainly to sportsmen. McCollom's, especially during its early years, was one of the latter type, and it fully deserved its ranking as one of the few places where a reasonably competent fisherman or hunter was seldom disappointed. Once it had firmly established its reputation, there were many nights during the hunting season, which began in August in those days, when nearly as many nimrods were put up in the barns as in the crowded bedrooms.

The trout fishing was just as exceptional. Rice, Barnum, Mountain and Osgood Ponds; Hayes Brook, the Osgood River — all these then and rarely even now, yielded spectacular catches. The rapids of the Osgood, which is Meacham Lake's main inlet and less than half a mile from McCollom's, was glowingly extolled by W.C. Prime in his very readable book, *I Go A-Fishing*. This author, a recognized connoisseur of trout water, considered this to be his favorite Adirondack stream.

Amiel G. McCollom, better known as Uncle Mac in later years, had apparently heard about the wonderful game country to the south while he was working on the Ogdensburg end of the newly-built railroad which later became the Rutland. When the job was finished in 1849, he decided that the Burnt Lands (fire ravaged), as they were called, were exactly the place for him and his family.

Mac's new home, a large log structure originally built by Amos Rice, had quite a bit of extra space, so very soon the likable Scotsman became the first hotel keeper in the town of Brighton. By farming, hunting, trapping, and guiding his growing number of guests, he soon made McCollom's a place well worth the bone-jarring journey to reach it.

McCollom was rated the best trainer and judge of deer dogs in the northern Adirondacks. Prior to 1897, when that method of hunting was made illegal, deer were driven by the dogs into the lakes and rivers and were then either harried until they drowned, clubbed to death or shot at close range by the so-called "sportsmen."

Since the success of the hunt depended almost entirely on the tracking skill and training of the dogs, usually hounds, the best of these were valued highly. Not to be overlooked were the fringe benefits in the form of bets which they won for their owners, who also got double the going wage for guides — or five dollars per day. Violent arguments and frequent fights often erupted, thus adding an extra fillip to the day's sport.

A.G. McCollom, since he had settled in the area a full ten years before Apollos (Paul) Smith moved over from Loon Lake to Lower St. Regis in 1859, considered the latter to be an upstart and a johnny-come-lately. The fact that Paul was also one of the very few Democrats in the region and put on the proverbial "dog" occasionally as he became more prosperous did not exactly endear him to Mac. Separated by a short seven miles and often taking parties to the same lakes, they saw somewhat more of each other than either would have preferred.

The most memorable of their clashes took place on the narrow road between the rival hotels. Uncle Mac, driving a buckboard drawn by a single horse, had taken his wife on a shopping trip to Brandon, then a thriving little lumber town with three hotels and numerous saloons and populated by some 800 souls. It was also a station on the New York and Ottawa Railroad, so many of the guests for both resorts detrained there.(Later on, Smith built his own private electric spur line from the New York Central station at Lake Clear.)

Their shopping done, the McColloms started home. They had not gone far when a stage coach came into sight far down the road. Mac recognized it immediately as the six matched horses came closer. Leather creaked and twin clouds of dust arose as the gap between them closed until both teams were stopped short. Sitting beside the driver of the other conveyance was Paul Smith, who yelled out, "Pull over, Mac!"

Mac, usually pleasant and obliging, was in no mood to comply. He called back, "Pull over yourself!"

"Pull out, I say!" blustered Paul.

"I won't!" was Mac's rejoinder.

Although McCollom was ordinarily entitled to half the highway, road courtesy dictated that the small wagon should yield ground to the bigger, more top-heavy vehicle. But Mac was more ornery than usual.

"Now you pull out!" was the final command of the angry Apollos. "I've got the President of the United States with me." And he really did have Grover Cleveland as his special passenger that day.

That settled it. If Mac had entertained even fleetingly any intention of giving in, he was doubly sure that he wouldn't budge an inch for the despised Democrats. Therefore his next retort was heartfelt and typical. "I don't give a damn if you've got the King of England with you! *You* pull out!"

Paul, being in a hurry and knowing that he had been outshouted and outdone (which was very seldom) ordered his driver to take to the ditch in order to get by. . . .

The lean years were pretty well past by that time. By 1873 business was flourishing at McCollom's so Mac decided to get someone to help with its management. After a brief and unpleasant experience with a man named Harkness, he met just the right fellow at Schroeder's hopyards in nearby Duane. Clarence MacArthur, the second of the Macs, was a knowledgeable young man who also knew a lot about hopgrowing, a sideline which the older man was seriously considering at the time. The two men worked well together right from the start and their friendship was well founded. Because the younger Mac had some of that blood in him, the older one affectionately referred to him as his "Little Frenchman."

The hop venture was doomed from the start. Since McCollom's has an altitude of 1800 feet, frosts came early and ruined the crop. Several disappointing seasons and that unprofitable undertaking soon became only an unpleasant memory.

Another enterprise, however, was far more successful. By that time there were many so-called camps, actually imposing log lodges, which had been built on the St. Regis Chain of Lakes on land sold at fantastically high prices by the astute Paul Smith to his wealthy former guests. The occupants of these luxurious "camps" required a daily supply of milk, other dairy products and poultry, so the Macs decided to cater to those needs. A lengthy itinerary was soon set up which entailed a start from Paul Smith's soon after midnight. Ira Bassett was one of the first of a long succession of deliverymen, which included Robert Stevens and Earl MacArthur, son of the second Mac and eventual owner of the third hotel at McCollom's.

These men would make the rounds in the early morning hours, ladling out the milk from the large cans in the boats into containers held by sleepy-eyed servants. Then, rinsing the dipper in lake water, they rowed to the next dock on the list of bluechip customers, which featured names such as Carnegie, Durkee, Forest, Hotchkiss, Howe, James, McAlpin, Morton, Palmer, Reid and others.

When Dr. Edward Trudeau, one of the customers, happened to observe the more than slightly unsanitary method of dispensing the milk, he readily talked the partners into starting a model dairy, the first in the Adirondacks, and thereafter the customers drank their milk with more assurance of its purity.

The herd of cows did not belong to the hotel owners. The Macs cannily concluded that there would be little left of the profits if they had to feed the cattle during the long winter months. They got around that problem by contracting with Romanzo Joy and several other Bangor farmers who agreed to provide 50 to 60 cows for the summer season at $5.00 per head per month. It took three days for the bovines to plod the 40 odd miles along hardly more than a trail via Duane and the dense Meacham Woods to their destination.

The blueberry season provided another cash income for the Macs. Each August whole families would arrive at the far-famed Burnt Lands to pick the vast supply of berries. Some of the people came from places 30 or 40 miles distant, and a tent village would appear on the plains near the hotel. Some pickers slept in the barns or in or under the wagons. The practically inexhaustible supply of berries was picked when they were half ripe so they would keep better. Large wooden scoops were used to speed up the picking operation. Although many of the berries were sold on the spot, there were always plenty to take home.

Naturally, many of the berry-pickers were also eager consumers of McCollom's marvelous milk punch. This was a potent potation guaranteed to warm the body and fortify the ego. The ingredients were rum, a chunk of maple sugar, a dash of nutmeg, and the rest was milk. Stirred well and sipped slowly, the imbiber would relax and soon become expansive. When repeated, this seemingly innocuous nectar made the whitewashed walls of the hotel barroom seem like Parian marble, and life became indeed wonderful.

The driver of the stagecoach which brought the guests from Brandon would signal, as he drove over the brow of the hill a half mile away, to Uncle Mac, who was usually sitting on the front porch at that time of day. By his raising the whip once for each punch ordered by his passengers, the host would know exactly how many to have ready for his new arrivals. They insisted that he must have been psychic to come out right every time.

By the late 1880's Uncle Mac, who had begun to slow down considerably, turned over the operation of the hotel to his younger associate, who built a much larger structure.

Years earlier McCollom's three children had all died young, victims of virulent epidemics. This triple tragedy and his own declining health made him willing to take things

Deer Harvest at McCollom's

Camp on Hayes Brook, McCollom's

easy. Then, in 1890, his wife also died, and Mac's death, at the age of 74, came soon afterward in 1893. The McColloms were all buried in the little cemetery on the knoll a few hundred yards west of the hotel.

Another amusing story about Paul Smith is related in John Titus' *Adirondack Pioneers*. Paul and O.D. Seavey of Hotel Champlain had gone to McCollom's for a few days of Fall hunting. One day Clarence MacArthur, acting as guide, took them to Rice Lake, only a little way from the hotel. Mr. Seavey went across the lake with MacArthur to watch and Paul went in another direction. Before long a deer came in, not far from Mr. Seavey, and he began shooting. Paul started out toward them and had not gone far before in some way he tipped over the boat and went down out of sight. He soon came up and pushed the boat to where he could touch bottom. He stood there for some time with only his head and shoulders out of water. Mr. Seavey and Mr. MacArthur saw it all, and when they got to him, they asked him how it had happened. He said he jumped out on purpose, as the bullets were flying around — and he thought he would rather be under water out of the way of them and that he would rather be drowned than shot!

Clarence MacArthur, the second Mac, took over the management of the hotel. All went reasonably well until the fateful morning of March 15, 1906. About three a.m. of that day fire broke out in the cellar. The owners, who were asleep in their rooms on the second floor of the three-story building, had a narrow escape and saved themselves by jumping from the windows. Although no lives were lost, the building and its contents were a total loss, which was only partly covered by insurance.

Another bigger hotel was built from lumber cut on their own land and sawed in their own mill. The MacArthurs were back in business again. The place maintained its popularity for the surrounding forests, lakes, and streams continued to provide excellent sport. By this time, too, many improvements had been made including a nine-hole golf course and tennis courts. Additional service buildings and a row of housekeeping cottages were built on the property, which by then consisted of 600 acres of farm and timberland.

During this period Earl MacArthur, the third Mac, assisted his father in running the hotel. He also knew and loved the woods and waters as few men ever do. After his graduation from Franklin Academy, 30 miles away in Malone, he went to Yale, where he attracted considerable recognition as a football player. He later became a master at the Peddie School, Hightstown, New Jersey. For several seasons he was also in charge of the school's summer camp at Osgood Pond, near McCollom's. From 1910 to 1936 he was head coach of football at Peddie. His teams won numerous New Jersey state prep school championships, and his star players went on to further acclaim and gridiron glory. Among these was Larry Kelly, Yale's great end who became Mac's successor after the latter retired in 1936. Mr. Mac the third wrote an interesting article about his outstanding coaching career for the November 12, 1938 issue of *Saturday Evening Post*. Having served as interim president at the newly-founded Paul Smith's College, he was later on the faculty of Keuka College in the Finger Lakes region. He died May 26, 1965.

When Clarence MacArthur died in 1913, Col. William Skinner of Hartford, Connecticut, bought McCollom's from the creditors. Robert Stevens, who later was in charge of the Meacham Hotel, was its manager for four years. Then, in 1920, Earl MacArthur regained ownership and operated it during the summer season. His mother and sister Gladys ran it during the rest of the year.

For the next five years, the hotel was a moderate success. Automobiles were still far from numerous, and people still spent all or nearly all their vacation time in one place. The desire to travel farther and see more of the country had not yet sealed the doom of the smaller resorts such as McCollom's, which was still largely dependent upon the business of hunters and fishermen.

Early in the morning of June 11, 1924, disaster struck again. Fire broke out in a shed adjoining the kitchen. Women employees who discovered the blaze spread the alarm, and all the occupants of the hotel were able to escape a flaming death. Most of the people lost practically all their personal effects.

The flames were so high and the smoke so heavy that both were plainly visible at Meacham, six miles away. Robert Stevens, manager at Meacham, phoned the observer on DeBar Mountain, who reported that McCollom's was burning furiously. A large group, including Mr. and Mrs. Stevens, started at once to give whatever assistance they could. They helped save the barns, garages, cabins, and some of the parlor furniture. But within 45 minutes after the fire had been discovered the hotel itself was in ashes. The replacement cost for the building and contents was estimated at $50,000.

Since the structure was under-insured, the loss to the owner was very heavy, and no thought was given to rebuilding. For many years thereafter the MacArthurs managed the cabins, which stand on the ridge overlooking the Osgood River. (These have now deteriorated badly).

The next owner, Francis Oehmke, took possession in 1955. The present owners of the small 350 acre estate are Dr. Lawrence Sherman and Dr. Thomas Brown of Plattsburgh, who bought it from the Oehmkes in 1969. The former manager's cottage has several apartments for married Paul Smith's College students. No other accommodations are provided.

The success of an Adirondack resort hotel business always depended on at least two of its assets — the beauty of its setting and the personality of its owners. Amply endowed by nature with eye-pleasing vistas of friendly mountains and far horizons, McCollom's more than adequately satisfied the first criterion.

The three Macs — Amiel McCollom, Clarence and Earl MacArthur — each in his own way and each an unusually strong and colorful personality — gave McCollom's its enviable ranking as an outstanding sportsmen's resort. All three were industrious, genial and memorable, but the story-telling prowess of Earl, the last of the line, has become legendary in the northern Adirondacks. Assuredly these were men to match the mountains.

Chapter 8

The Banner House

What is now known as the Banner House on Lower Chateaugay Lake is one of the oldest resort hotels, if not the oldest, in the Adirondacks. The first proprietor was Jonathan Bellows, who came from South Charlestown, New Hampshire, and settled in the present town of Constable, Franklin County, sometime between 1805 and 1813. He was a direct descendant of John Bellows, a passenger from London, England, on board the good ship *Hopewell* in 1635. Like so many other restless, adventurous people of that time, a later generation of the Bellows family had moved from Massachusetts to New Hampshire, then on again through Vermont to northern New York in search of greater freedom of opportunity in that vast northern Adirondack wilderness region known as the Shattagee (Chateaugay) Woods.

Soon after his arrival in Constable, Jonathan established a series of trap lines, one of which followed the Little Trout River southward and then across to the Chateaugay River, the outlet of the lakes of the same name. Continuing upstream, he found on the lower lake the hunter's shack which the Drews family of Gilmantown, New Hampshire, had occupied in 1816, before building their own cabin on the opposite shore.

Bellows bought the shack and 50 acres of land from Gates Hoit, who was the agent for several non-resident landowners. Not long afterward Bellows replaced the shanty with an enlarged, comfortable, permanent home for himself and family.

By the early 1830's he was providing accommodations for occasional hunters and fishermen. Their accounts apparently attracted the attention of more sportsmen, for by 1837 an appreciable number of guests, most of them from Montreal, began to arrive and Bellow's Lake House had become a popular resort. Since indoor space was limited, many of the arrivals brought their own tents and equipment. Bellows or one of his sons took care of the guiding.

When the Northern Railroad, later known as the Rutland, was completed in 1850, the small hotel prospered even more. Except for the Saranac region, this locality was the only section of Franklin County that sportsmen sought at that time.

Undoubtedly the most famous guest ever to stay at the Lake House was Arthur F. Tait, the artist, whose superb paintings of hunting and fishing scenes were lithographed by Currier and Ives. At least two of his pictures were painted there in 1854 and 1855. These were called "Ice Fishing on Chateaugay Lake" and "Arguing the Point." The latter work features Jonathan Bellows and his son Franklin.

Tait was described by H. Perry Smith, author of *Modern Babes in the Woods*, as "a

Trout Fishing on Chateaugay Lake [Lower] Tait Currier & Ives print

Deer Shooting on the Shattagee. Currier & Ives print

jolly Englishman, a good sportsman and a great lover of nature." Wallace's *Guide to the Adirondacks* called him "a master hand in throwing the fly, floating for deer and making a canvas glow with life."

Two other celebrated artists, Chester Harding and Louis Maurer, also stayed with Bellows during the mid-1850's. So far as is known, Harding, who is renowned for having done the only portrait of Daniel Boone, did not paint any of the local scenes. Maurer's work, like Tait's, was made world famous through the medium of Currier and Ives prints. He probably painted his "Deer Shooting on the Shattagee" somewhere along the shores of Lower Chateaugay Lake.

After Jonathan Bellows' death, his son Lewis added on to the original structure of the Lake House and continued to operate it. In 1891 Millard Bellows, son of Lewis, sold the hotel to J.S. Kirby and A.M. Bennett. Shortly afterward, when the former became sole owner, he changed the name to the Banner House, signifying his intention of making it an outstanding hostelry.

Mr. Kirby, the son of Charles A. Kirby, one of the area's oldest residents, owned a large farm and had been a partner with O.F. Chase in a mercantile firm in nearby Brainardsville. He spent all of his 75 years in the town of Belmont and was closely identified with the Banner House for a generation before selling the business to F.W. Adams, his son-in-law. He spent the rest of his life at the hotel, however. At the time of his death on April 16, 1921, the *Chateaugay Record* described him as a well-informed, cultured person and an interesting conversationalist. He liked the life of a hotel owner, and his guests responded to his friendliness with equal warmth. Being interested in local history, he wrote many papers which he read to fellow members of the Franklin County Historical Association.

The Banner House's next proprietor, Mrs. Louise Adams Chase, was the third-generation owner. She and her family moved to the Banner House when she was three years old. She graduated from Chateaugay High School and taught in rural schools for several years before her marriage.

Mrs. Chase inherited her grandfather's interest in local history. She wrote a series of articles entitled "This I Remember" for the *Chateaugay Record.* Like her grandfather, she also had a warm personality. Her guests soon became her friends and they sought her company often. Willingness to listen, prompt attention to their requests, her conversational skill, and her interest in her guests as people — these were her most obvious traits and personal assets.

Banner House has always catered to families. Kids seemed to enjoy being there and sensed that Mrs. Chase liked to have them around. She was seldom too busy to listen to their youthful tales and problems and was quick to respond with encouragement and advice.

The following incident illustrated the informal atmosphere of the place. the late N.H. Botsford, who was treasurer of the *New York World,* had vacationed there many years. He was a very dignified old gentleman with one notable idiosyncrasy: he seldom carried much money. He usually did not have even enough cash to tip the help, so Mrs. Chase would pay them and add that amount to his bill, which she would send him after his return to New York.

One day, when he was all ready to leave for the city, he drove around to the front porch, where Mrs. Chase was sitting and talking with a woman guest who had just arrived. Botsford got out of his car, walked over to Mrs. Chase, kissed her goodbye, and returned to his car. From there he called out, "When you get around to it, Louise, send me my bill!" Then he drove away.

John S. Kirby in 1915

Mrs. Chase, Her Family and Guests

The bewildered guest remarked, "I've done a lot of traveling and stayed at a lot of places, but this is the only place I've ever been where the guests kiss the owner goodbye and then leave without paying their bill!"

After Mrs. Chase died May 13, 1971, her daughter Pauline, who has more than a modicum of her mother's understanding of people and management talent, took over the business. She represents the fourth generation of Banner House proprietors.

Many of the Banner House guests have been returning year after year. Of one family four generations have been guests there. Much of the hotel's appeal can be traced to its location on a knoll which commands a pleasant panorama of lake, wooded shores, and a long line of medium-sized mountains. It is also far enough from centers of population to ensure quiet nights and restful days but still within less than an hour's drive from Plattsburgh and Lake Champlain. As in its earliest days, Banner House continues to draw guests seeking quiet relaxation.

Banner House on Chateaugay Lake

AN ADIRONDACK VILLAGE — WAITING FOR THE STAGE

From Frank Leslie's Popular Monthly Sept. 1890

Chapter 9

Early Adirondack Roads

David B. Hill, while governor of New York State, described the Adirondacks as "the nation's pleasure ground and sanitarium and yet, prior to the construction of the Adirondack and St. Lawrence Railroad in 1891-2, this region was for the most part inaccessible except to a comparatively few hunters and fishermen who were willing to undertake long trips by stage or buckboard or still longer and more arduous journeys through lakes and streams and over numerous portages or carries. An Adirondack Park had even been talked of (first by Verplanck Colvin in 1872) and even created (May 20, 1892) but there was no way for the people as a whole to get out and enjoy it. It was very much as if a great city had a park with a wall around it."

This was an accurate appraisal of the primitive transportation system of the time and points out one of the main reasons for the slow development of the region. On the other hand — and providentially so for many of us — the very remoteness and relative inaccessibility also delayed the inevitable despoliation and destruction that frequently accompany the inroads of progress and change — terms that have currently acquired numerous ugly connotations.

There were three so-called Old Military Roads carved out of the Adirondack wilderness by 1825. Although, understandably, the communities later connected by these early routes preferred to nourish the romantic delusion that they had been built by soldiers in and for the War of 1812, all available evidence points to the contrary. In at least one instance — the Northwest Bay-Hopkinton road — it is quite probable that the original designation was the Old Military *Tract* Road; by abbreviation and attrition tract could conceivably have been omitted.

Interestingly enough even the adjective old was not part of the official name and is entirely of popular origin. It started when the State later set apart another block of land in central New York for the purpose of satisfying bounty claims to compensate resident militia-men willing to protect the Canadian Border. Moreover, it is noteworthy that no part of the *Old* Military Tract's 665,000 acres — located in Clinton, Franklin and Essex Counties — was ever awarded for bounty purposes; eventually all of this huge holding was sold by the State as "wild lands" because apparently no Revolutionary War veteran ever showed enough interest to take up one of the available tracts, but settled in less hostile sections of the State instead.

The first "roads" westward were blazed trails, then bridle paths and at length rude tracks passable in Winter at least by ox team. Brooks and rivers were swum, forded or crossed by long stringers on which small poles had been placed close together. The frequent swampy areas were made passable by bone-jostling corduroy.[1]

The three "Old Military Roads," visible on the Eddy map of 1818 and the Andrus map published in 1830, crossed the Adirondacks from widely-separated points. The earliest or northern road, also known as the North West Bay Road started at Westport on Lake Champlain and terminated at Hopkinton in St. Lawrence valley. The second to be built connected Chester (Chestertown) in Warren County and Russell, (later extended to Canton) both in St. Lawrence County. The third route, the most southerly, was first constructed in 1812 between Sir William Johnson's Fish House lodge on the Sacandaga River and Wells. The remaining section was probably completed that same year. Of considerable historic interest is the fact that this road quite logically followed the old Indian trail from the Sacandaga to Raquette Lake which was used by Sir John Johnson and his Tories on his 19 day flight from Johnstown to Canada in May, 1776 to escape certain retribution by Mohawk Valley patriots.

According to Mary MacKenzie, Town of North Elba Historian, there is solid evidence that the North West Bay Road was in use before 1800 and so appeared on an 1804 regional map. The first to cross the mountains, many parts of it were incorporated into present highways. Built by the wealthy landowners of the huge Macomb's Purchase in St. Lawrence County to provide access to the thriving Champlain basin, it was taken over by the State in 1810 and thereafter greatly improved. Unquestionably, Roswell Hopkins, an influential legislator, certainly wasn't exactly opposed to getting a better road to his home in Hopkinton and was the first to travel it in 1801. Obviously, Archibald McIntyre, State comptroller,

A Solved Traffic Problem near Keene Valley — Stoddard Photo

---

1. Corduroy has an interesting origin: it derives from cord du roi, king's cloth whose use was limited to royalty with sure death as the penalty for misuse.

was also well aware of the need for better transportation facilities to his ill-fated iron enterprise on the Chubb River plain in North Elba.

Incidentally, the scenic six-mile, now-abandoned stretch between Keene and North Elba is still locally called the Old Military Road. From the top of Alstead Hill overlooking Keene, it moseys through the picturesque pass between towering Pitchoff Mountain on the south and the gently serrated Sentinel Range to the northward. This was the most difficult section of the entire route for teams and stage-coaches and required all-out effort by the horses (passengers walking at times) and a long six hours to cover. It eventually degenerated so much that in 1858 the State built a parallel route, now Route 73, through Cascade Pass. Although travelers thereafter used the ice-bound lakes for Winter travel, many area people still preferred the old rutty, high-crowned, treacherous, pock-marked, primitive wagon trail in Summer.

Incidental historical significance is enhanced by the fact that the dauntless John Brown of Ossawatomie very nearly prematurely ended his headlong, hectic career along this rugged highway in 1850. Walking home to North Elba from a mid-winter trip to Keene in order to save the coach fare, exhausted by lugging a heavy satchel, he came within a proverbial whisker of freezing to death in a snowbank before mustering sufficient reserve strength to flounder onward to the welcome haven of the nearest neighbor. Nine years later — on Dec. 7, 1859 — his body passed this way again en route to its final resting place at the foot of the huge boulder on the Plains of Abraham.

Although the North West Bay Road had already been built through North Elba and Averyville to Saranac Lake, by 1810 the rest of the route — through Harrietstown, Paul Smith's, McCollom's, Meacham and along the East Branch of the St. Regis River to St. Regis Falls and on to Hopkinton — was not completed because insufficient funds had been appropriated for the entire job. Finally in April, 1816 a supplemental act was passed by the State Legislature, work was started on each end and the project was completed.

By law the commissioners were empowered to assess each town served by the North West Bay-Hopkinton route the sum of $75.00 to help underwrite the State's grant of $8,000 distributed over several years.

This road was used extensively for nearly 40 years as almost the only outlet for the region through which it ran. About 1850 the Ogdensburg and Lake Champlain Railroad (later a branch of the Central Vermont and still later part of the Rutland system before becoming a link in the New York Central before it went kaput) was begun.

For many years from 1850 on the western end of this famous old road was seldom used and eventually became practically impassable. But, at the same time, the eastern section became increasingly popular with the development of Saranac Lake and Lake Placid as hunting, fishing and health resorts. Stagecoaches ran on daily schedules and numerous inns sprang up to accommodate the travelers.

Besides the three mis-named military highways there was still another road which crossed the region at an early date. This one also had Hopkinton for one of its termini; on the other end was Port Kent on Lake Champlain. Called the Hopkinton to Port Kent Turnpike and legislated in 1824, it required four surveys to lay out a satisfactory course which eventually led from Port Kent to Keeseville, then northwesterly to Franklin Falls, Alder Brook, Loon Lake, Duane, Dickinson and on to Hopkinton, the end of the line. The distance was about 75 miles, of which more than 50 traversed virtually unbroken forestland.

In 1829 the State appropriated $25,836 to pay for this project and authorized a tax levy of $12,500 more on adjacent lands. Later on the Legislature loaned Clinton County

$5,000 to build a road via Redford and Goldsmith's to hook up with the Turnpike near Loon Lake; in 1832 an added $3,000 was granted to complete this branch road to the foot of Loon Lake hill.

For many years toll was charged at intervals along this route and most of the steepest hills had hemlock-plank surfaces. During the period from 1835 to 1860 an enormous amount of teaming passed over it. These were the boom years of the lumbering industry, when clear-cutting the forests and subsequent fires in the slash left many Essex and Franklin County mountains and plains completely denuded.

Curiously enough, while the lumbering business poured large amounts of money into such villages as Jay, Keene, Keeseville, Clintonville, Duane, Saranac and St. Regis Falls, ultimately most of the timber kings lost money and some of them died bankrupt. The same was true of the iron industry's big names who did not diversify their investments and optimistically put far more into their mines than they ever took out of them.

In the heyday of the Turnpike, especially in the Fall and early Winter, long lines of wagons and sleighs made their slow way eastward with heavy loads of wheat, corn, pork, hides (deer and cattle), wool and potatoes from the fertile fields of western Franklin and St. Lawrence Counties and later returned with lighter but more valuable cargoes of fine flour, cotton cloth, tools, better-grade staples and such luxury-type goodies as they could afford.

An article in the Malone *Farmer* provides a factual idea of the slowness of travel in those unlamented, long-gone days. In 1802 it required six days to go from Malone to Plattsburgh on steer-back; in 1820 it took two days to travel from Moira to Ft. Covington, 20 miles away. Moreover, the trip, made in June, was with a yoke of oxen and sled because the road was impassable for wheels. In 1840 letters and newspapers required from six to eleven days to reach Northern New York from Albany and as late as 1857 Malone newspapers needed two weeks to reach subscribers in Saranac Lake. [Editor's note: things haven't really improved much in 120 years, have they?]

The central road — the one that ran from Chester (today's Chestertown) in Warren County northwest to Russell and extended to Canton, county seat of St. Lawrence County in 1834 — was authorized in 1807. From its eastern terminus it followed the North Branch of the Hudson River into and across Essex County before veering west through the north-eastern corner of Hamilton County, where it crossed the outlet of Long Lake. From there it penetrated the extreme southeastern corner of Franklin County, then went into St. Lawrence County at the southern end of Big Tupper Lake. From there it headed into the home-stretch section to the Grasse River and on to Russell. Folder No. 20 *Four-Track Series*, which provides an excellent map of the central Adirondack region, labels it as "the Old Military Road built in 1812, from Ogdensburgh to Lake George."

Besides perpetuating the persistent legend that it was a military highway, built by soldiers for the stalemate War of 1812, the road was actually begun four years earlier. Nor did it connect the two places cited although the necessary extensions were made later.

The southerly route, the Fish House-Russell road, was laid out in 1812 or 1813 and ran in a northwesterly direction from Fish House, Sir William Johnson's lodge in what is now Fulton County, to Russell. It was a prolongation of an earlier road projected or cut on orders by Johnson, probably for military purposes, from Albany through Schenectady and on to the site of his rural retreat. Often called the Albany Road because of its original starting point, this extension is therefore the only one of the three so-called Old Military Roads which could justifiably rate its name.

The 18 mile stretch from Fish House to Wells was built in 1812; the rest of this wilderness roadway was supposedly finished that same year. After leaving Wells, according

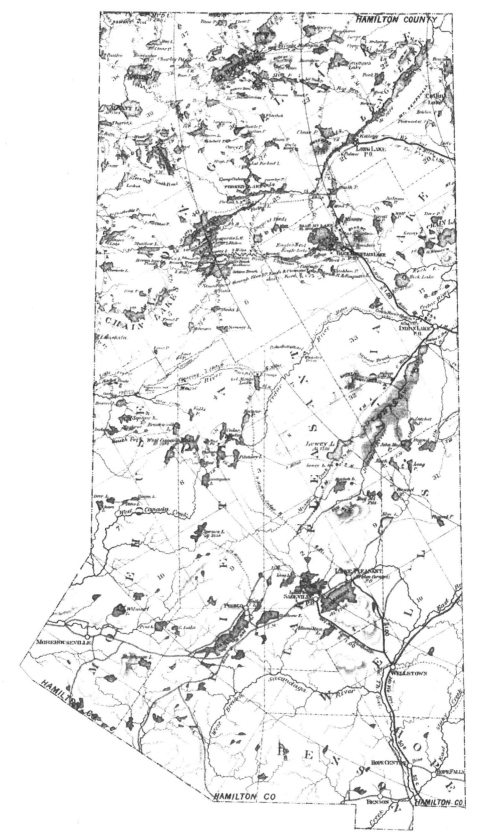

Stoddard 1883 Map Showing Albany and Carthage Roads

to Donaldson, the route skirted the north shore of Lake Pleasant, passed along the south shore of Raquette Lake, continued to the outlet of Albany Lake (named after the road but now known as Webb's Ne-ha-sa-ne). From there it crossed the northeast corner of Herkimer County into St. Lawrence County, where it joined the St. Lawrence Turnpike about ten miles south of Russell.

Stoddard's 1883 map plainly shows that after leaving Lake Pleasant this road crossed the headwaters of Jessup's and Cedar Rivers, passed to the east of the Cedar Lakes, skirted Little Moose Lake, then went on by way of Sumner and Shedd Lakes to the mouth of the Raquette Lake's South Inlet, where the Johnson party discarded their snowshoes — and, still farther along the escape route, their two canoes.

There was a later development which helped reinforce the road's military origin myth: in 1937 two iron cannon made before the Revolutionary War were found about five miles apart on the south shore of Big Tupper Lake on property then owned by Col. William Barbour but later sold to the American Legion. The larger of the two pieces was five feet long and weighed 1300 pounds; the smaller, 54 inches long, weighed 700 pounds. When discovered they were sunk so deeply into the ground that only their tops showed; the carriages had long since rotted away. One of the wheels had fallen off and a beech tree, more than two feet in diameter, had grown up inside the circle, indicating that the cannon had lain there for well over a century.

The weapons had been spiked to render them useless if found by pursuing colonists hell-bent on capturing Johnson and his band of 300 Tories in retaliation for his bloody raids all along the Mohawk Valley.

On Sept. 20th of 1937 the cannon were donated to the Johnstown Historical Society and returned to their former stations outside Johnson Hall.

There was yet another ancient highway through the central Adirondack region. This was the Champlain to Carthage route, authorized by the Legislature and laid out about 1837. According to Borden H. Mills, Sr.'s articles in the January-February and March-April issues of the *Ad-i-ron-dac* (1949) the route was traceable as follows: "the Carthage road (called at its western terminus the "Old State Road") ran from Crown Point to Root's on the Schroon River (just north of Frontiertown). From there it went westward on along what is now known as the Blue Ridge Road to Tahawus Post Office (Lower Iron Works); then it followed present Route 28N to Long Lake Village. From there it slanted southwest along the Lake to Deerland, followed the south branch of the Raquette to a point half a mile west of Buttermilk Falls, then swung to the south and west, roughly paralleling the Raquette River and Forked Lake (at about a mile distant) until it turned northerly and crossed Raquette Lake outlet east of "Cary's."

Continuing westerly it then swung northerly along the west bank of Brandreth Lake outlet stream, crossing at the outlet itself and skirting the easterly shore of the lake; then it turned due west between North and West Ponds to and across Shingle Shanty Brook to what was formerly Little Rapids Station, south of the present Ne-ha-sa-ne Station of the Adirondack Division of the New York Central Railroad, earlier known as Webb's "Golden Chariot Route," or the Mohawk and Malone Railroad.

From there it followed a westerly course not indicated on the Geological Survey Map as surveyed in 1900-1902, past what is known there as the Beaver River Flow (sometimes called by early writers the Stillwater) to Fenton's Number Four. From that point it followed the Beaver more or less to Belfort, thence through Croghan to Carthage.

Harold K. Hochschild in his monumental *Township 34* suggests that from Raquette Lake to Ne-ha-sa-ne the route followed the then-abandoned Fish House-Russell road.

Mr. Hochschild also notes that although the road was projected in 1837 there is reason to believe that the section between Brandreth and Long Lake was not opened to traffic until 30 years later. Between 1840 and 1870, when big plans were being made for developing both roads and railroads, mapmakers often failed to differentiate between those built and those proposed. For example, the Carthage Road appears on Merritt's 1860 map as already operative in that section, while on Burr's map of 1840 (Colton, publisher) the entire stretch between Crown Point and Beaver River Flow indicates completion. The much more reliable Burr map of Hamilton County, published by Stone and Clark of Ithaca, and making use of Prof. Emmons' surveys of 1839-1840, shows the road from Tahawus as splitting into two routes — one marked "Richard's route old road" and the other labeled "Chandler route new road," which lead into Long Lake village. In other words both roads are indicated as ending at the east shore of Long Lake, which may also be construed as anticipated rather than actually built.

All of these old highways were of course very primitive projects. More like what lumbermen called woods roads, merely wide trails along which trees had been cut down and the roadway filled in somewhat, corduroyed and crudely graded. "Passable in Winter, impassable in Spring and impossible in Summer" is Donaldson's apt description. Hough in his *History of St. Lawrence County* stated that the two Russell roads were already (1853) rapidly falling into disuse and decay and having been virtually abandoned soon after construction. Historically speaking, the only "Old Military Road" that ever amounted to much, and the one that was constantly being maintained and periodically improved, was the North West Bay Road from Westport to Hopkinton.

Before 1900 wagon roads were never hard-surfaced — except for the infrequent planked stretches — but were made of dirt or gravel, whichever was handy. Corduroy (logs placed sideways across the soft spots) was frequent. The only vehicle that could take the punishment was the buckboard — a springboard with a seat constructed amidships and supported by axles on each end. Much of the driving had to be done at night and always with a strong team of horses. In Winter most people used a Canadian pung, a low-slung sleigh with wide solid runners and often built like a toboggan so that it could pass over or through deep snow with greater ease. It also had a high dashboard and rear, which acted as windbreakers and made the journey far more comfortable.

Since the average speed over snow-covered roads was about five, occasionally six miles per hour a trip from Santa Clara or St. Regis Falls to Malone would require a long day of travel from daylight until late at night. When a blizzard roared in with the prevailing westerly wind, the traveler would tie the reins to the whipsocket or dashboard, snuggle down on the bottom, draw his buffalo robe and carriage blankets around him and let the faithful horses take over.

The rest of the year the ubiquitous buckboard was the customary means of travel over the dusty or muddy roads, according to conditions.

Two eye-witness accounts of the miserable travel conditions of the time provide graphic descriptions that are hard to top. The first of these is S. R. Stoddard's exaggerated spoofing of a memorable stagecoach ride on a snowy Oct. 7, 1873 between Paul Smith's caravansery on Lower St. Regis Lake and William Martin's snug haven on Ampersand Bay of the Lower Saranac. "Soon we became conscious that we had left the main road and were on one which required some little attention on our part to keep from doing injury to the interior of the coach. It was a good road — for a dyspeptic or one troubled with a poor appetite. The driver was apparently in somewhat of a hurry. The ride cost us $6.00 (14 miles), but we sure got our money's worth. There was much variety to it. It was a good coach too and we, being the only occupants, had choice of positions so we tried several. We braced ourselves up in the corners. We rattled around. We shot from side to side, made some good runs, caromed into each other and pocketed ourselves under the seats. We couldn't get knocked out because the sides — excepting a lookout hole — were buttoned down and the roof was firm. We were satisfied of that because we tried it. Sometimes the Professor (Charles Oblenis, S.R.S.'s brother-in-law) would rise up to go over a big stone and immediately he would start for me. I had striven with him and remonstrated against such frequent and energetic calls and unceremonious visitations — but to no effect. Retribution was sure to follow, however, for when his side went down, I would sail majestically over and land on him. That vehicle meandered playfully over stones and stumps and into holes. It would bounce over logs when we, rising like young eagles, would soar away toward the roof. Now we like to soar, mind you, but to alight was something else!

"Our conveyance would drop down into deep holes and stop in such an emphatic sort of way that we would involuntarily feel our heads, fully expecting to find our backbones sticking up through our hats. When at long last we reached Saranac Lake, it was with a feeling of genuine goneness peculiar to those who have been without food for days and days on end."

The second testimonial came in an article by a Charles Fenton entitled "Still Hunting on Vanderwacker Mountain," published by *Forest and Stream* on May 27, 1876: "After five days of bouncing over the Catamount or Carthage Road in a wagon containing supplies for a two-months' hunt, we finally reached the little hamlet of Pendleton (now Newcomb), where lived four or five families. The road had been given up as impassable several years before so we asked a grave-looking man what our chances were of getting over it. He shook his head doubtfully. Then we turned to our teamster.

"Well," quoth he, "I hev druv this here old team in the woods for 20 years and I hev never seed anyplace so bad that I couldn't git thru somehow!" And so we moved on and that our faith in him was well founded is soon proved.

"The 'road' continued to get progressively worse so we finally came to a place where the corduroy was all broken up and the mudholes seemed unfathomable. Our party was walking some distance ahead and, wishing to see how our doughty driver would handle the situation, we hid in a roadside thicket and watched. Well, as soon as he came to the quagmire he stopped, scanned the scene, glanced ahead to see if we were still in sight, then settled back on his seat, took a firm grip on the reins — and plunged in.

"Down, down went the horses into the muck and broken logs, he swinging his whip lustily and loudly urging on his trusty and trusting steeds. No use. They floundered around until they made it about to the middle of the mess, then one became so entangled that it fell over on its side. The poor beast put out its utmost effort but only got itself bogged down even deeper.

"In the meantime our dauntless driver seeemed not in the least discouraged. He simply dismounted, patted his horse on the head, told it to take it easy and that he'd soon be back to help him. He then sat nonchalantly down on a log, pulled out his pipe, charged it and starting puffing away as though he hadn't a care in the world.

"After awhile he got his axe from the wagon, cut a stout pole to use as a lever, adjusted a fulcrum, ran his lever under the horse's belly and started prying him up.

"At this turn of affairs we could hold out no longer so revealed ourselves by uproarious laughter. Then we went to the rescue, helped extricate the critters and proceeded on our way, rejoicing."

Highways spelled travel — travelers meant business — and business brought innkeepers. Since the settlements in the very early days were far apart and travel pace was slow because of the seasonal obstacles of snow, mud and sand, there was an obvious need for taverns and wayside inns. Some of these were built as such while others were originally fairly roomy private homes whose owners frequently had to accommodate storm-bound or benighted travelers and later decided that they might as well go into the business. While most of the inns were located in the trading and manufacturing centers, there were others spaced about a day's travel apart along the turnpikes and highways.

The turnpike inns were opened mainly to accommodate teamsters and the occasional business-men and, what was equally important, the stabling for the many horses employed. Rates at these taverns were certainly modest enough — 25¢ for a meal and the same for lodging and for stable charges. Many of these places consisted of one large room which served as kitchen, dining and sitting purposes, invariably a taproom and a small bedroom for owner and wife on the first floor. Above this and usually reached by a ladder was the dormitory where the guests slept.

Of course the only heat was that provided by a huge fireplace. The light came from "tallow dips," while the teamster who arrived late was given a perforated tin lantern with a candle stuck inside which enabled him to see well enough to stable his team.

The proverbial old-time hospitality undoubtedly can be traced to the sense of loneliness and isolation which made each chance guest a Godsend to the news-starved dwellers in the wilderness.

One of the most pathetic stories of that era happened in just such a remote tavern — that owned by Harry Hatch six or seven miles north of Loon Lake on the North West Bay Road. One winter a Canadian arrived at the little log waystation in the early evening. By morning he complained of being very sick but nevertheless continued his journey. Several days later Mr. Hatch developed small-pox and soon died of the disease, undoubtedly contracted from the indisposed visitor.

For a week prior to Hatch's demise there had been a heavy snowfall of blizzard proportions. The road being blocked the widow was unable to contact relatives or neighbors, the nearest one six miles away. Not wanting to keep the corpse in the house she dragged it into the dooryard and buried it in the deep snow where it remained for several days... A small clearing now marks the spot where the tavern formerly stood.

Those inns which acquired the greatest popularity were run by unusually industrious and knowledgeable people and often it was a family affair with the jovial husband acting as host-bartender, the wife managing the kitchen and the grown children doing their shares as waitresses, maids and errand boys.

Understandably, it would be impractical to provide a complete list of the regional hostelries but the following would be representative: The Fouquet House (owned in the 1880's by Paul Smith) in Plattsburgh; the Chasm and Lake View Houses at Ausable Chasm; the Adirondack at Keeseville; the American at Au Sable Forks, the Owl's Head at Keene; French's at Franklin Falls, the Crystal Spring House at Bloomingdale; the Tahawus and Crawford's at Keene Valley; the Windsor and Deer's Head Inn at Elizabethtown; Root's at North Hudson, Bliss's and Whiteface Mountain House at Wilmington; The White House on the Blue Ridge Road; Aiden Lair Lodge (Mike Cronin's place); Lyons' and Scott's at Averyville; Ayers Hotel and Red Tavern Inn both at Duane; Hunters Home on the North Branch of the Saranac River, where Paul Smith got his start in 1852. Others were Littlejohn's at Merrillsville, Aunt Polly's at Newcomb, Kellogg's Adirondack Hotel at Long Lake etc., etc. Probably the most famous pair of them all, both on the fringes of the Adirondacks, were the Half-way House between Glens Falls and Lake George and the

Half-Way House between Glens Falls & Lake George 1879 — Stoddard Photo

On the Road from North Creek to Blue Mountain Lake 1888 — Stoddard Photo

94

renowned Wayside Inn at Lake Luzerne. All these were stop-over spots and not resort establishments, which were in a class by themselves.

Most of the early pioneers had hacked out their farms along the highways shortly after they were opened for traffic. As soon as possible they were raising corn, rye and wheat — the first two to distill into whiskey, which was considered essential to life in those days. Debts were often paid off in spirits and in some cases even the permanent and itinerant preachers accepted it gladly as part of their pay. Money was almost unknown and the barter or swapping system was the only means of trade known. Potash or black salts was practically the only cash crop they had and a way had to be found for getting it to market, so the roads had to provide the outlet.

Although many travelers had their own teams, far more journeyed by stage-coach. Between 1815 and 1888 the first coaches, drawn by four or six horses, depending upon the type of terrain, "cooled" along by drivers using large fans, appeared on such turnpikes as the Ogdensburgh to Plattsburgh. According to the late Marjorie L. Porter, one Jonathan Thompson made two round-trips a week from 1823 on; he began carrying mail in 1837. After his death a nest-egg of $60,000 was found in the cellar of his home. Thompson's brass stage lanterns had Redford glass, among the most sought-after types now being collected.

A. F. (Fitz) O'Brien, McManus and Will Hutchins were well-known stage drivers in the Saranac Lake area, as was another driver named Harper farther east. George Meserve, probably the most publicized driver of them all, carried 3367 passengers from Bloomingdale to Paul Smith's without a single accident. Meserve, who later became President Cleveland's personal horse chauffeur, claimed that he could start his six-horse team from a standstill in front of Paul Smith's hotel and have the animals going all-out by the time they reached the first bend in the road — a relatively short distance. He handled his 16-foot whip so expertly that he could flick a fly off the ear of his lead horse without frightening the equine. Smith's stages were drawn by six white horses in the daytime, six blacks on night trips.

Standard equipment for all drivers was a big horn which they would wind (blow through) as they neared the village limits and again as they pulled up with a dusty flourish in front of the inn or tavern. At that point hostlers would sprint out to wipe the lather off the steeds and Mr. Harper, togged out in a white Stetson, custom-made suit, snappy vest crossed by a huge chain attached to an onion-type watch would put his highly polished black boots on the wheel of the coach and, brandishing his whip-stock, would step down to the ground. Grandstanding of course but everyone loved it.

The stagecoaches themselves were real eye-catchers. Those owned by Peter Comstock on his Red Bird route between Whitehall and Plattsburgh were painted vermilion while others were yellow or blue or combinations of colors - all ornately decorated and displaying the company name.

Some of the earliest coaches were long, narrow, box-shaped wagons slung on leather thoroughbraces, or on the bare axle, with tops made of leather or painted canvas. Accommodating 10 to 15 passengers by using jumpseats inside and all the available space on top, these contraptions were anything but comfortable and convenient.

Many improvements were made later on, especially by Abbott and Downing of Concord, New Hampshire, whose firm started business as early as 1802. The celebrated Concord coaches had a bulging back, seats facing each other inside and hinged stool-seats between. On pleasant days the premium seats were those on the upper deck and particularly those alongside the driver, for which there was an extra charge for the privilege of enjoying his conversation and company, tour-guide status.

Often the roads crossed hogbacks or narrow ridges with steep shoulders and deep ravines on either side. At these danger points the driver of the stagecoach would often call to the passengers — "Lean to the left or lean to the right!" as the situation called for. Otherwise — and it sometimes happened — the stage and occupants would become unbalanced and hurtle down the wooded embankments. Particularly dangerous were the narrow, often shifting in rainy weather, so-called roadbeds of the Chapel Pond and Cascade Lakes thoroughfares.

Most people are familiar with the term turnpike, which meant that certain sections of the roadways were owned by companies or private parties who charged a fee for the use and maintenance of the road. Such tolls could be avoided if the traveler detoured around on a bumpier side-road called a shunpike.

Besides the gaudy stagecoaches and tallyhos there were many other types of traffic. On early thoroughfares slow-moving oxcarts and bullteams were common. Droves of cattle and their drivers moseyed along to market; sheep and even geese were herded along; big, high-racked charcoal wagons pulled by horses or oxen plodded down from the sideroads to the forges. Peddlers, either on foot burdened with their 80-100 pound loads, or if more prosperous, driving their well-designed and heavily-loaded carts. Groups of laborers, traveling preachers, itinerant artists and artisans (tinsmiths etc.) and even strolling players and an occasional band of gypsies and horse-traders — and during the dark hours probably a horse thief or two — such as Sile Doty of Bangor or Alonzo Clark of Dickinson, in haste to widen the gap between them and their pursuers....

The completion of the Chateaugay Railroad from Platttsburgh to Saranac Lake in 1887 and its extension to Lake Placid in 1893 combined with the building of the Adirondack and St. Lawrence Railroad (Webb's "Golden Chariot Route") in 1892 (sold to the New York Central the next year, it became their Adirondack Division) provided rail service from population centers of the Northeast directly to Montreal. These lines quickly superseded and replaced the stagecoach runs in much the same manner that autos in their turn outmoded and outdrew the railroads. Once more traffic is brisk over the old roads but what a different mode of travel it has become!

This represents a rather superficial picture of the early roads, the people who traveled over them and the relatively slow development of an adequate system of land transportation in Northern New York. Moreover, one does not have to be a Methusaleh to have seen much of the progress in his own lifetime — at least the decline of the railroad and the growth in the reliance on the automobile. Actually it is still quite hard to realize that even up to the end of World War I there were virtually no paved roads such as we know them today. Personal recollection dredges up the fact that it was not until 1912 that the first concrete surface, an experimental quarter-mile ribbon of cement, was laid down just south of Duane Center. It stood the test well and prompted the State and County highway departments to construct more of the same.

Although there were of course other ardent advocates of improved highways, there were two in particular who deserve much credit. The first was the versatile S. R. Stoddard of Glens Falls who, besides being a prolific photographer, guidebook writer and map maker, also produced the first really thorough and popular automobile chart of the North Country in 1906, and followed it up with up-dated annual editions for ten years thereafter.

The second active promoter and lobbyist was Malone's Jack Flanagan, who was so obsessed by the potential economic and political benefits to be gained that he became noted statewide as "Good Roads" Flanagan. Moreover, he was no prophet crying in the wilderness because he really got results.

On the Road to Blue Mountain Lake c. 1895

Early Road Through Chapel Pond Pass 1880 — Stoddard Photo

The Fiend of the Road. Currier & Ives print

What's On the Sign Board?

Life Mag. Aug. 1, 1912

When we tool along the Northway even at the legally allowable rate of 55 miles per hour, it is hard to realize that less than 100 years ago it often required a full day to cover even a minor fraction of that distance. I for one keep thinking of the "Old Military Road" stretch from Keene to North Elba and the snail's pace speed of one mile per hour. Almost like hiking through the Seward Range Blow-down — and just about as exasperating. Frankly, even though I feel that I missed a few things by not living a century or so ago — the less-ulcerous tempo of living for instance — I still have no hankering whatsoever to retrogress back (redundant but more emphatic) to the days of primitive travel.

Chapter 10

Era of the Early Adirondack Railroads

The early half of the 19th century saw several schemes for building railroads either into or through the Adirondacks. They were usually part of a package deal which included somewhat grandiose proposals to construct navigation routes connecting the larger lakes and rivers into a continuous waterway system through the mountain region.

The first New York State railroad was chartered in 1826, the first train chugged over the ten-mile stretch between Albany and Schenectady in 1831, but by 1845 there were only 700 miles of track in operation in the entire State. Nevertheless, there were already proposals in the planning stage for the building of roads in the Adirondacks.

Chronologically, the first of these projects dates back to 1834, when the Legislature passed an "act to incorporate the Manheim and Salisbury Road," changed three years later to the Mohawk and St. Lawrence Railroad and Navigation Co. This authorized the building of a railroad and canal from Little Falls on the Erie Canal to the St. Lawrence River. The 1838 pamphlet and map put out by the embryonic company indicated the proposed railway but not the parallel canal. Supposedly it would start at Little Falls, head northeasterly along the East Canada Creek to the west side of Piseco Lake in Hamilton County and then northerly to the south end of Raquette Lake. Unfortunately — if you want to call it that — this never got any farther than the old drawing board.

As related in Donaldson's *History of the Adirondacks* a survey report was made in 1838 for a right-of-way between Ogdensburgh and Lake Champlain but this too died a-borning. Of the suggested alternate routes the southern one would have started at Port Kent and crossed the northwestern neck of the woods, whereas the other would have terminated in Plattsburgh avoiding the formidable Adirondack terrain entirely. Like the other this scheme also went kaput but, revived seven years later, became the actual course of the Northern Railroad between Ogdensburgh and Malone in 1850.

In 1846 still another attempt was made — this one "to provide for the construction of a railroad and slackwater navigation from or near Port Kent on Lake Champlain to Boonville in Oneida County. The plans called for the railway to hit the Saranac River at McClenathan Falls, now known as Franklin Falls, then proceed by river, canal and lake navigation through the River and Saranac series of lakes — Lower, Middle and Upper — thence up the Raquette River to Long Lake, Crochet (Forked) and Racket (Raquette) Lakes, the Fulton Chain and on down through the Moose River Valley to Boonville. Even though this far-out plan was extravagantly promoted it too never got off the ground.

Interestingly enough this doozy of a plan was mainly at the behest of the enterprising

Amos Dean, one of the project's commissioners and the owner of much acreage in the Long Lake area. Chalk up another disappointment for the developers.

The first railroad to come near the Adirondack Park was the Whitehall to Plattsburgh line, constructed in 1868 between the latter place and Point of Rocks or AuSable Station, a steamboat stop on Lake Champlain. This twenty-mile section was extended to AuSable Forks in 1874 but never got any farther. A railroad spanning the entire distance from Plattsburgh to Whitehall had been agitated for years previously, but the actual construction plans became the swirling storm center of a notorious political squabble which eventually and effectively killed the proposed undertaking.

The Adirondack Railroad

By far the most ambitious railroad project of the earlier era was the plan to put down trackage between Sacket's Harbor, in Lake Ontario, and Saratoga. Incorporated in 1848 and headed by some of the most prominent men in the country, this expensive effort over a twenty-three year period still carries all the elements of a fascinating drama. Highlighting the enterprise was the preparation of two surveys stretching from the upper Hudson Valley through the heart of the Adirondacks to the shores of Ontario. The northerly route — 182 miles via Raquette Lake and either the Beaver or Moose River, then along the valley of the Black River to Lake Ontario — was finally decided upon.

The estimated cost of $576,000 was softened considerably by the granting of an option to buy upwards of 250,000 acres of prime real estate for 5¢ per acre. To further sweeten the deal, this acreage was matched by private owners and all of it was declared exempt from taxation for an appreciable period.

If ever there was a railroad more needed or favored by the sovereign state of New York, a railroad conceived and managed by energetic and influential men, it was this one — and yet the promoters' dreams were never realized.

After 30 miles of track had been built the company exhausted its capital, got nowhere and, in 1863, the property was acquired by New York Central capitalists and Dr. Thomas Clark Durant.

Durant, previously prominent in the planning and building of the Michigan and Southern, Chicago and Rock Island, Mississippi and Missouri railroads, was the most active advocate of the Union Pacific Railroad from the start of construction in 1861 to the driving of the last spike. During that period he was vice-president, general manager and acting president most of the time.

He immediately reorganized and renamed the company and gave its investors land, mineral, timber and manufacturing rights. Its western terminus was changed to Ogdensburgh, its stockholders were granted complete tax-exemption for twenty years and its holdings were enhanced by the acquisition of the MacIntyre Iron Company at Tahawus.

Although prospects were definitely rosy and in spite of Dr. Durant's well-known ability and abundant resources, only 60 miles of track — from Saratoga to North Creek — were ever laid. Black Friday of 1873 came up, British and American capital dried up, and the owners of thousand-dollar bonds had to settle for $210.00 each. Later the railroad was sold at foreclosure proceedings to William West Durant and William Sutphen for $350,000. Finally, in 1889, the line was signed over to the present owners, the Delaware and Hudson Company. Much of the original property gradually was acquired by corporations and private owners.

The Chateaugay Railroad

The first railway to cross the "blue line" and enter the mountains was the Chateaugay Railroad, which ran from Plattsburgh to Saranac Lake. The first train over the line was run on Dec. 5, 1887.

This road dates back to 1878, when legislation was passed in Albany "authorizing the construction and management of a railroad from Lake Champlain to Dannemora State Prison." Construction authority was delegated to the Superintendent of Prisons; all the work was done by convict labor. Not long after its completion in 1879, Smith A. Weed of Plattsburgh and a group of business associates needed an outlet for their iron ore being smelted at their forges at Popeville, near Lower Chateaugay Lake. They decided to lay a track from Lyon Mountain to Dannemora and thus connect with the line already running to that place. Soon afterward in May, 1879, they organized the Chateaugay Railroad Company and leased the Dannemora line from the State. On Dec. 17th of that year the first regular train went over the entire line and on Dec. 18th the first shipment of ore reached Plattsburgh.

The Chateaugay Railroad was later extended from Lyon Mountain to Standish, then to Loon Lake and finally to Saranac Lake in 1887. On January 1, 1903 the Delaware and Hudson Railroad Company bought the Chateaugay and broad-gauged it.

In 1893 the Saranac Lake and Lake Placid Road was put down and operated between the two villages. Fare for the 10-mile trip was $1.00. Like the Chateaugay this short line was also narrow-gauge but since three rails were laid, broad-gauged rolling stock bound for Lake Placid could be accommodated. This road was sold to the New York Central and eventually to the Penn Central.

Hurd's Road

The next railroad to penetrate the "blue line" was built in stages by the flamboyant timber tycoon, John Hurd. Entirely in Franklin County this line wound through the forest and entered the Park at Le Boeuf's, about ten miles south of Santa Clara.

About 1882, Hurd, Peter MacFarlane and a man named Hotchkiss bought some 61,000 acres of land and already existing mills at St. Regis Falls. From that point they built seventeen miles of track to Moira, a station on the Northern Railroad (later the Rutland), which ran from Ogdensburgh to Malone.

Soon afterward Hurd became sole owner, chartered the Northern Adirondack Extension Company and built another twenty miles of track — first to Santa Clara (named for his wife) and then to Brandon in 1886. The last link, the twenty-two mile section to Tupper Lake, was finished in 1889. The total length of railway, some sixty miles, was never much more than a logging railroad in Hurd's time.

Hurd's destiny was determined to a very large extent by his precarious relationship with the Dodge-Meigs Co., which later became the Santa Clara Lumber Co., unquestionably one of the few really important companies of its kind operating in the northern Adirondacks. The company, which started just after the Civil War with Titus B. Meigs, and Norman and George Dodge as partners, also had extensive interests in Georgia, Pennsylvania and elsewhere. Through a Henry Patton of Albany in the late 1880's the firm was introduced to John Hurd, who at that time controlled large tracts of timberland in northern Franklin County. Shortly afterward the interested parties were granted a 50-year charter under which they contracted to meet the following stipulations: "to make an earnest, determined effort to prevent and extinguish forest fires; to plant trees, grown largely in their own nursery; to ross (debark) pulpwood in their own mills and sell same; to utilize the so-called waste and sell it as chips for chemical pulp."

Capital investment was reckoned as 4,000 shares, with par value of $100.00 — of which Dodge, Meigs & Co., owned 2,200 shares and John Hurd, 1800. The company's operations were limited almost entirely to Franklin County, where it owned and cut over nearly 100,000 acres and supplied mills at St. Regis Falls, Santa Clara and Tupper Lake. Its principal products were soft and hardwood lumber, rossed pulp, wood clapboards and box shooks, hemlock bark, spruce and hemlock lath, and chips and fiddle butts — selected logs used in the manufacture of piano sounding boards.

Relations between the swashbuckling Hurd and his more sophisticated partners were none too cordial from the very beginning. Two years after the formation of the company hard feelings were created when Hurd installed foundation piers for an enormous sawmill (the Big Mill on the site of Municipal Park, Tupper Lake) in direct violation of an agreement that gave the company the right to choose the railroad terminus. After a great deal of conniving and legal maneuvering young Ferris Meigs acquired the title to property on which Hurd had already spent thousands to improve.

Old John was understandably furious at this skullduggery and the battle began. Hurd had borrowed large sums of money from the Franklin Trust Co., of Brooklyn on shaky security. Meigs, only 23 at the time, was given sole authority to handle the case for his part of the firm with instructions to get the money due them from Hurd but without revenge or profit. The latter apparently lost what little cool he had and became abusive but had to concede to a settlement. Final arrangements were made not by Meigs but by Mr. Dodge, who botched the deal and weeks of remedial work were needed to square it away formally to Dodge & Meigs Co. Apparently the firm had also been forced to cover notes on which Hurd had defaulted on previous occasions.

Even though Hurd lost out no effort was made to exploit the wide-open opportunity to send him to the cleaners and Titus Meigs passed up an offer of $50,000 for the millsite.

This misfortune, plus the even more costly encounter with Webb, hastened the financial downfall of the old giant.

"Uncle John" Hurd, as the hard-driving, blustering and dynamic man was called, was a reckless speculator and much-talked-of person during his heyday in the region. After his twin disasters he returned to Bridgeport, Connecticut, where he died in poverty on August 5, 1913 at age 83 having "looped the loop of spectacular success as an Adirondack lumber-king," as Donaldson commented.

According to the publisher-editor of the Malone *Farmer* Hurd was unquestionably one of the most courageous and determined men who ever operated in the northern Adirondacks.

The thriving villages of Dickinson Center, St. Regis Falls, Santa Clara and Tupper Lake are actually monuments to his memory. With his associates he developed (clear cut) the lumbering industry in western Franklin County and did not rest until he had completed his Northern Adirondack Railroad up steep grades and over very difficult terrain. All this after he had passed his prime of life.

The building of Webb's "Golden Chariot Route" unquestionably contributed to the collapse of the Hurd Line, which was sold in 1895 to a syndicate which proceeded to extend the line across the Canadian border to Ottawa. This resulted in the eventual changing of its name to the New York and Ottawa. Through service was established in the fall of 1900. In 1906, at a foreclosure sale held in St. Regis Falls, the railroad again changed ownership.

Snow-Bound. Currier & Ives print

This time it became part of the New York Central system.

Even after the New York Central System took over from "Uncle John" Hurd and renamed it the New York and Ottawa, train travel in Winter was often anything but pleasant. For instance in the files of the Tupper Lake *Herald* for March 13, 1908 is the account of a blizzard that must have been a real doozer: "The old reliable New York and Ottawa, which has pulled through some bad storms had to succumb to the force of last Friday's blizzard. The train left Ottawa in the afternoon and struggled ahead until it stalled in the drifts between Dickinson Center and St. Regis Falls. The engine was detached from the train in an attempt to force a way through and it proved to be impossible to get it back again. The cars, stranded without heat, became frigid and the passengers suffered acute discomfort until after midnight, when two teams from Bishop's Hotel got through and took them back to the Falls. Thanks to this assist by old-fashioned horse-power the hapless passengers had a chance to rest and thaw out before their train was dug out and rolling again. It arrived in Tupper Lake at 2 P.M. — about twelve hours late."

However, the N. Y. & O. was not the only one to have trouble during that same storm. The south-bound New York Central train, due in Tupper at midnight was stalled near Beauharnois, P.Q. when it plunged into a huge snowbank in which a freight train had previously suffered the same fate. The snow was five feet deep on the track and the wind was fierce. The trains were soon unable to move in either direction. A snowplow was sent to the scene and the freight cars were finally hauled out one at a time. The passenger train reached Tupper at 2 P.M. Sunday. If you had to travel in the Winter in this region back in 1908 you had to go by train because there was no other way.

Undoubtedly Hurd's greatest achievement was creating the village of Tupper Lake. Before his time, there was nothing much in that vicinity but pasture land and clearings belonging to the early settlers. But when Hurd built the Big Mill on the site of the present Municipal Park, the place boomed and prospered as a lumber town. The lively, rough-

Dr. W. Seward Webb, Pres. Adirondack & St. Lawrence Railway Co.

looking settlement was almost entirely wiped out by the holocaust of July 29-30, 1899, when 169 buildings were reduced to ashes within a span of only three or four hours. The first proved to be the proverbial blessing in disguise because more substantial and attractive structures were gradually built as the village recovered its confidence and sense of purpose.

Webb's "Golden Chariot" Route

Aside from the obvious desirability of opening the Adirondacks for the enjoyment of the general public, this region represented the only route not already pre-empted for trade between New York City, Canada and the Northwest. Furthermore, there has always been keen competition between different parts of the Dominion as shipping points and communication centers. The only open ports in Winter are Halifax and St. John, Nova Scotia and to reach these harbors from the Canadian Northwest necessitates a long haul by railroad, whereas a shorter route would place Canadian commerce within direct contact with the port of New York. Efforts to provide such a mutually advantageous route were given top priority on both sides of the Border in the 1880's and '90's.

At that time the profitable carrying trade was about equally divided between the Delaware and Hudson and the Rome, Watertown and Ogdensburgh Railroads. The latter line avoided the formidable Adirondacks by using a longer route which skirted its western slopes, while the D. & H. monopolized the narrow Champlain Valley.

Therefore, any other railroad company seeking Montreal trade would necessarily have to build directly through the mountains, a tremendous undertaking.

By 1890 there had been much newspaper agitation in metropolitan papers on the desirability of such a road and the fact that the New York Central was not in direct competition with the smaller lines. Persistent pressure became so strong that the Central took the preliminary steps toward building a road which was to parallel the Rome, Watertown and Ogdensburgh in whole or part. Such was the general situation when Dr. W. Seward Webb, the son-in-law of William H. Vanderbilt, stepped into the spotlight.

Webb, who had always been an Adirondack addict and sportsman, was a charter member of the Kildare Club, north of Tupper Lake, as well as the owner of some 115,000 acres in Herkimer and Hamilton Counties, became enthusiastic over the possibility of constructing the desired railroad even though his father-in-law did not share his interest nor furnish financial backing. The New York Central, however, showed considerable interest in the proposed railway at that time.

The projected railroad depended primarily on the acquisition of several smaller lines, the first of which was the Herkimer, Newport and Poland Co., constructed in 1883. Next he annexed the Mohawk and Northern Company, opened for operation in 1890. By merging these he now headed the Mohawk and Adirondack Railroad, which later was expanded into the Mohawk and Malone Railroad Co., made possible by the building of the Remsen-Malone section in less than two years.

Since the New York Legislature, because of skullduggery and delaying tactics on the part of lobbyists and lawyers for the rival D. & H., refused to provide any help, Webb went ahead anyhow and provided the necessary money, men and machinery.

In early 1891 George C. Ward, an engineer who knew the Adirondacks well, was hired to make a survey of the route from Remsen to Paul Smith's and from there to Malone. In the reconnaissance party was Lem Merrill of Merrillsville, who was even better acquainted with much of the projected right of way than was his boss. Lem walked the entire length of the line during the surveying operation.

At that point the Rome, Watertown and Ogdensburgh agreed to lease its line to the New York Central, which thereafter had no official or financial interest in the new enterprise.

Webb's next move was to negotiate with John Hurd who, though hard-pressed for money, refused the former's offer of $600,000 - considerably more than the poorly-built line was worth. Dickering broke off and Webb spent the Summer in Saranac Lake in order to take personal charge of his project.

Hurd late reconsidered, a deal was made and papers were ready for the signatures the next morning. That night, however, a Mr. Payne of the Pope-Payne Lumber Co., visited the horse-trader type Hurd in his New York hotel and offered to raise his (Webb's) bid by $50,000 if Hurd would give him a short-term option. The next day, instead of signing the papers, the wily "Uncle John" just dropped in to tell Dr. Webb that the deal was off once more.

Later that morning Payne appeared in Webb's office and tried to sell him the option for a sizeable profit. The furious Webb told him in well-selected language exactly what he thought of the pair and informed them that he (Webb) would parallel the Hurd road within a year — and kept his word.

It was now full speed ahead as Webb's crews went into action at both ends simultaneously. The work was pushed feverishly both Summer and Winter until completion. Many seemingly insurmountable problems were encountered. Summer rains made such bogs of the supply roads that in certain southern sections six-horse teams sometimes arrived with a load consisting of one bale of hay — not even enough to feed the team. Backpacking was often required to feed men and horses in some of the more distant camps. Since it was impossible to bring in modern equipment, progress was frequently both exasperatingly slow and expensive. Building rights across the restricted Forest Preserve lands were gained by swapping right-of-way acreage for other land of equal or greater value.

Negro workers, recruited in Tennessee, also compounded the difficulties. Some arrived barefooted and with only overalls for clothes. Even after they had been outfitted properly, many of them still didn't like the climate and wanted out. Some did and upon reaching New York started an editorial agitation in the Yellow Sheets (tabloids) which led to unjust criticism of Webb, who had had nothing to do with the hiring of the men, that having been done by the contractors. A would-be blackmailer was trapped in Boonville by use of a primitive dictograph, a stovepipe hole in the ceiling of the hotel room.

An example of the loyalty engendered by Dr. Webb was demonstrated in early 1892, when the northern operation reached Loon Lake. There Chief Engineer Roberts received a telegram from Webb stating that he (Webb) had promised to build a temporary spur line to the Loon Lake House so that President Benjamin Harrison could take his invalid wife to Chase's. The job had to be finished by the next day. After protesting that it could not be done in that short time, Roberts started work immediately. His crew graded and put down a mile of track in 24 hours and everything was ready when the special train pulled in.

On another occasion one of Webb's detectives notified him that the engineers and draftsmen at Herkimer were loafing and had not reported for work until late morning. The Doctor then asked, "What morning are you talking about?" The man told him. "Oh," said Webb, "you should have been there the night before!"

There were many earbenders told about the building of the road. One of the most characteristic featured the frenzied rivalry between the crews of St. Regis Indians on the northern section and the Negroes working to the south. Daily progress reports were posted each night and the men worked furiously to outdo each other. One resourceful boss got extra effort out of his men by placing a keg of beer far enough ahead to guarantee a big day's work and then let them celebrate when they had reached that goal.

Finally, on October 12, 1892, about a half mile north of Twitchell Creek Bridge, the two ends were joined and the last spike driven. This honor was given a young assistant engineer, a better engineer than track-layer, who missed his target a round dozen times before he finally connected — much to the disgust of the assembled Negroes and Indians.

While work on the Adirondack and St. Lawrence road, as it was later known, was nearing completion, Webb concentrated on a section even farther north, the Malone to Montreal phase. Completed as far as Valleyfield by Jan. 17, 1892 this line was extended to Coteau, where it connected with the Grand Trunk, later called the Canadian National. Starting on Oct. 24, 1892, when the Herkimer and Malone line was placed in service, through trains were run from New York City to Montreal via Malone and Coteau.

On June 1, 1898 Webb entered into an agreement whereby the New York Central, now actively interested, took over the operation of this line without sharing in its profits or losses. This pact continued until Jan. 1, 1905, when the Central bought all the outstanding capital stock of the Webb route, and the builder retired from his last association with an enterprise which he had brilliantly and successfully placed in full operation within eighteen months from the start of the survey. It is doubtful if such a record and under such almost overwhelming difficulties has ever been duplicated.

The Raquette Lake Railroad

Unquestionably the greatest promoter in the kaleidoscopic history of the Adirondacks was William West Durant (1850-1934), the son of Dr. Thomas Cole Durant, the leading proponent of the Union Pacific and several other important western railroads. Like his father W. W. was a geared-up visionary whose wide-ranging plans for the development of his company's vast Adirondack properties (variously reported as between 500,000 - 700,000 acres), eventually turned sour and he died in decidedly straitened financial circumstances. Bedeviled with personal and family problems he nevertheless established a solid reputation for his generosity, his magnificent "cottages" and his flamboyant manner.

Preliminary Grading near Malone for Adirondack & St. Lawrence Railway Co.

Construction Work near Malone for Adirondack & St. Lawrence Railway Co.

First Station at Mt. View, c. 1892 — Courtesy of Robideau Studios

Old Forge Railroad Station and Steamboat Dock -- Photo by Hodges

Like his father also he became engrossed in construction of the Raquette Lake R.R., an 18-mile ribbon of steel built in 1899 mainly to serve the Raquette and Eckford Chain of lakes (Utowana, Eagle Nest and Blue Mountain Lake) and because the wealthy property owners in the area wanted to make their forest estates more accessible.

According to a quote by Dennis Dillon in Harold K. Hochschild's fascinating *Township 34* the Raquette Lake R.R. was "conceived by a woman - Mrs. Collis P. Huntington, who was so pompous and so glorious that she didn't want to be dragged from the mainline train of the Adirondack Division of the Central at Old Forge up through the Fulton Chain in those small steamboats, get out and travel to another boat with all the inconveniences and length of time it took, and she said she wouldn't come there (Camp Pine Knot) again until he could (her husband) build a railroad, and that if he could build one from New Orleans to San Francisco, California, he could build that little short road for her and he started out to do it!" [Whew, quite a mouthful!]

The incorporators of "that little road" were Huntington, Morgan, Webb, Whitney and Dix; Robert Bacon, F. G. Smith, Harry R. Whitney and J. Harvey Ladew, all of New York City; Samuel Callaway, president of the New York Central; Chauncey M. Depew; Charles E. Snyder; Edward M. Burns, W. W. Durant and Dr. Arpad Gerster. Most of the little line's $250,000 capital was put up by the first four men; the others put in smaller amounts.

"For its size," wrote Donaldson, this little road undoubtedly had the wealthiest board of directors in the country."

The new railroad was opened for business on July 1, 1900 and throughout its 33 years of existence its summer schedule consisted of two trains each day in each direction — a day train and a Pullman section at night. During the same period the only forest fire along its right-of-way was an easily extinguished small blaze.

The Winter of 1902-1903 was a rough one for the railroad as far as public relations were concerned because the officers applied for permission to suspend service entirely from Jan. 1 to May 1. The result was a torrent of objections from many directions, including a mild protest from Lt. Gov. T. L. Woodruff, owner of Kamp Kill Kare.[1] C. D. Adams, a lawyer representing Charles Bennett and other Raquette Lakers filed stronger squawks and the application was denied. Next step was a petition demanding the resumption of daily service, a move that smelt of skullduggery because many signers were summer residents who had no intention of ever using it during the winter.

The end of the line for the line came in 1933 but during that comparatively brief period it acquired a special aura or patina because of the twenty-four carat social status of its plethora of world-renowned passengers. Definitely a glamor era in Adirondack history....

One of the principal causes of forest fires during the days of wood-burning engines was of course smokestack sparks which ignited combustible material along the right-of-way. Later on when coal became the fuel there was always the danger of fires being set when the firemen stoking the big boilers dumped white-hot coals on the roadbed. Fires were so frequent during the dry season of the early years that laws were passed requiring spark arresters in the stacks. Sometime later wood was outlawed except in Winter. Coal

---

[1] Lt. Gov. Woodruff pulled off a beautiful ripoff in acquiring his Lake Kora property. In 1897 the State Forest Preserve Board, of which Woodruff was a member, bought 24,000 acres of W. W. Durant property on the south shore of Raquette Lake. Curiously enough this deal did not include 1,000 acres plus or minus around Lake Kora. Not long thereafter Woodruff obtained it and the reason for non-acquisition by the State became obvious. By this connivance Woodruff wound up with a choice forest domain entirely surrounded by State lands, thus insuring relative privacy. Interestingly enough Gov. Black was an occasional guest there; his wife a far more frequent visitor.

eventually gave way to oil and the problem was minimized.

Other precautions included powerful pumps and reels of hose. Best prevention of all were special trains with tank cars, shovels, axes and other firefighting equipment held in readiness at strategic points.

The Adirondack line generated very little local freight business other than lumber. In the early days of the line millions of board feet of finished and unfinished timber products passed over the rails.

Very likely the only really embarrassing situation which the famous little spur line (R.L.R.R.) had occurred near the Clearwater (Carter) end of the trackage. One day the oil-burning engine ran out of water and therefore couldn't generate the steam needed to operate the boiler. This created a temporary predicament for the engineer who had tried to get as far as he could before putting on the brakes on a slight upward grade.

Just then he noticed a farmer and his horse in a nearby field and, since he had no other option, asked the farmer for a tow. The farmer agreed, unhitched his horse as the engineer uncoupled his conked-out engine from the rest of the train. Since the engine was much smaller than the ordinary type the horse had no difficulty whatsoever hauling the locomotive the quarter-mile distance to the nearest water tower. Having tanked up, the engineer back-tracked to the rest of his cars and proceeded the rest of the way to Raquette Lake Station.

Veteran railroad men claim — or don't care to admit — that they have ever heard of a similar situation. The moral of the story seems obvious; one horse power can be of a greater value than any disabled locomotive.

Paul Smith's Electric Railroad

There was still another small railroad which certainly rates inclusion in the list of early Adirondack Railroads although it was built as late as 1906. This was Paul Smith's electric line which ran the seven miles between Lake Clear Junction and the hotel. The wealthy Paul (Apollos) having seen many of his guests arrive at the Junction in private railroad cars decided that they might just as well pull in at his hotel and over his own private line. Some of his New York Central official friends pooh-poohed the idea — said it couldn't be done — called it a paper railroad — commented that it wouldn't even be able to pay surveying costs etc., but he just let them have their fun.

At the time he made up his mind to go ahead with the project, he had packed his bags and was about to leave for California. So he just unpacked them, started the men at the biggest cut and went on from there. When the job was done, Brown of the Central came and wanted to ride in on the maiden trip with regular locomotive and heavy car. Paul was afraid the whole roadbed would collapse and tried to talk him out of it. But Brown insisted that he wanted to try out the "paper railroad" so Smith said, "Well, O.K. Go ahead!" — and they made it without trouble.

When they reached Lake Clear Junction on the return trip, Brown took off his hat, shook Smith's hand and exclaimed — "Paul, I give up! You've done it and I'm sure that you're the only one who could. But it must have cost you a lot of money!"

"Oh well," answered Paul, "that's all right. 'Twas my money and every foot of that road is on my own land!" Shortly afterward the Central offered to buy it but Smith turned them down.

This electric railway — actually a one-car affair — fitted with modern conveniences plus baggage department, carried passengers, hauled Pullmans, private cars and

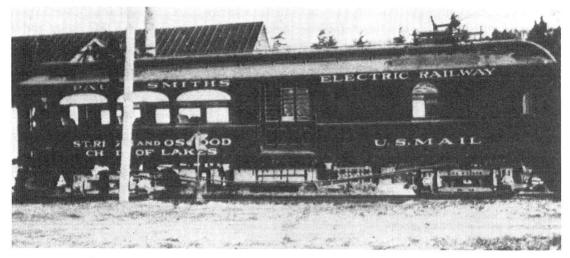

Paul Smith's Electric Railway — Courtesy of Dr. Chester L. Buxton, Paul Smith's College

Paul Smith, Sept. 22, 1878 — Stoddard Photo

freight between Lake Clear and the Hotel. It ran until 1921, when increasing use of automobiles made it dated and unnecessary.

The early — and many later railroads took a great deal of journalistic abuse, much of it deservedly as its revenues and quality of service declined simultaneously, but the prize-winning piece of sarcastic reporting which follows is certainly in a class by itself; I doubt if the Adirondack lines ever deteriorated to this extent:

"Slowest Railroad — Oswego to Syracuse

A railroad, 36 miles long, runs between Oswego and Syracuse. I rode it recently and can testify that if you wanted a draft in your face you had to ride backward. Never any hot

111

journals on that road — greatest danger is that the stuffing and gravy around the axles will freeze. The whistle screech is like the low, very faint-like warble of a four-year-old boy blowing through the knothole in a board fence. It's capable of giving a grasshopper a mild thrill of alarm but won't scare a cow worth a leather cuss. The conductor, engineer and fireman always walk on ahead to look for broken rails and cows run on ahead of them to keep out of the dust. I tried an experiment just out of curiosity: two trains were passing each other in opposite directions so I stuck a match out of the window, let the head rub against the side of the passing car, but they were going so slow that I couldn't even strike a light.

If anyone ever plans to take a trip over that line he should be sure to take along a lot of clothes, a whole ham and a barrel of cornbeef or else he'll starve to death enroute.

Letter to the New York Sun 1870"

The End of the Railroad Era

Throughout the nation but particularly in the thinly-populated regions such as the Adirondacks the railroad industry has suffered from the progress of the times. From the days of the Great Depression in the '30's down to the late 1950's the companies started a systematic program to abandon their more economically anemic branch lines along with curtailment or even cessation of passenger service.

Although most of the lines were generously subsidized, they still could not — and in many instances did not make any serious effort to counter the growing competition from the trucking businesses. All too often the owners of the iron horses indicated a deliberate and sustained attitude of "the public be damned", when the customers began to complain loud and often about the steady deterioration in the services provided for both passengers and shippers.

A clear example of the degree of decline is furnished by the June 20, 1913 issue of the Tupper Lake *Free Press* which carried the schedule of the Adirondack Division of the Central plus these noteworthy remarks: "To older residents who listen in vain for the lonesome sound of a steam locomotive whistle echoing through these hills, it recalls an era when 90% of the travel in and out of the North Woods was by rail, and the arrival of each train at Tupper Lake Junction touched off a busy scramble, with scores of passengers boarding or leaving the cars, express crews bustling around and "busmen" for the Altamont, the Iroquois and the Holland House vying for fares.

There were six trains scheduled north and six south daily back in 1913. The Montreal Express pulled in at 5:05 A.M. It was followed at 6:15 by the Adirondack and Montreal Special and at 7:18 the Tupper Lake Local was due...The southbound parade was equally impressive.

During the 1920's and '30's approximately 20 regularly-scheduled passenger trains operated daily on the Adirondack Division in and out of Lake Placid. There were also four to six freight trains each day. On Labor Day weekends as many as 10 to 14 sections of Pullmans left Placid for New York City and points west of Utica. Tom Kyle of Saranac Lake, who started his railroading career in Grand Central Station of Fun City, recalled that there were usually five sections headed for Lake Placid every Friday night, which meant 10 to 12 cars and 350 to 400 people.

During this same period the large area hotels were enjoying the boom years. The fashionable resorts such as the Loon Lake House, Paul Smith's and Saranac Inn flourished because of the excellence of railroad service. In those days wealthy families stayed the entire

Union Station, Saranac Lake, N.Y. c. 1905

season in one place. The wives, children and servants usually arrived about July 1st and departed just ahead of the Labor Day weekend. The husbands would leave their city offices on the Friday night sleepers and wake up the next morning in time for breakfast and the prospect of two full days of recreation. Early Sunday evening they would return to the City aboard a Pullman which pulled into New York at 7:30 a.m., which allowed ample time to get set for another week's work. Very convenient!

Since the Adirondack region has many summer camps for children, the railroads also got that business as well. Camp specials were scheduled with whole cars reserved for just one place such as Moss Lake Camp, near Big Moose Lake or the Adirondack-Florida Summer School, near Onchiota. It was quite a sight to watch several hundred youngsters, their trunks and other belongings and — in the case of the former — their horses and gear being unloaded from the special boxcars.

From an engineering standpoint the worst spot on the line was the steep grade at Big Moose, 2040 feet above sea level. Frequently even in Summer, two steam locomotives — one pulling and the other pushing were needed to handle that stretch of track. Purgatory Hill was aptly named because the firemen had to grunt, sweat and shovel to coax the 10-car train over the crest. In Winter, when the mercury plummeted almost out of sight at the bottom of the tube (40°-50° below zero) even 3 engines were put in service because the rarefied air made it difficult to generate steam. I can recall one 56° below night when the train was six hours late on a six-hour run from Malone to Utica. Later on when the big diesels came into use the trip was a comparative cinch. However, after having been accustomed to the unforgettable sound of a steam engine whistle as it cut loose at crossings, arrivals and departures, I never could be impressed by the far less sonorous wail of a diesel roaring through the night.

During the Depression years the Central tried to keep the tourist business alive by promoting and scheduling the use of ski trains, which proved to be very popular.

Daily freight trains added to the traffic which kept the steel bright on the Adirondack Division just prior to World War I.

Fifty years later there were only two passenger trains serving the Tri-Lakes area. One left Lake Placid at 9:30 P.M. and reached New York City at 7:15 the next morning. This was the only passenger train going south on the Division. The only northbound train left New York City at the ungodly hour of 11:45 P.M. (for those riding in the daycoach) and arrived in Lake Placid at 9:55 A.M.

The process of gradually working toward the elimination of all traffic to the North Country area began about 1950, when the New York Central petitioned the Public Service Commission to remove some of its trains.

The next phase featured the closing down of the stations. Those between Lake Clear and Malone were closed in May, 1956 and later torn down. Before the final closing of the Gabriels station a few had remained open during the Summer months, but closed in the Winter. In the Fall of '56 a Kentucky salvage company tore up the tracks from Malone to Gabriels and thereby removed all reminders of railroad traffic to this part of the mountains.

After 1956 Lake Clear Junction became the freight center and ticket office for the eliminated stations. Mail for the surrounding villages was unloaded there and carried the rest of the way by truck.

In 1959 the P.S.C. allowed the Central to drop the two day trains but made them keep the night trains in operation. That same year the Lake Clear station was closed and its business moved to Saranac Lake. The Central continued its efforts to discontinue its passenger service completely but, even though it succeeded in modifying its service each time, it could not get permission to pull out altogether. In 1961 the freight office operation was moved to Tupper Lake where it functioned until very recently, when Penn Central stopped operations altogether.

Residents of the Tri-Lake area did not hesitate to express their concern and even indignation about the obvious objective of the railroad officials. Area Chambers of Commerce fought a sometimes bitter delaying battle in order to protect their vested interests and growth potential, which is predicated upon good transportation facilities. Public hearings were held in Saranac Lake and other communities at a cost of several thousand dollars each in order to force the railroad to stay in operation at least until the Northway was completed.

The trend of the final meetings illustrated a lack of any real interest on the part of the railroad to seek any solution besides discontinuance. Its method was to make its so-called service so bad that it was used less and less. Eventually the people in the area supposedly being served no longer really cared whether or not the railroad pulled out since they were just about reconciled to the eventual adjustment. Then came the end of an era: on April 24, 1965 the last passenger train, with Floyd Fullerton at the throttle of the big diesel, pulled out from Saranac Lake station. Many people, nostalgically inclined, gave the engineer a big send-off.

The Central then proceeded to cut down freight service and refused to handle shipments of less than carload bulk. This especially embittered the area merchants but the New York Central and later the Penn Central, its successor, apparently were not interested in trying to increase the freight loads through promotion and improved service.

For a while one freight train a week went through on a rather casual schedule, depending on the nature of the cargo. The former Sunmount State Hospital, Ray Brook State Hospital and several area firms in Saranac Lake and Placid were still being supplied

Easy Rolling

A Wreck near Horseshoe [Tupper Lake area] in 1920's

wholly or partly. Then came strong rumors and stronger indications that the Penn Central would end its operation in the fairly foreseeable future. Railroading, particularly passenger traffic, was no longer a paying proposition in most of the nation.

Then, within the last two years, the Penn Central finally did go and a great deal of glamor of a sort went with it. The railroads played such a significant part in the development of the region that their passing has already been sincerely missed — at least by those who rode the trains in their heyday. The sound and smell of escaping steam, the waving of the brakeman's signal lanterns, the "All Abo-a-r-r-r-d" of the conductor after he had consulted his vest-pocket Hamilton watch, the slow pumping and pounding of the huge well-greased driveshafts, the whirling and grinding of the big wheels as they sought to get traction; the slightly nauseating odor of the plush seats, the ubiquitous orange and banana peels, the newspaper and candy "butcher," the solicitous conductor, the cinders and smoke billowing in from the open windows — each is part and parcel of a composite pattern which will linger long in the memories of the older North Country generations....

Right now in the midst of the energy crunch there are indications of a possible new lease on life for many abandoned or about to be abandoned railroads. The high price of gasoline and automobile maintenance would seem to justify the return of the iron steeds. There is much talk in Albany and Washington about the benefits of mass transportation as a booster shot to the sagging economy of the hinterlands and resort areas. Projects such as turbo-trains from Utica to Montreal, using the Penn Central right-of-way, have periodically surfaced but so far nothing has jelled. In whatever form it eventually takes a restoration of railroad service — passenger and freight — would be a definite asset to the Adirondacks in particular and the whole state in general.

But for the present at least, in view of the fact that spikes have been pulled and rails removed for salvage purposes, this nostalgic little item seems very appropriate.

Abandoned — Olin Lyman
I
The old Branch line with its rusted rails
    Winds on through the ancient hills;
The shadows creep as the sunlight fails,
    Then the calls of the whippoorwills
Sound in the thickets where verdure lies
    Shading the green of the grass-grown ties.

II
The night is born and the stars awake
    While the moon ascends the sky;
A ghostly wind stirs a lonely lake
    To the wail of the loon's weird cry,
And the vines creep up to the broken door
    Of a station where man will come no more.

III
Midnight and hush — then the phantom roar
    And the clang of a ghostly bell
And an eerie whistle, while pistons pour
    Their wraiths of steam....the knell
Intones again....past the stunted pine
    The ghost train rolls on the Memory Line.

There's an old saying that it's always darkest just before the dawn. Apparently that's the situation right now in respect to railroad service in the Adirondacks. Just when everyone had become stoically reconciled to the very plausible conviction that the railways had been permanently and irrevocably assigned to uneasy and unnecessary oblivion, the news came out of Albany on Wednesday, April 17th that Gov. Malcolm Wilson had authorized Transportation Commissioner Raymond T. Schuler to proceed with the acquisition of the property including the rails and structures under the 30 Million Dollar Essential Rail Preservation Appropriation recently enacted by the Legislature regarding the rehabilitation and the restoration of the line from Remsen to Lake Placid and the restoration of service to the region.

According to the Governor: "Our goal is to preserve the right of way and the opportunity for its continued service as a transportation facility in the best way possible for environmental, energy, tourism and other economic reasons important to the people of the North Country." As yet no price has been set and no word received whether the acquisition would be by condemnation or negotiation.

State Attorney General Louis Lefkowitz and North Country legislators Stafford, Harris and Ryan, along with many organizations including the Adirondack Park Agency, the Adirondack Park Assn., and the Adirondack Mountain Club had been persistently petitioning the Assembly, Senate and Governor for months in order to prevent the further dismantling of tracks and bridges under a salvaging contract issued by the bankrupt Penn Central Railroad.

Appeals were made to the Federal District Court in Philadelphia, which has jurisdiction over the disposition of the railroad's assets, to hold off the destruction of the line until the New York State voters could decide on the fate of last November's billion-dollar transportation bond issue, which included funds for the purchase of the railroad. After the defeat of the issue the Ohio-based salvage firm resumed its job of pulling the rails, a project stopped by the onset of Winter.

The Adirondack Park Agency, headed by prestigious Richard Lawrence of Elizabethtown, then interceded and issued an order against the salvage outfit to cease and desist on the grounds that the operation constituted a regional project and was therefore subject to Agency review. However, the Pennsylvania Federal Court overruled the A.P.A. and further ordered the State of New York and its agencies to refrain from any further actions to halt the dismantling of the line.

Roger Tubby, ex-president of the Adirondack Park Assn., had noted in a very persuasive letter to Gov. Wilson that the purchase of the railroad called for a "now or never" decision because the option would be in all likelihood lost forever if immediate favorable action were not taken.

Among other benefits the line is considered to be the prime access route to Lake Placid should it get the 1980 Winter Olympics.

Mr. Tubby also pointed out that the resumption of service would provide an environmentally acceptable way to open up remoter sections of the Adirondack wilderness to future generations, especially those areas of Forest Preserve lands now sealed off by large private holdings such as Brandreth, Whitney and Webb estates. These back-country state lands are all located at a distance from major highways.

Another aspect of the welcome acquisition would be the restoration of the line from Lake Clear Junction to Malone and the Canadian Border in order to tap the very profitable freight business from central and western United States to Montreal and eastern Canada markets. During the peak years of the New York Central's Adirondack Division (later sold to Penn Central) as many as 1,200 freight cars a month went over the line, so it has a rosy potential which could provide competition to the more expensive trucking business, which filled the gap left by the discontinuance of freight service about 1972. Moreover Malone — my old hometown — could certainly use the booster shot of increased business activity.

So, for a variety of reasons, things seem to be looking up for the North Country people of all persuasions — hotel and motel owners, sports equipment dealers, real estate and insurance agents, bankers, merchants and just plain residents. Most of them are at present quite pleased and comforted by the prospects of more people and more business — a feeling tempered by an almost too good to be true but let's wait and see reaction. Others, here and elsewhere in the region, would be even more elated if the bringers of that business would just send up the money instead — and stay home. Fortunately for the region, this inbred, inhospitable, unintelligent, short-sighted and somewhat hostile attitude is anything but representative and should therefore be taken not with a grain but a whole shakerful of salt. If it pans out and the Adirondack Division is actually brought back from oblivion, the entire North Country will be the beneficiary and will share the certain results of this long-deferred and urgently needed economic transfusion.

John Cheney — Stoddard Photo

Old Mt. Phelps — Stoddard Photo

Alvah Dunning
— Stoddard Photo

Mitchell Sabattis

Chapter 11

Four Great Adirondack Guides

In addition to the allure of its obvious natural assets, much of the fame of the Adirondacks can be traced directly back to its old-time, outstanding guides. By the middle of the last century at least four of these men had already become living legends.

Yet, however remarkable their talents were, it is quite certain that Cheney, Sabattis, Phelps and Dunning would never have acquired more than a local reputation had it not been for the strong impression each made on one or more of the prominent writers of their time — Todd, Hoffman, Chittenden, Headley, Lanman, Lossing, Street, Mather, Murray, Warner and others. All extolled their exploits and their characters and thereby created much of the color and glamor that has since become an appreciable part of the lore of the Adirondacks.

While such distinguished regional writers assured the guides their immortality in prose, another of their contemporaries, a camera artist named Stoddard, provided them with an equally graphic form of fame by picture and by print.

The purpose of this article, mainly a synthesis or composite of the early sources, is to *Chauffer la gloire* — rekindle the renown of the great guides, the men who wrote about them and the man who caught their likenesses on film.

John Cheney (1800-1887)

The first of the Adirondack guides to become a celebrity was John Cheney. Born in New Hampshire he lived both there and in Ticonderoga until he was thirty. Then, as that place became too settled to suit him, he moved to the vicinity of Adirondac, the mining village southeast of the High Peak area of Essex County. There he was employed by the ill-fated McIntyre Iron Works for about twenty years.

Since this work, mainly as a hunter and guide, was mostly seasonal he had ample time to hunt and range through that densely-wooded, mountainous, game-filled region. When the Emmons-Redfield party made the first recorded ascent of Marcy on August 5, 1837, Cheney and probably Harvey Holt were the guides. In 1839, he also guided Prof. Benedict when that scientist established the height of Marcy as 5344 feet, a figure verified by Colvin in 1872.

Probably the most tragic event in Cheney's life occurred at Calamity Pond, near Lake Colden, on Sept. 3, 1845. On that fateful day David Henderson, the dominant influence in the management of the Iron Works, accidentally shot himself and died less than fifteen minutes later. The following year, when he was guiding Rev. J. T. Headley, Cheney

David Henderson, Dominant Figure at Tahawus

Henderson Monument at Calamity Pond — Stoddard Photo

120

pointed out a log alongside the trail which had been widened to enable him and a group of other guides to carry out Henderson's body. "There," he said, "I sat all night and held Mr. Henderson's little son in my arms. It was a dreadful night."

During the years when the McIntyre Iron Works (called Adirondac Iron and Steel Co., after 1848) was in operation, Cheney was frequently sent to Albany and Jersey City on company business and often was entrusted with large sums of money.

The first of many noted writers to become strongly influenced by Cheney's hunting prowess was Charles F. Hoffman, who in 1838 described him in *Wild Scenes in Forest and Prairie* as a "slight-looking man of about seven and thirty, a man that lived winter and summer in the woods - honest John Cheney, as staunch a hunter and as true and gentle a practicer of woodcraft as ever roamed the broad forest." That author, crippled since youth when a leg had been crushed, was bitterly disappointed when he was unable to climb the final steep slopes of Marcy, which he called Tahawus (the cloud splitter).

Hoffman's sincere and purple praise was only the first of other similar descriptions. Headley, for whom he guided in 1846, devoted a whole glowing chapter to him in *The Adirondack; or Life in the Woods*. Two of his exploits are noteworthy and characteristic of the man. The first of these incidents which the old hunter eventually told to many eager listeners featured a panther which was about to pounce on him. Before the crouching animal could make its leap, however, a bullet through the head deterred the beast forever.

"And how did you feel," asked the author, "When you discovered such a creature ready to spring upon you?" Instead of a detailed emotional analysis he got this straight-forward reply:

"I felt as if I should kill him."

Headley was remarkably impressed by his guide's personality. "Cheney has none of the roughness of the hunter, but is one of the mildest, most unassuming, pleasant men you will meet with anywhere." Another author, Henry Dornburgh, in his pamphlet on the Adirondack Iron Works,[1] stated, "John was loved and esteemed by all."

Still another author, Charles Lanman, allotted a whole chapter in his *Adventures in the Wilds of America* to Cheney, the Adirondac hunter. He too was struck by the seeming contrast between the woodsman's appearance and his hunting skills. "I expected, from what I had heard, to see a huge, powerful, hairy Nimrod. Instead I found him small in stature, bearing more the appearance of a modest and thoughtful student, gentle in his manners and as devoted a lover of nature and solitude as ever lived."

Lanman's book featured nine pages of thrilling experiences which Cheney told him during a summer vacation devoted to fishing and the ascent of Tahawus. These include encounters with a hibernating bear, wounded moose and deer, panthers and wolves. Full credit was given by the guide to the devotion and courage of his dogs.

In a letter to S. R. Stoddard in 1873 Cheney narrated his most memorable hunting trip. "One day I was chasing a buck on Cheney Lake. I was in a canoe and had put my pistol down by my side. Somehow the pistol slipped under me and discharged, the ball striking me half way between knee and ankle. Being 14 miles from any habitation at the time and alone, I only stopped long enough to see what harm had been done. Then I seized the oars and started after the buck again as the thought struck me that I might need that deer now more than ever. I caught up with him and made short work of it, took him ashore, dressed and hung him up. But I soon perceived that if I ever got out of the woods I must lose no time. By then my boot was full of blood and my ankle began to pain me bad, so I cut two crotched sticks and with their help (as crutches) I managed to get out of the

---

1. Dornburgh, Henry, *Why The Wilderness is Called Adirondack*, Glens Falls, 1885, 14 pp.

woods in about eight hours. I only stopped to set down once because it was so hard to start again."

The pistol was especially made for him. The stock was carved from a birch root, and the barrel was eleven inches long. This favorite weapon, sold at auction for $100.00 to give him badly-needed funds, is now reputedly in the Geological Room of the State Education Building in Albany.

During his first thirteen years in the wilderness this modest man who never hunted on Sundays killed 600 deer, 400 sable, 19 moose, 27 bears, 7 wildcats, 6 wolves, 30 otter, 1 panther and a beaver.

Cheney, probably the most interesting of the early Adirondack guides, died in Newcomb in 1887. His name is perpetuated by two ponds and a mountain near Lake Sanford.

Mitchell Sabattis (1801(?) - 1906)

The name of Sabattis figures prominently in the history of the North Country. Captain Peter Sabattis earned his title by service in both the Revolution and the War of 1812. He had been one of Col. Benedict Arnold's guides in late 1775 on that well-conceived but poorly-executed, unsuccessful expedition against Quebec by way of the swampy wilderness of northern Maine. The older Sabattis was said to have been a noble specimen of a man, mentally as well as physically, and lived to be a reputed 108.

Mitchell, the best known of Peter's three sons, was born in Parishville, St. Lawrence County, probably in 1801. Like Cheney, whom he strongly resembled in size and manner, he was gentle and unassuming. But, despite their small stature, both men possessed remarkable strength and endurance. The Indian's inherited knowledge of woodcraft, sharpened by constant practice, amounted almost to animal instinct.

The younger Sabattis first saw Long Lake when he was about eight. Apparently the family, as was customary with many of the northern New York Indians, spent the short Adirondack summers hunting, fishing and raising a crop of corn for winter use. When he was 13 Mitchell dropped his first deer with a blast from an old muzzle-loader braced against a log.

Before settling permanently at Long Lake, Sabattis lived at Pendleton, now a part of Newcomb. There in 1859 B. J. Lossing, the noted historian, met him and his German wife and family. The author stated in his classic *The Hudson from the Wilderness to the Sea* that the Indian was "by far the best man in all that region to lead the traveler to the Hudson waters and the Adirondack mountains." Sabattis and another guide named Preston took the Lossing party on the well-narrated trip to Marcy and a few days later to the lower end of the legendary Indian Pass. Mrs. Lossing, who was a member of the group was told afterward by Cheney that she was the third woman to have climbed Tahawus; Phelps inferred that he guided the first two.

There were other writers — Rev. J. T. Headley and L. E. Chittenden — who also recorded their indelible impressions of the great guide. In his *Adirondac; or Life in the Woods,* the former had this to say about Sabattis as they parted: "I shook his hand with as much regret as I ever did that of a white man. I shall long remember him. He is a man of deeds and not of words — kind, gentle, delicate in his feeling, honest and true as steel."

Chittenden in his *Personal Reminiscences* wrote two chapters featuring Sabattis: "Adirondack Days" and "The Story of Mitchell Sabattis." These are based on a five-week trip to Long Lake in the late 1850s. During that halcyonic holiday the Professor from Burlington had two experiences which illustrate the almost incredible keenness of senses

Sweeney Carry between Raquette River and Wawbeek, Upper Saranac Lake — Stoddard Photo

that centuries of wilderness life have developed in the Indians. Wrote Chittenden: "I wanted to have the experience of floating for deer. On a rainy, foggy night Sabattis and I went to Moose Creek to try for them. The marshes were overflowed. Just when we were ready to give up, we heard a deer. It was standing in the shallow water. Mitchell stopped the boat opposite it, so near that we could hear the animal chewing the pads. It was impossible to get a sight of it, however. If we made any disturbance, it was certain to disappear instantly in the darkness.

"For five minutes we stood endeavoring to pierce that black curtain with our eyes. Then I estimated as well as I could its height above the water, aimed where the chest ought to be and gave it one barrel. Away it went floundering across the marsh to solid ground.

"Well, we've lost him" I said, greatly disappointed.

'How can we lose what we never had?' was the guide's pertinent reply. 'But we will have him yet before daylight. He is hard hit and will not run very far.'

"And that was exactly how it turned out. The Indian's ear had detected an injury to one of the animal's front legs. In the dark and rainy night by jacklight he found the deer's bloody path out of the marsh, followed it over fallen trees and through heavy brush a mile or more up the steep hillside until he overtook the wounded deer. Then, holding the light in one hand and the gun in the other, he fired the finishing shot. Such a story seems incredible and, had I not seen the results, I would not have believed it."

The second incident concerned trout fishing. Having been disinclined to fish for several days for a variety of reasons, Sabattis finally decided that all the weather conditions were just right. He rowed Chittenden to the mouth of Cold River and indicated the spot to make the first cast. The author obeyed and a trout responded almost instantly. "As I checked the trout he rushed past the boat within reach of Mitchell's landing net. He made one sweep and a five-pound speckled trout lay panting in the boat, my first fish in the

123

Adirondacks. What followed was mere repetition. Every time the fly struck the water a half dozen trout leaped for it. In a short half-hour five brook trout, weighing more than 20 pounds, were taken. But that short half-hour was an era in my life."

S. R. Stoddard, who met Sabattis in 1873, provided still another proof of the latter's fearlessness and hunting prowess. He told the famed photographer that he had, up to that time, killed nine panthers. He had driven one of these great cats along a narrow shelf on the face of a ledge and into a crevice. Sabattis then proceeded to dislodge the formidable creature by poking it vigorously with a sharp stick so that his companion could get a shot at it. When, for some unaccountable reason the other hunter failed to do so, Sabattis coolly dispatched the beast himself.

In his earlier days moose were plentiful in the woods and the hunter killed more than 20 of them. Whatever the quarry it apparently was rare indeed when more than one bullet was required.

Besides being an unexcelled hunter and guide Mitchell Sabattis, after his celebrated conversion from John Barleycorn's influence, became a pillar of the Methodist Church, first at Newcomb and later at Long Lake. Dr. Todd, author of *Long Lake*, spoke of him as "a noble young Indian man whose violin leads the music in public worship." In 1865 Sabattis raised $2,000 toward a new church by speaking before the congregation of city ministers whom he had guided.

The interesting story of the Indian's redemption from drink is told in *Personal Reminiscences*. Chittenden had solved a domestic crisis in the Sabattis family by buying the mortgage in time to prevent bank foreclosure. He did this in exchange for a promise by Sabattis to swear off drinking forever and to meet him the next August at Bartlett's.

About midnight one evening the following February the Indian's benefactor was pleasantly surprised. Sabattis, in a home-made sled pulled by two borrowed horses, had driven the 150 miles distance from Long Lake to Burlington. The sled's cargo consisted of the choice sections of 25 deer, the carcasses of two black bear, ten dozen grouse, 100 pounds of trout and the skins of a panther, marten, mink and foxes. Since there was far more game than he could possibly use, the author arranged for the sale of the surplus and the proceeds, plus the money Sabattis had brought, were more than the balance of the mortgage. The rest was used to build an addition to their home and to buy furniture.

Twenty-five years later, the loan having been fully repaid long before, Prof. Chittenden returned to Long Lake and found that the old guide had never broken his promise. The writer described their reunion as follows: "The next morning I heard a light step on the uncarpeted hall and a knock on my door. I opened it and Sabattis entered. He was as glad to see me as I was to grasp his true and honest hand. But I was profoundly surprised. Had the world with him stood still? He (84 years old) did not look a day older than when I last saw him. The same keen, clear eye, transparent skin with the play of the muscles under it, the same elastic step, ringing voice and kindly heart. His eye was not dim nor his natural force abated. We spent a memorable day together — at nightfall we parted forever. Not long afterward (1906) he died full of years, full of honors, that noblest work of God, an honest man."

Orson (Old Mt.) Phelps (1817-1905)

Although "Old Mountain" Phelps justly deserved having his name bracketed with those of Cheney, Sabattis and Dunning, his fame was based on a more unusual talent. While each of the others was celebrated as a mighty hunter, resourceful woodsman and highly competent guide, the trait that set Phelps apart was his intense love of the mountains — especially Marcy (which he called Mercy) — and his inordinate desire to climb them.

Other guides took their "sports" on hunting and fishing trips. Phelps took his to clamber up the peaks surrounding Keene Valley and he made those trips memorable by expounding picturesquely and quaintly about the beauties and sublimities of his mountain world. More than anyone else he deserves the credit for popularizing the sport of climbing.

Phelps was born in Wethersfield, Vermont in 1817. About 1830 he and his father, a surveyor, moved into the Schroon Lake country — within view of that alluring serrated skyline to the northwest. An even closer attachment to the mountains was formed when he worked for several years at Adirondac Iron Works, just south of the High Peak area.

In August 1849, accompanied by Henry Estey and Almeron Oliver, he made his first trip to Tahawus (Marcy). The next month he moved from Schroon and settled in Keene, that loveliest of valleys. That same year he blazed the first trail from the east to the summit of Marcy, going in from Upper Ausable Lake via Haystack and the head of Panther Gorge. About 1850 he guided two women safely up Marcy and back and thereby gained considerable prestige.

That reputation was given an even greater impetus in 1878 when Charles Dudley Warner's essay "The Primitive Man" (later called "A Character Study") appeared in the Atlantic magazine. This tribute not only pleased the shaggy old woodsman immensely; it also made him famous overnight.

As Donaldson expressed it in his *History of the Adirondacks* "Phelps was lassoed by a literary halo. It was a big halo and it got around his feet and tripped him up now and then." Although his description was accurate enough, the charm of Warner's style made "Old Mountain" far more alluring than he actually was.

S. R. Stoddard, who met the venerable guide in 1873, described him thus: "A little man, about five feet six in height, muffled up in an immense crop of long hair and a beard that seemed to boil up out of his collar band. Grizzly as the granite ledges he climbs, shaggy as the rough-barked cedar, but with a pleasant twinkle in his eye and an elasticity to his step equaled by few younger men. He likes to talk and delivers his sage conclusions and whimsical oddities in a cheery, chirrupy, squeaky sort of tone — away up on the mountains as it were — an octave above the ordinary voice, somewhat suggestive of the warblings of an ancient chickadee."

This "Primeval Man," jokingly or not, once declared that no water had struck his back in 40 years. "I don't believe in this etarnal sozzlin'," he maintained; "soap is a thing that I hain't no kinder use for."

Some of his other remarks, as recorded by Warner, were extremely expressive as well as tortured. A "reg'lar walk" meant over a marked trail; a "random scoot" meant a bushwhacking trek; a "reg'lar random scott of a rigamarole" meant a tight spot in the woods such as a seemingly impassable swamp. His classic contribution to the language was his reply to a question about the next day's itinerary: "Waal, I callerlate, if they rig up the calerlation they callerlate on, we'll go to the Boreas."

Marcy, which he climbed more than a hundred times, was by far his favorite peak. For him it was a holy place and it gave him a sense of "heaven up-h'isted-ness." He had no patience with people who did not share his reverence for "Mount Mercy" and once became so disgusted with a group of girls who gabbed about fashions on his sacred summit that he afterward remarked, "I had a good mind ter kick the silly things off my mounting!"

When Otis Estes, a Keene Valley neighbor, was praised for being a religious man, "Old Mountain" commented: "Otis probably is the piousest man in town, but I enjoy religion more."

Besides the influence of Horace Greeley's "Try-bune," which Phelps read avidly, his association with three prominent clergymen was next in importance. The Reverends Bushnell, Shaw and Twitchell frankly enjoyed his friendship; moreover, they treated him and were treated by him as equals.

C. D. Warner, who also admired Phelps greatly and would have no other guide, summed up his impression of the old man in these graceful, memorable words: "There were other trappers, and more deadly hunters and as intrepid guides: but Old Phelps was the discoverer of the beauties and sublimities of the mountains. I suppose that, in all that country, he alone had noticed the sunsets and observed the delightful processes of the seasons, taken pleasure in the woods for themselves, and climbed mountains solely for the sake of the prospect. He alone understood what was meant by scenery....

"In his solitary wanderings and musings, the primitive man, self-taught, had evolved for himself a philosophy and a system of things. When the outer world came to him, perhaps he had about as much to give to it as to receive from it; probably more, in his estimation, for there is no conceit like isolation."

During his sunset years, before the old guide had become too feeble, he pieced out his slender income by making packbaskets, keeping store in a haphazard, contemplative way, and selling Stoddard guidebooks and photographs of himself.

Orson (Old Mountain) Phelps died in 1905 at the age of eighty-eight. A mountain named after him by Colvin and a picturesque waterfall help keep alive the fame of Phelps in Keene Valley.

Alvah Dunning (1816-1902)

Alvah Dunning, the famous hermit guide of the Raquette Lake region, was in every respect the Adirondack version of the primitive man. By his very nature he seemed to revert toward earlier eras and he deeply distrusted the inroads of progress. He sought only food and solitude in the woods, not beauty as did Old Mountain Phelps.

Like so many other strongly-marked personalities he had his share of staunch friends, mostly among the sportsmen he served, and more than his share of enemies, these chiefly among his fellow guides who envied him for his uncanny ability as a hunter and trapper, his anti-social nature, and his frequent outbursts against superfluous slaughter. His well-publicized feud with the celebrated Ned Buntline was probably the highlight of his eventful career.

Born in June, 1816 at Lake Pleasant, Hamilton County, Alvah began to hunt and trap with his father when he was only six. In his eleventh year he shot his first moose; in his twelfth he guided the first outsiders into the Raquette Lake area.

His father, who had seen service as a scout under Sir William Johnson, was considered to be every bit as formidable and ruthless an Indian fighter as his famous friends, Nick Stoner and Nat Foster.

While still a youngster and living with his family. Alvah's father got word one day that company was coming to spend a week or more. Since they needed more fresh meat to take care of their guests and themselves, young Alvah was sent out to get a deer. He rowed his boat up the lake to the inlet, where he shot a large doe; after dressing it he loaded the animal into the guideboat and headed for home.

There was a strong wind that day so he kept as close as possible to the east shore. When he had covered about 1½ miles in good time his course skirted the foot of Steep Rock, a

Panther,

now Extinct in Adirondacks [?]

huge ledge protruding straight out of the water. His keen ears caught a scratching sound overhead. As he glanced up he saw the tawny shape of a painter (panther) twitching its tail as it got ready to spring. Not having taken his usual precaution to reload his old muzzle-loader after killing the deer, the frightened boy had no weapon handy except for an oar which he raised as the big cat made his move.

Just as the panther launched itself into space Alvah instinctively felt that he needed help, so he shouted, "Oh Lord, save me! And would you believe it? That cussed painter turned a complete somerset in the air above me — [as Alvah told it many times in after-years] and landed smack dab right back on that same rock!" Talk about answered prayer!

The son inherited his father's keenness of vision, stealth, endurance and economy of motion. These talents enabled him to become one of the most resourceful and successful hunters the Adirondacks have ever produced. Only Mitchell Sabattis, John Cheney, Caleb Chase and possibly Elijah Simmonds were as nearly deadly shots and only the Indian possessed "Snake eye's," (Dunning's) instinctive skill in woodcraft.

Harry Radford in the Winter 1902 issue of *Woods and Waters* described a shooting match between Dunning and Caleb Chase, of Newcomb. The target was a carpet tack on a whitened plank; the range was forty yards. Each man sent the first four of his allotted five shots within a hair's breadth of the tiny target. On the fifth Dunning scored the only bullseye. It is noteworthy that the winner was over sixty-five at the time.

His lifetime tally of trophies included, besides countless deer and bears, nearly a hundred moose and slightly more than that number of panthers (102). His biggest catch of fish was made in 1833, when he pulled 96 pounds of trout out of Piseco Lake in two hours.

For many years Alvah lived at Blue Mountain Lake but in 1865, when people started arriving there in ever-increasing numbers, he moved to Raquette Lake. During the next twelve years he had that lovely lake all to himself in the Winter and had little reason to complain about being crowded in the Summer.

In 1865, when W.H.H. (Adirondack) Murray made the first of many annual trips to that region, Dunning became his guide. Later on, of course, he was succeeded by "Honest John" Plumley of Long Lake. Dunning also guided Verplanck Colvin on his ascent of Mount Seward in October 1870.

He liked and respected Murray but his scorn of the men he later guided was expressed in these remarks to Fred Mather: "These woods is a-gittin' too full o' people fer comfort. — They're a-runnin' all over here in Summer a-shootin' an' a-fishin'. They do git in the way, an' they ain't got no business here disturbin' the woods."

"They pay you well for workin' for them, don't they, Alvah?"

"Yes, they do, durn 'em or I wouldn't bother with 'em; but I druther they'd stay out o'my woods. They'll come anyhow, an I might as well guide them for if I don't someone else will. But I druther they'd keep their money an' stay out o' the woods. I can make a livin' without 'em but they'd starve to death here without me. They're the durndest lot of cur'osities you ever seen an' many of 'em's fools!" [From *My Angling Friends* — Fred Mather]

When he agreed to guide a party he gave his employers full value for his wages. Several times when his "sports" were unsuccessful through no fault of his — he even refused their money. "Won't take it, ain't done nuthin' to earn it!" he would declare.

His first home was a rough shack on Indian Point; the next was a closed in lean-to on Osprey Island, also on Raquette Lake. In spite of a stubborn stand there he was finally dispossessed by Dr. Durant, who wanted the property for one of his family. The eviction action was made somewhat more bearable by the acceptance of a hundred dollars.

From there he found temporary seclusion at Eighth Lake of the Fulton Chain but, when others settled there too, he felt forced to return to Raquette Lake, where he built a hut on Brown's Tract Inlet. Even there he could not escape from either people or progress. This time it was the Raquette River Railroad; again he was partially compensated for the inconvenience of his reluctant departure.

"I guess I've lived too long." (83) he said, "I sorta hoped I could die in peace in the wilderness where I was born. But if I don't slip my wind pretty quick, I guess there ain't goin' to be no wilderness to die in. I've heard tell that the Rockies are bigger. Guess I'll go out yonder and hunt for a quiet corner out o'reach of tootin' steamboats an' screechin' en-jines."

A year later he was back at Raquette Lake — this time at Golden Beach, near South Inlet. From that time on he hunted and fished a little and spent his Winters with relatives in Rome or Syracuse. In March, 1902 he went to the Sportsmen's Show in New York City as a guest of the Whitneys. On the return trip he spent the night at the Dudley House in Utica. The next morning he was found dead in his bed. Unused to illuminating gas he had apparently blown out the light — as he would a lamp or lantern — not turned off the jet.

Fred Mather devoted a chapter to Dunning, who had been his guide on many trips. A renowned outdoorsman himself and a competent judge of people, the author had this to say about the old hunter while he was still alive: "Let the old man alone. If he lives for twenty years, he will never do as much harm to the fish and game as the so-called "sportsmen" … The game laws are all right but no right-thinking man should use them to oppress an old hunter whose only larder is the woods in which he was born. The strict letter of the law need not be enforced on the man whose whole life has been spent in a struggle for existence in the forest and who could not live out of it. Put yourself in his place."

Despite some grumbling in official circles he never was prosecuted, for Jack Shepard, an old-time Fulton Chain guide who had known Dunning for 30 years, summed up for Mather this opinion of Dunning: "He was an honest and hospitable man of the old style, all of whom looked on game laws as infringements on the rights of men who live in the woods. He was the last of a type that has passed. He killed deer when he needed it, caught trout out of season to bait his trap, firmly believed it a sin to kill wastefully and destroyed less game than many who cried out against him."

So lived and died Alvah Dunning, one of the greatest of the Adirondack guides, and every bit as unusual as Cheney, Sabattis and Phelps.

Chapter 12

The Adirondack Lean-to

The lean-to, like the packbasket and guideboat, would certainly lose much of its connotative quality and most of its character if it were not coupled with that other almost inseparably related, romantic, redolent, remarkable and ruminating word — Adirondack (a term as you will recall which was insultingly used by the Iroquois to revile the bark-munching seasonally resident tribe whose food supply was often uncertain). Moreover, in each instance and over the years these felicitous word pairs have gradually acquired such a pleasantly evocative, reciprocal relationship that it would seem somewhat presumptuous if not practically impossible to satisfactorily disassociate or improve them. How's that for a frankly chauvinistic opener?

Historically speaking, the memorable mountain region north of the Mohawk cannot of course be given all the credit for first conceiving the three-sided structural concept now so well-known to innumerable devotees of Adirondack trails. Somewhat similar shelters have of course been built since the proverbial time immemorial to provide temporary or even semi-permanent protection from the whims of the weather for all God's creatures — human and sub-human alike — wherever and whenever needed.

But the familiar basic design now known everywhere as the Adirondack lean-to — round spruce logs, sloping and over-hanging roof, plank floor and balsam bedding — did originate in the Adirondacks. Back in the early '90s resourceful guides such as Ellsworth Petty (Bill Petty's father) used this pattern in building the first such typical shelter for the Lyon family on Deer Island in Upper Saranac Lake. The Conservation Department, recognizing a good thing when they saw one, merely standardized the dimensions and added such desirable improvements as fireplace, garbage pit and comfort station.

Over the years there have been many terms used to describe the now renowned lean-to. One last-century designation was open shanty (or shantee), which usually indicated an improvised crotch-pole framework covered with brush, hemlock or spruce bark, evergreen boughs and occasionally with split, hollowed-out sections of medium-sized trees — the so-called Yankee trough type of roof. Certain other guides and woodsmen referred to such welcome stop-over spots as camps. Summer people, who were often generically and even contemptuously called sports by most of the memberhip of the guides' guild, persistently employed the term open camp until well into the middle of the present century. Interestingly enough, the most recent Conservation Department brochure diplomatically uses both open camp and lean-to when referring to that distinctive structure.

In a somewhat similar sense a low-key but long-lived dispute has been waging over the

Yankee Trough Roof of Camp on Upper Au Sable — Stoddard Photo

terms portage and carry. Although the former designation is always used in Canada, there are also perceptive people south of the Border who have adopted it as an Adirondack expression. However, perhaps because they consider resorting to any foreign word as being undesirable as well as unnecessary, most Adirondackers steadfastly refuse to employ any word other than carry.

In each instance the plainer and more meaningful term has just about driven out the more formal nomenclature.

Dr. Paul Jamieson, in his well-researched and excellent article on the Adirondack lean-to, which appeared in the February-March 1965 issue of *The Conservationist,* commented that although the Conservation laws of 1885-1894 established and thus preserved the Adirondacks, one of the last great wilderness regions of the East, very little effort was made to make it accessible for recreation. Even though the legislation which created the Adirondack Park in 1892 declared that it would "be forever preserved, maintained and cared for as ground open for the free use of all the people for their health and pleasure," successive Conservation commissioners were both hesitant and hampered because of pre-existing Forest Commission edicts which prohibited felling trees and girdling or peeling bark from standing trees. Fallen timber only could be used for firewood and camp construction." Since the legality of building shelters in places where live timber would have to be used for building materials was thus open to question, the Conservation Department played it safe and built no lean-tos until 1919, when it put up the venerable, small economy size edifices at the Four Corners and near the Feldspar-Opalescent confluence. Things speeded up in 1920, however, when 18 such shelters were erected in the region.

Although the Conservation Department wisely or otherwise dragged its collective feet in the matter of lean-to construction, as early as 1897 private organizations such as the Adirondack Trail Improvement Society, consisting of Ausable Club (St. Hubert's) members and others, and the Camp and Trail Club, founded by the Lake Placid Club members in 1912, opened up and maintained new trails from the east and north sides respectively of the High Peaks section.

Dr. Godfrey Dewey and the late Harry Wade Hicks of the Lake Placid Club, with the ever-ready assistance of perennial club president Henry van Hoevenbergh, were the prime movers in the organization and subsequent success of the latter society. Sno-Bird and Gothics open camps were constructed by them, by permit from the State agency, during the period from 1913-15.

Sometime previous to 1890 van Hoevenbergh had already built Mt. Jo and at least two other strategically spaced shelters for the convenience of his guests at the ill-fated Adirondack Lodge, which was devoured by fire on June 3, 1903.

By latest count there are — or were — 235 such structures in the Adirondacks; of this number 134 are in the High Peaks area (including canoe routes). There are 23 in the Colden-Flowed Lands sector and several more, including at least two additional organizational (double size) shelters, are planned in order to accommodate the ever-increasing numbers of hikers and outing club members who are annually attracted to this alluring region. On double holidays such as Dominion Day and July 4th as many as 800 people have checked in at Colden Ranger's cabin. Many others, of course, neglected to sign the register, so according to the recently resigned Chet Rafferty,[1] there may well have been as many as 1,000 reasonably happy wanderers who have occupied the lean-tos and available tent space — besides the woodshed and adjacent bivouac area — on a major holiday or a College Weekend.

Just another proof of the ever-mounting pressure on lean-to facilities and the necessity for additional accommodations was contained in a recent newspaper article which reported that during the relatively short period from early May until early July more than 6,000 people had checked in at Marcy Dam. That's what is known as downright saturation use of that portion of the Preserve.

Add these thousands to the hundreds of thousands of tent and trailer campers who flock to the more accessible areas and campsites and the conclusion is obvious. A visit to any of the populous campsites, such as Sacandaga, Meacham or Golden Beach, provides an instant answer to the question of why so many venturesome and crowd-allergic people periodically indulge a yen for the less luxurious but esthetically far more rewarding spell of lean-to occupation. Adirondack literature abounds in passages delineating and extolling unforgettable and unforgotten evenings spent either under the shelters or the stars.

One of the earliest accounts, which appeared in *Knickerbocker Magazine* in 1856, described a camp in this Victorian prose: "Built of hemlock bark it was entirely open in front and about two feet high in the rear. That for the ladies was within three feet of the lake with a screen of evergreens between it and the gentlemen's, which was about fifty yards off. The floors were of fresh hemlock boughs which were also to serve as beds. For pillows the gentlemen had their carpetbags; the ladies, cushions stuffed with moss."

Still another graphic description of lean-to construction is available to the interested reader and researcher. Moreover, it probably provides the most details to be found in Adirondack literature. Entitled "A Visit to the John Brown Tract" and written by T.B. Thorpe, it appeared in the July, 1859 issue of Harper's *New Monthly Magazine*."

"And here let me say that the building of these rude but comfortable quarters in the wilds of John Brown's Tract is among the interesting incidents of backwoods life; and the practical good sense of the guides, displayed in extemporizing comfortable lodgings, justly

---

1. Now deceased.

causes admiration. With an axe and plenty of hemlock trees they seem to be quite omnipotent. The place once selected for the hotel, as these shanties are generally termed, the first thing done is to cut down the brush for some 18 or 20 feet square — care being taken that a fallen tree shall form the southern boundary of the clearing.

"While the hunters are doing this the guides select some hemlock trees in the vicinity and, with their sharp axes, soon girdle them a foot or two from their base and then again as high as they can reach. This accomplished they slit down the section parallel with the trunk and insert into the incision, with but comparatively little labor, a sharpened rail. The beautiful covering of the tree first starts reluctantly then yields and is torn off in an immense sheet. Several of these sheets are procured when the frame of the shanty is speedily formed. A few rough poles, with rafters inclined toward the fallen log, are all that is necessary. Then the hemlock bark is stretched over the frame with all the facility of so much well-tanned leather.

"In a very short time a comfortable lodge has been completed; earth is thrown around the base to keep off currents of air and leave a drain in case of a flooding rain. In the front are piled huge logs which are set on fire for the double purpose of rarefying the night air and keeping off all insects and other varmints . . . The "floor" is next covered with hemlock boughs of two or three feet thickness. Upon these boughs is placed a blanket, the hunter rolls himself up in another, the guides make a tremendous fire and thus all comfortably lounge away the evening hours which precede luxurious sleep."

In Hoffman's *Wild Scenes in the Forest*[1] a far cruder camp in the Indian Pass was depicted: "It was nothing more than a shed of boughs open on the side nearer the fire. It promised sufficient protection from the rain so long as the wind should blow from the right quarter . . . 'Well,' said Cheney, 'You see there's no place but what if a man bestirs himself to do his best, he may find some comfort in it. Now many's the time that I have been in the woods on a worse night than this and having no axe nor nothing to make a fire with, have crept into a hollow log and lay there shivering until morning. But here now and with such a fire as that _____'

"As he spoke a sudden puff of wind drove the smoke from the green and wet timber full into our faces and filled the shantee to a degree so stifling that we all rushed out into the rain that blew in blinding torrents against us.

'Tormented lightning!' cried John, who seized his axe and plunged into the darkness. In a moment or two a large tree came crashing down with all its leafy honors, bearing with it two or three saplings which fell at our feet. With the green boughs he made a wall around the fire to shut out the wind, leaving it open only on the side toward the shantee. The supper was now cooked without further interruption . . . .

"After a story-telling session the piles of brush which encircled the fire suddenly kindled into a blaze which for a moment or two threatened to consume our wigwam. The wind at the same time poured down the Pass in shifting, angry blasts which whirled the flames in reeling eddies high into the air and brought the gray cliffs into momentary light. The cold rain changed into a flurry of snow which accompanied the smoke into the innermost parts of our abode. . . . . Sleet and smoke alternately dampened and stifled every effort at conversation until finally all was still except for the roar of the elements. . . .

"I wrapped myself in my cloak and placing my mouth upon the ground to avoid choking from the smoke, I was soon dreaming as quietly as if in a curtained chamber at home. The last words I heard John say, as he coiled into a blanket were — "Well, it's one

1. Hoffman, C.F., *Wild Scenes in Forest and Prairie*, London: Richard Bentley, 1836 Vol. p. 65.

comfort: since it's taken on to blow so, I've cut down most of the trees around us that would be likely to fall and crush us during the night."

That is what could be called an amazing and not altogether credible adjustment to a rather precarious situation. Although every hiker can undoubtedly recall remotely similar circumstances in kind if not in degree — all of us can understandably appreciate not having to periodically subject ourselves to many such unenviable overnight ordeals.

Presumably every 46er has his own private stock of stories about unfortunate individuals who found it well-nigh impossible to adjust to life in the lean-to. Overcrowded quarters, close confinement caused by seemingly endlessly dreary hours or even days of remorseless rain, personality clashes (cabin fever) precipitated by bad planning and worse luck — all these factors are often part and parcel of nearly everyone's exposure experience. But undoubtedly the most unusual and for the couple concerned, the most regrettable example of misfortune I have ever heard of took place in just such an Adirondack setting. A friend, Watson Harding, was an interested and even fascinated witness of the following course of events.

Sometime in the 1920's Harding and a companion named Woodford were on a fishing trip at the Flowed Lands, a trouty stretch of water then as now. They had been there several successful days when, rounding a bend in the trail, they were mildly astonished to first hear then see a strange procession approaching them. Three decidedly out-of-place characters came closer and then materialized as a girl, a man and a chauffeur in full regalia. The attractive female and her escort were dressed to the nines as though they were on their way to a country club reception. The chauffeur was festooned like a clothes tree with hampers, hat boxes and assorted suitcases and obviously was having a stumbling, hard time peering through and around the assorted paraphernalia in a commendable effort to keep not only vertical but on the trail.

Following the customary exchange of greetings and while the fishermen's eyeballs retracted back into their momentarily vacated sockets, the intrepid trio disappeared from the sight but not from the minds of the astounded pair. Gradually the gay voices died away in the distance giving Harding and Woodford time to shake their heads and rub their eyes repeatedly just to rule out the possibility of their having tangled with an Adirondack-style mirage. However, after comparing notes, they both decided that they had indeed seen what they had seen — and were convinced that there would shortly be noteworthy developments as well as an interesting explanation . . .

By following at a discreet distance the trout fanciers found out that the party had taken up quarters in two of the lean-tos close to the Opalescent. Later that day the inquisitive pair managed to meet the chauffeur, who satisfied their curiosity about the rest of his party. The light-hearted ones were of course newly-weds who were helping establish a tradition started by the bride's parents, who had apparently enjoyed a halcyonic honeymoon blessed by perfect blue and silver skies and warm, delightfully aromatic nights in an incomparably scenic setting.

According to the chauffeur the groom had shown considerably less than all-out enthusiastic approval before finally agreeing to follow his determined young wife's wishes. Further explanations were abruptly abbreviated by shouted orders for the liveried one to build a fire, cook and serve the first evening's meal . . .

That night, shortly after a silvery, large economy-size moon had provided a romantic respite, ominous sights and sounds punctuated and punctured the idyllic interlude. A grade A dilly of a line storm roared in from the west, an endless array of scudding clouds dumped their cargoes of dew and power-packed winds pulled out all stops. Harding and his

Indian Pass

friend, comfortably ensconced in a well-protected, well-roofed shelter, occasionally speculated about their neighbors' less intact ceiling which, they knew, had numerous knot holes. While these admittedly provided better ventilation they nevertheless also permitted a more than adequate amount of aqua to enter.

Instead of following the usual Adirondack meteorological pattern of cloudburst followed by almost immediate clearing, the storm continued practically unabated all night, and well into the next a.m. Then the torrential downpour was replaced by a steady, relentless drizzle which made things unpleasant for Harding and Company but downright distasteful for the honeymooners.

Having decided to keep as up-to-date as possible on developments elsewhere, Harding saw to it that he somehow managed to time his trip to the river to coincide with the chauffeur's arrival there. Thus he learned that the pathos-evoking pair had spent an indescribably dismal and sleepless night as far back in their lean-to as possible — but unfortunately could never escape the nerve-jangling, clammy, inescapable ordeal by water.

The chauffeur also confided that the endearing expressions got fewer and farther between as the tempest progressed. Eventually all of the customary and heretofore automatic social amenities were curtailed and then finally replaced by the heartfelt but heartless bludgeon-like terms characteristically flung by less-endowed couples.

The rest of that day, and that night as well, featured unrequested encores in the form of almost incessant and alternate downpour and drizzle . . . .

Shortly after daybreak the chauffeur again briefed Harding anent the hapless honeymooners. No longer on speaking terms the two had consumed the rest of the goodies which the hired help had hauled in. During one lull in the storm he (the uniformed one) had

Avalanche Pass

managed to get a feeble fire going. The bedraggled bride, momentarily cheered by the flame, had emerged from the lean-to. That precipitated the climactic scene. Apparently motivated by something done or said by the blanket-bound husband, the exasperated, fed-up female had cut loose with several soul-searing curses. Next she yanked off her wedding ring and heaved it into the fire. For an encore she then hurled her engagement ring into the ashes and angrily withdrew into her sodden corner of the lean-to.

Not long after that the trio appeared, outward bound and moving fast. In the lead, trying to look as self-controlled and dignified as she conceivably could under the circumstances, was the badly-disillusioned and disheveled girl. Fifteen or twenty yards behind, the man tried his best to appear as presentable as possible.

Bringing up the rear and still burdened with the residue of the dunnage came the intrepid chauffeur, who nodded knowingly as he passed the sympathizing and only slightly amused trouters who had discovered that the difference between comedy and tragedy apparently depends solely upon the point of view.

Although the prose writers who visited the Adirondacks during the early years appreciably outnumbered the out-and-out poets, the versifiers nevertheless also recorded their own often ecstatic appreciation of their wilderness sojourn. Outstanding among these lyrical outbursts, besides such gems as Ned Buntline's "My Wildwood Home", A.L. Donaldson's "Tahawus" and John Burnham's "My Highland Home," is Homer Sweet's "Twilight Hours in the Adirondacks" (1870).[1]

1. Sweet, Homer D.L., *Twilight Hours in the Adirondack,* Syracuse, Wynkopt & Leonard, 1870, P. 19.

The opening stanzas of this memorable poem pay well-deserved tribute to a section of the High Peaks region — the Colden-Flowed Lands. Apparently the Tahawus Club, successor to the eventually unsuccessful Adirondack Iron Works, maintained several shelters on the shores of the Flowed Lands besides several on the less distant Preston Ponds.

Sweet, as have many far more recent receptive visitors and lean-to dwellers, commemorated his stay there in rather rhapsodic terms:

"Our camp is made on Opalescent River,
Just where a little branch comes in from Colden,
These meet, embrace and fairly seem to quiver
With fresh delight, within the glorious, golden
Sunlight that tinges every wave with amber,
In imitation of a naiad's chamber.

The stream is small — some thirty feet — not wider,
And moves mid many maple-sugary stones
With just the flash and color of boiled cider —
Its ripples giving out in faintest tones
The sweeter music, with the gentlest motion
That smoothes the senses like lethean potion.

Our cabin, partly made by two huge boulders,
Whose moss-grown sides give many a varied hue,
Though rough, is higher than man's shoulders;
The third side, logs piled carefully and true;
The fourth is open — this we all love dearly —
It gives a prospect to the south-west clearly.

The roof is bark of spruce, peeled from the trunks,
And gives balsamic odor to the air;
The smudge in front, built of decaying chunks,
Sends up its curling wreaths like incense rare,
And drives from us the gnats, flies and musketoes (sic)
Much more effectual than bar and vetoes.

Before this parlor cabin, twelve by twenty
On rustic seats or lounging on log couches
Are grouped my friends, for this occasion plenty,
Who, late returned, are emptying their pouches
Their bags and baskets, for they each have hoarded
Some wealth the hills or rivers have afforded"

Another delightful passage in a less rapturous yet readily identifiable mood, can be found in a renowned prose classic of the northern wilderness — J.T. Headley's *The Adirondack or Life in the Woods* (1849).[1] In a letter dated Long Lake, Aug. 1 (1848) the estimable author recounts another and more typical aspect of open camp occupancy:

1. Headley, Joel T., *The Adirondack or Life in the Woods*, New York: Baker & Scribner's, 1849.

"Dear H--:

My last (letter) left us yawning and stretching around our camp fire a little after daylight in the morning, looking and feeling stupid and heavy but a fresh wash in a mountain rill near by restored us to life, while the answers to the inquiries how each other had slept brought back the merriment that seldom flags in the woods. 'Well, R-ffle, how did you sleep?' 'Pretty well, only H- kept punching me to keep me off him.' 'And how did you sleep, H-?' 'As I'll never sleep again. I was on the lower hillside and served as a block to the whole of you. You rolled down against me and wedged me in so tight that I couldn't, with my utmost effort, turn over to save my life.'

'Mr. W-d, was you broke of your rest?' 'No, I slept pretty well considering the circumstances.' Turning to Mr. P., I remarked, "Well, Mr. P., I saw you get up once when I rose to put some wood on the fire. You lay rolled up in your blanket like a mummy, while the sparks fell in a shower around you. I thought that you would find it rather too hot before morning.'

'I don't remember getting up at all,' he replied; 'probably the roaring fire you made *did* cause the smoke to choke me. No, I never waked but once, and then I was startled by the sound of an axe. I opened my eyes and saw you splitting down the stump — the root of which was my pillow — directly over my head.'

"This of course I stoutly denied, amidst the uproarious laugh of the company. I then remembered the frightened look he had given me as I was cutting into a stump nearby him, and in the next moment rolled rapidly in his blanket down the hill. The suddenness and oddity of his movement surprised me at the time, but now it was well explained. In his half-wakened state he saw the bit of my axe gleaming in the firelight and thought it was descending directly on his skull. No wonder he had performed those sudden evolutions."

The previous quotations from the realm of Adirondack literature have dealt primarily with more or less straightforward delineations of lean-to construction and occupancy delights. But quite conceivably the very choicest passage of all are those which enliven the pages of *The Aristocrats,* a comparatively little-known collection of letters by Gertrude Atherton which was published in 1902. Besides its charming dedication the irresistibly clever book contains what must be the most amusing account ever written about the pleasures and problems of life in a lean-to:

"Have you wasted any time, my dear, imagining what an 'open camp' is like? I hope not for it would be a waste of good mental energy. The briefest description will fit it. Three sides and a sloping roof and all of bark. The front "open" is the exactest interpretation of the word. Inside — nothing. Twelve feet long and not quite the depth of Mr. Meredith Jones, who is six feet two.

"This mansion stood on the edge of a clearing, across which lay a big felled tree. Against this we immediately all sat down in a row. Beyond was a charred ruin and near the log a rude table. Does this sound romantic? I wish you could have seen it. But we all laughed and were happy, and we women, even then, did not realize the true inwardness of the situation. The forest, the beautiful forest, rose on three sides of us; beyond a stream, concealed by alders, was a high sharp ridge of mountains — and we were hungry . . .

"When luncheon was over Mr. Latimer made poor Miss Page a comfortable couch of shawls, with a small packbasket for a pillow and she soon fell asleep. The guides washed the dishes, then immediately felled two young spruce trees and, with the help of Latimer and Mr. Meredith Jones, shaved off the branches and covered the floor of the cabin. This was our bed, my dear, and it was about a foot deep. When it was finished they covered it with

A Full House at the Campfire — Stoddard Photo

Summertime on Upper Au Sable Lake — Stoddard Photo

138

carriage robes and all preparations for nightly comforts were complete.

"By this time it dawned on Mrs. Meredith Jones and myself that we were *all* going to sleep under that roof. Opp had examined the sky and predicted rain before morning, and Miss Page was not equal to a return journey — "doubling the road," as they say here — even if any of us had contemplated such a thing.

'Tom and I will sleep in the middle, said Mrs. Meredith Jones reassuringly to me, after an earnest conversation apart with her husband, but I was immensely amused at the whole situation. We were as helpless against certain circumstances as if we did not possess sixpence between us; for it would have taken nearly a day to build another camp and the guides were too tired to think of such a thing. We were all stranded out in space, and there was nothing to do but make the most of it . . .

"Miss Page turned to me a perturbed face, 'I cannot believe it is possible that we are all going to sleep in there,' she said. 'Why it is shocking! I begged Mr. Van Worden to put up a partition but he says it is quite impossible, that there won't be room to turn over as it is. I wish I hadn't come. Suppose it should get out? Why, people would be horrified!"

"Really," I said, "I think you take an exaggerated view. We are all going to bed with our clothes on, the camp is open, there are nine of us, and our chaperones will sleep in the middle. We may not be comfortable, but I think the proprieties will take care of themselves."

'I think it is shocking!' she said, 'perfectly shocking. It seems so coarse and horrid. I'll remember it as long as I live.'

I felt like shaking her, but she looked so distressed that I said soothingly: "Please don't worry. I will sleep next to Mrs. Meredith Jones and you can tuck away in the corner where no one can see you and you will be quite forgotten."

'Yes,' she replied quickly, 'I insist upon having the corner — particularly as you don't mind.' She added apologetically, 'You are quite different from my idea of English girls. I should have thought that you would be simply horrified.'

"Perhaps we are more matter-of-fact than you are," I said drily. "Where a thing can't be helped it can't, and we are sensible about it. Now, I am surprised at you. I had always supposed that American girls--"

'Oh don't!' she exclaimed. 'You are going to judge us all by those horrid things you met in Europe and in novels. I can assure you that Southerners — *gentlewomen*— are as particular as English girls — more so I reckon. Do you realize that you are going to sleep in the same room with six men?'

"I don't look at it that way at all," I said tartly. "And for heaven's sake make up your mind to the inevitable and think no more of it."

"After supper the guides built a high fire of great logs, and we all sat about and the men "spun yarns" of the days when the panther and the bear roamed the woods, and finished with stories of the beautiful red deer that alone claims the forest today. Of course the men smoked and we were all very happy and comfortable until we went to bed. Mr. N. sat as close to me as he decently could and — I will confess to you, Polly — under the encouragement of the shadows which covered a part of me and all of him he held my hand. I could not struggle — well —

"About ten the men all marched up the hill in single file, singing, and we had the camp to ourselves for a half hour. We took off our boots, corsets and blouses, put on dressing sacks, tied our heads up in silk handkerchiefs and our night toilet was complete. Miss Page had evidently made up her mind to accept the situation but she was so manifestly uncomfortable that I tied nearly all of her face up in her handkerchief and tucked her away in the corner with her blanket up to her nose. She turned her back upon us and regarded the chinks in the bark in silent misery. Mr. Van Worden had brought three extra pairs of socks and these he had directed us to pull over our stockings as the night would grow chilly.

"We had been in bed nearly twenty minutes and had already learned something of its hardness when the men returned.

'Now,' said Opp, 'You must all lie on the same side and when one of you wants to turn over be sure to sing out and then we'll all turn over together.'

"His was the only remark. The other men pulled off their boots and crawled into bed without a word looking rather sheepish, and ostentatiously refraining from glancing in our direction. Men are certainly more modest than women in certain conditions and Mrs. Meredith Jones and I almost laughed out loud — especially as the other guide went to bed with his hat on!

"For about a half hour we were as quiet as the sardines we must have resembled. Then my side — the one I was lying on — began to ache from my neck to my heel, and from the numerous sighs and restless jerks I inferred that we were all affected in the same way. At all events Opp sang out, 'Heave over, hey?' and we all turned like a well-regulated machine. I whispered to Miss Page but she would not answer me.

"It was just after that we became conscious that the temperature was about ninety. The fire was not three feet in front of us and blazing more violently every moment. I had been endeavoring to forget my discomfort in watching the black masses of the treetops thrown by the blaze into extraordinary relief against the dull sky and tarnished stars, when I heard Mr. Van Worden whisper fiercely, 'What in heaven's name did you build that red-hot fire for? It's hot enough for three camps and we won't sleep a wink!'

"Opp replied apologetically: 'I thought it was goin' to rain and it was best to have things well het up, but I guess it tain't. It's hot and no mistake.'

"I saw Mr. Latimer fighting to get out of an extra sweater without attracting attention and I, by the same herculean effort, managed to reach down and get off my stockings and those socks. But still the heat was insupportable and the bed grew harder every moment. Our pillows, too, were logs under the spruce, and I am used to a baby pillow that I double under my neck and face. How I longed for it!

"Finally Latimer slipped out of bed and went over to the edge of the clearing and lit his pipe. The guides followed immediately, then Mr. Meredith Jones, and they sat along the log in dejected silence. Mrs. Meredith Jones heaved a deep sigh. 'I really can't stand it, girls,' she whispered, and followed her husband. Of course we went too and Mr. Van Worden was left alone.

"For a half hour we sat about in an almost complete silence, waiting for that wretched fire to burn down. Opp separated the logs and finally, as we were all too sleepy to hold our heads up, we crawled back to bed, one by one — all except Mr. Latimer, who stretched out on the table, and Mr. Nugent, who made a bed for himself on the ground. That gave us a trifle more room in the camp, and we could turn without 'singing out.' In a few minutes, hot as it was, I fell asleep.

"I suppose it was two hours later that I awoke. The fire had taken a fresh start and was blazing more merrily than ever. I felt as if I were in a Turkish bath and as Miss Page was no longer in front of me I inferred that she had been forth again. Then it occurred to me that she could not have budged without Mrs. Meredith Jones and I turned about quite suddenly. Mrs. Jones was not there! Nor Mr. Jones nor the guides. O Agatha! Agatha! I was alone in bed with Mr. Van Worden!

"The situation was humorous, but somewhat embarrassing. I hardly knew whether to pretend sleep or not, for I did not feel like going out and sitting on that log again. I could see the dark figures in various dejected attitudes. Mrs. Meredith Jones and Miss Page were sitting back to back with their heads hanging; while Mr. Meredith Jones stood with his hands in his pockets glowering at the fire. Latimer was sitting on the table smoking his pipe and Mr. N. was digging his heels viciously into the earth. As for the guides they lay flat in the distance, tired out, poor things. Only Mr. Van Worden looked serene. He, too, lay on his back, his hands clasped over the greater part of him. I supposed that he was asleep, but he remarked genially, 'Hot, isn't it, Lady Helen?' I'm afraid one camping experience will do you for the rest of your natural life.'

"I assured him that I never had been so much entertained, and we conversed as naturally as if it had been noon-day until I was reminded of the irregularities of the situation by a gasp from Miss Page. She nudged Mrs. Meredith Jones, whispered hurriedly, and in another moment I was chaperoned on either side.

"It was at least another hour before the fire burned down and the temperature cooled. Then the men crawled back to bed, one by one, and in a few moments they were all sleeping and as quietly as kittens. It really was quite remarkable."

Admittedly this has been a very extended excerpt but, in my opinion, justifiably so because, over the years, the same droll passage has brought much delight to countless readers who have been fortunate enough to know of its existence. Moreover, the quality of the selection is indicative of the consistently high level of entertainment provided throughout the entire minor masterpiece, whose dedication is equally remarkable: "To All Lovers of the Adirondack Peaks and Forests and Lakes this little volume is dedicated by an Alien but Ardent and Grateful Admirer, H.P."

The sub-title itself is also noteworthy: "Being the impressions of the Lady Helen Pole during her sojourn in the Great North Woods as spontaneously recorded in her letters to her friend in North Britain, the Countess of Edge and Ross."

In the same literary league but not blessed with anywhere near the same risibility factor is the book saddled with the uninspiring and uninspired title *Letters from the United States, Cuba and Canada*. In missives 17, 19 and 29 Lady Amelia Matilda Murray recounts her well-publicized water-route trip through the heart of the Adirondacks in 1855. Since very few visitors and certainly no prominent women had preceded her into the region, her account furnishes valuable impressions and reactions to Gov. Seymour's celebrated guided tour.

"In the woods you must expect to pay a certain price in discomfort for a very real and very deep pleasure." So wrote Stewart E. White in his eminently readable book "The Forest". He was referring to insect pests and in doing so established a strong rapport with every hiker who has knowingly or otherwise done some of his climbing during the late Spring and early Summer when the winged hordes are really on the prowl. Co-existing with them on the trail is torture enough but lying helplessly in a lean-to can be pure hell.

Perhaps the insect repellents on the market today are more effective now than they were ten years ago, but I can vividly recall slopping on just about every known brand name before testing out the most pungent and effective dope of all — Nessmuk juice, which is a head-clearing conglomerate made from 3 ounces pine tar, two ounces castor oil and one ounce pennyroyal oil. Simmer over a slow fire and the resulting goo will last a full season. Believe me, it really works.

The only hitch is that nowadays the first and third ingredients are almost impossible to locate. Moreover, unless the brew is concocted outdoors the aroma is so penetrating and potent that it is guaranteed capable of testing the durability and endurability of a marriage.

White comments that the question of flies in its wide embracement of mosquitoes, sandflies, deerflies, blackflies and midges is one much mooted. One writer claims that blackfly bites are but temporary inconvenience of a pinprick. Another tells of boils lasting a week as the invariable result of their attentions; a third concentrates his anathemas on the musical mosquito while a fourth descants on the maddening midge.

As for the truth it is at once in all of them and in none of them. The annoyances or after-effects from a sting depend entirely on the individual's physical makeup. Some people are so poisoned by mosquito bites that three or four on the forehead will entirely close the victim's eyes. On others they leave only a small red mark without swelling. Black-flies, the most industrious of all the winged nuisances, can literally make the blood stream down the faces of their prey. But this biter at least stays still long enough to give the bitten a chance to murder him in retaliatory glee.

Midges, punkies or no-see'ums — call them what you will, — have been known to drive people so frantic that they have jumped into the river clothes and all just to get rid of their relentless pursuers.

Nessmuk[1] remarked that a two-day exposure to the pests caused one young man to come out of the woods with one eye entirely closed and the brow hanging over it like a clamshell, while his face and hands were almost hideous from inflamation and puffiness. The St. Regis and St. Francis Indians, although born and reared in the woods, by no means make light of the blackfly.

The same writer remarked that it took the man (W.H.H. Murray) who could shoot Phantom Falls to find out that "The blackfly's bite is not severe nor is it ordinarily poisonous. There may be an occasional exception to this rule but beside the bite of the mosquito, it (the blackfly's) is comparatively mild and harmless. 'Gnats', according to Murray, "are much worse than the blackfly or mosquito."

After noting that only the female of each of the insects cited does the jabbing, Kephart in the Book of Camping and Woodcraft furnishes further data on the depredations of mosquitoes. "Deer and moose are killed by mosquitoes which settle on them in such amazing swarms that the unfortunate beasts succumb from literally having the blood sucked out of their bodies. Bears are driven crazy, are totally blinded, mire themselves in the mud and starve to death."

These are of course rather direful details that present the possible extremes which can plague the early season climber. Usually by pickling oneself in a smudge or swaddling his entire carcass except for a tiny nasal outlet, one can sweat out a seemingly week-long night. By bolting down a couple of tranquilizers or even stronger pellets a person can assure himself of a deep if unnatural slumber in the innermost recess of the lean-to.

When the climber is able to hit the trail in the late Summer or early Fall, when the low temperatures have practically eliminated the insect plagues, the days and nights can be pure pleasure. The soul-stirring combination of cold air and warm sun, the visual and aural delights provided by the kaleidoscope of color and the unforgettable and unforgotten sounds of Autumn combine to form a panorama of impressions that never cease to soothe and stimulate the spirit.

Although the cavalcade of colors is an undeniable annual visual treat, it is the perennial sounds of nature that seem to linger longest in at least one person's memory, — like the loons at the Duck Hole which kept a certain pooped-out ('dechine' the French would call it) person ungrudgingly awake most of the night as he listened to their wild

---

1. Nessmuk (Geo. W. Sears) *Woodcraft*, New York: Field and Stream Publishing Co., 1884.

A Pair of Loony-Birds

tremulous cry which always seemed far distant, like the last faint pulse of echo dying over the waters of the Preston Ponds; and in the pass between the Santanoni Range and the McNaughton-Henderson ridgeline.

As James R. Lowell aptly described the voices of the loons, "It is one of the few sounds that, instead of disturbing solitude, only deepen, confirm and enhance it."

Another such eerie, essentially and characteristically natural sound is the quavering vocal outbust of a pack of coydogs, which one full-moon night some dozen years ago, were relentlessly closing in on a harried deer not far to the east of the later burned-out Scott's Clearing lean-to. The reverberations from the nearby shoulders of McIntyre and Street intensified and prolonged the excited yipping of the pack until the sounds of the chase gradually died out in the distance.

Still another haunting and pulse-quickening sound occasionally heard by lean-to occupants in the remoter sections is the low-pitched, drawn-out calls of a pair of big owls — probably the great horned or barred variety — as they concentrate on flushing smaller birds — particularly easily panicked robins — from their roosting places. Several times I have heard the potential prey confer frantically before fear finally put them to flight. One evening I heard the air rushing through the wing tips of a big predator as it swooped down to make successful contact with the victim — a fact confirmed the next morning by the sight of scattered feathers on the edge of a pond.

As the "dedicated" climber who is both heaven and hell-bent on reaching 46er status progresses through the aspiring and final stages, he has ample opportunity to sample the shelters in all sections of the High Peaks area. In doing so he inevitably rates each of the open camps according to its location and other environmental factors. Assuming that the structural conditions are basically comparable, he then scores it on such criteria as scenic qualities and the presence or absence of rapid water.

My favorite rustic retreats as listed in general order of preference are as follows: 1) Feldspar, 2) Uphill, 3) Wanika Fals, 4) Indian Falls (the shelter nearer the ledge), 5) the original Wallface 6) either of the Calamities, 7) Bushnell Falls, 8) Henderson, 9) Rocky Falls and 10) Caribou . . . What are yours?

Caribou Lean-to between Avalanche and Colden Lakes — Photo by Steve Slaughter

Obviously, these and many other similar if less picturesquely-placed shelters represent only a small fraction of the number which, in response to the irresistibly potent pressures generated by the population explosion will eventually proliferate along the present and future Adirondack trails. Those of us who have been very vocal in expressing our disapproval and deep disgust at the present competition for sleeping space and the occasional display of crude manners and even cruder personal habits can at least derive a degree of consolation from the knowledge that we had our fair share of lebensraum as well as elbowroom

"What oft was thought but ne'er so well expressed." This observation by Pope is pre-eminently illustrated by the celebrated passage by William James when he related what he called a Walpurgis Night spend in Panther Gorge in 1898. In it he epitomized what all of us have experienced but have lacked the power to communicate verbally. Moreover, it sums up most eloquently the mysterious impact that primordial natural influences make in varying degrees on various persons.

Writing of this night to his wife he said — "I spent a good deal of it in the woods, where the streaming moonlight lit up things in a magical checkered play, and it seemed as if the Gods of all the nature mythologies were holding an indescribable meeting in my

144

breast with the moral Gods of the inner life. . . . The intense significance of some sort, of the whole scene, if one could only *tell* the significance; the intense inhuman remoteness of its inner life and yet the intense *appeal* of it; its everlasting freshness and its immemorial antiquity and decay; its utter Americanism and every sort of patriotic suggestiveness, and you, and my relation to you part and parcel of it all, and beaten up with it, so that memory and sensation all whirled inextricably together. . . . It was one of the happiest lonesome nights of my existence and I understand now what a poet is."

A very fitting ending for an article about anything dealing with our beloved mountains but especially applicable to that distinctive, characteristic and memory-evoking feature of the Adirondack scene — the lean-to.

Quite often hikers and climbers in the High Peak area have shown curiosity about which lean-tos were built first and the order in which they were put up. The following data on the first 15 has been supplied by Bill Petty, District Director of Lands and Forest, State Conservation Department, Ray Brook Headquarters.

1) Four Corners 1919
(replaced by helicopter service 1967)
2) Feldspar 1919
(rebuilt in 1943)
3) Henderson 1920
4) Sno-Bird (built by Camp & Trail Club) 1921
5) South Meadows 1921
6) Calamity #1 1922
7) Gothic 1922
8) Ward Brook 1922
9) Moose Pond 1922
10) Whiteface 1923
11) Marcy Dam #1 1923
12) Cold River #1 1923
(re-roofed in 1964)
13) Avalanche #1 1923
14) Scott's Clearing 1924
(rebuilt 1947 following destruction by hunters)
15) Middle Saranac 1924

A Lapham Party of Glens Falls at Huntley Pond c. 1895

146

Chapter 13

The Macomb Purchase, Early Saranac Lake and the Lakes

One of the largest real estate transactions that ever took place in New York State was that known as the Macomb Purchase when, in January 1792 the State conveyed to Alexander Macomb and others nearly four million acres in Northern New York at eight cents an acre or about $320,000. This vast area was spread over six different counties — St. Lawrence, Jefferson, Lewis, Hamilton, Franklin and a portion of Oswego.

The surveyors divided this huge region into Great Tracts Numbers One through Six. However, there were more than 300,000 acres not included in this division and this area has always been referred to in conveyances as the Remainder in exactly the same manner as the others have been known as Great Tracts Numbers etc.

Great Tract Number One is entirely in Franklin County and contains 821,000 acres, subdivided into twenty-seven nearly equal parts of 30,000 to 32,000 acres, each of which are called "townships."

Over the years there has been considerable confusion over the terms "town" and "townships." In certain parts of the South, in other parts of New York State and in sections of New England, the two are identical but as used in the Macomb Purchase they were not synonymous terms, although some of the boundary lines correspond with the town lines.

Moreover, in some of the larger tracts or grants, the townships laid out by the surveyors are numbered but have no other distinguishing designation. For Franklin County and in other parts of the Purchase, the surveyors not only numbered the townships but also gave them names — probably supplied by the owners for sentimental reasons and usually those of family members or places in England, Ireland or elsewhere which had been their original homes.

The four and a half townships which comprise the town of Harrietstown — numbers 21, 23, 24, 26 and 27 were assigned names now seldom used: Harriet, Killarney, Barrymore, Tipperary and Covehill.

Although there were four men involved in the Macomb Purchase only his name was used. However, all of them were among the most prominent citizens of New York City and State. Macomb himself, born in 1848 in County Antrim, Ireland, was the son of John Macomb, an enterprising wool merchant who would have been conspicuously prosperous anywhere but in the Emerald Isle. Unfortunately for him he was caught in the middle of a wholesale effort by the English to destroy the Irish wool trade, whose products were rated the best in the business. Confiscatory export taxes and strictly enforced embargoes resulted in the destruction of that Irish business.

Alexander Macomb [left], William Constable [right]

Along with tens of thousands of their countrymen — names which later became famous in their new home across the Atlantic — went Carrolls, Barrys, Livingtons, Clintons, Dongans, Logans, Duanes, Constables, McCormicks — and Macombs, who emigrated from Ireland in 1755.

At that time Albany was the outermost limit of civilization, a frontier town close to the Indian country. Here the Macomb and Constable families settled and the sons became busy in the fur trade. Their friends and contemporaries were various Van Rensselaers, Schuylers and Alexander Hamilton. The business prospered so well that the sons persuaded their father to move to even more productive territory — Detroit, where they became very wealthy.

During his wide-ranging travels Macomb saw the alluring land that later made his name immortal because "so long as civilized government remains, historians, students and attorneys concerned with law titles will follow records back to Macomb's Purchase."

However, according to Donaldson, there is considerable evidence to show that Constable may have at least shared the honor of instigating the land purchase deal even though the final deed cites him as a purchaser under Macomb. McCormick's name appears as the original proprietor with said Macomb. Macomb supposedly persuaded his friends William Constable, by then a prominent merchant and Daniel McCormick, director of the newly-founded Bank of New York, to join him in the epoch-making transaction. Apparently they were readily convinced after a week-long idyllic exploratory trip up the St. Regis River from the majestic St. Lawrence.

Of interest is the fact that later on Macomb reserved for the use of the St. Regis Indians a six-mile square part of land where the river of that name flows into the St. Lawrence.

William Constable, born in Dublin in 1761, was the son of John Constable, a surgeon in the English Army. After his arrival in America he became a very prosperous merchant, reputedly the first to send trading ships to China. He died in 1803. The town of Constable in Franklin Country's St. Lawrence valley and the village of Constableville, along with his baronial home there in Lewis County help perpetuate his name. His brother James at one time owned five towns. Between them the brothers were by far the largest individual landlords in the State.

McCormick, also Irish-born and "the most polished gentleman" in New York City, who for many years was president of the St. Patrick's Society, lived at 57 Wall Street until it was destroyed in a great fire. He saw that part of the city change from residential to business and all his friends move uptown, but he preferred to remain where he was. Nor did his style of dress change with the years. He continued to wear knee-breeches, white stockings, buckled shoes and powdered hair. Honored and respected by all, he never married.[1]

James Duane, another of Macomb's associates, had a distinguished ancestry. His grandfather was the first mayor of N.Y.C., later a state senator and finally a prominent judge. Duanesburgh, outside Albany, and the Adirondack town of Duane were named after the family.

The first patents issued to Macomb on Jan. 10, 1792 were for Great Tracts IV, V and VI and the Remainder area, a total grant of 1,920,000 acres. Although a few relatively small sales were made shortly thereafter, the entire holding was transferred from Macomb to Constable on June 6th of that same year. Therefore his actual ownership of the vast property was of less than six month's duration and since he never did acquire title to Great Tract I, II and III, which he assigned to Daniel McCormick and who got title directly, Macomb legally was entitled to only about half the acreage covered by his name.

Macomb and his father-in-law, Philip Livingston of N.Y.C., were both intensely interested in the so-called "waste lands" of the Adirondack region as well as in the earlier Totten and Crossfield Purchase, which generated among wealthy speculators golden dreams of real estate bonanzas. The two men were also actually interested in the second allotment of the T-C Purchase as well as in other risk-taking deals. Macomb in particular was definitely a plunger and was not always exactly ethical in his get-rich schemes.

This was shown by his connection with the Company of the Million Bank of the State of New York. Its capital base was $1,000,000 divided into 2,000 shares but when the subscription books closed nearly 24,000 shares had been sold, which represented an excess of $11,000,000. This led to much cynical public reaction such as that in the New York *Journal and Patriotic Register* for Jan. 18, 1792: "By all which banks and fortunes, the stockholders and particularly the possessors of scripts and original subscribers, without a farthing, are soon to become richer than Eastern nabobs, and the favored city of New York like the Peruvian mountains."[2]

The sarcasm was well deserved because the big bubble burst soon afterward. In April of the same year Macomb was put into prison and it is very likely that his life was spared mainly because of the thick stone walls. About that time he declared himself bankrupt and started transferring his Northern New York holdings to his friend Constable.

One of Macomb's sons, Alexander, who became a general in the New York Militia, also had a hard time hanging onto money. Like his father he too became financially embarrassed, was sold out by a N.Y.C. sheriff and eventually moved to Georgetown, S.C. After the death of his wife Alexander sent for his aged father, and mother who had been reduced from affluence to poverty. There Alexander Macomb lived out his remaining ten

---

1 Barret, Walter, *Old Merchants of New York City.*

2. Donaldson, Alfred, *History of the Adirondacks* 2 vols., New York: Century Company, 1921.

years and died in 1831, leaving as his memorial a name that will never vanish from the Adirondacks...

Another fascinating but not totally unexpected aspect of the Macomb Purchase was the uproar it raised when the magnitude of the deal and its price became public information. Enemies of Gov. Clinton and his administration accused the land commissioners and him of not only dishonesty but also of complicity in a plot to sell the annexed territory to Canada. Although all concerned vehemently denied the charges and produced reams of supporting testimony, the basis for impending impeachment proceedings against the Governor were soon dropped after a supposedly thorough legislative investigation and its resultant whitewashing conclusion.

However, according to Donaldson, it cannot be denied that whereas Macomb and his associates paid only eight pence an acre for their land, adjoining tracts had been sold just previously to the Roosevelts for three shillings, one penny and to Adgate for two shillings per acre.

Still another facet that beclouds the transaction is the fact that in 1794 a law was passed setting the minimum accepting price for the remaining 2,000,000 acres of public land at six shillings an acre, thus enhancing greatly the value of the so-called Macomb Tract. Not so strange either, according to F. B. Hough in his *History of Lewis County*, is the conviction that the owners of that tract were the main proponents of that accommodating legislation.

Originally the Town of Harrietstown was covered with magnificent forests of white pine and spruce which attracted the lumbermen in the early days. Much of the timber was cut during the Winter months and floated down the Saranac River to Plattsburgh during the Spring drives.

In 1825, sixteen years before the town was formed by separation from Duane, Capt. Pliny Miller (1775-1859), a veteran of the War of 1812, and his friend Alric M. Bushnell, both of Sand Lake (Rensselaer County), acquired 300 acres of land for two dollars an acre in what later became the central section of the present village of Saranac Lake. Miller later bought out Bushnell, came and settled on his holdings and built a dam and sawmill on the site of what is now the Niagara-Mohawk building. In the late 1840's he built a small hotel on the lot now occupied by the village office structure; this was leased from 1848-1850 to William F. Martin and from 1850-1852 to Virgil C. Bartlett, two pioneers who later became prominently identified with their own resort hotels — Martin's (later Miller's) on Lower Saranac Lake's Ampersand Bay, and Bartlett's renowned little place on the carry between Round Lake (Middle Saranac) and Upper Saranac Lake.

Although Jacob Moody, who arrived from Keene, N.H., in 1819, was unquestionably the first settler in the region, his homes were in what is now Highland Park and, when legal title was unobtainable, in the pines near Moody Pond, where he cleared about sixteen acres and built a home.

The Moodys, the Millers, the Bakers and the Martins and shortly afterwards the Dupreys, Sweeneys, Daniels and the Rices became the family nuclei of the village and their intermarriages sired many generations of businessmen, hotel-keepers, store-owners and guides.

Nowadays, it is very difficult to realize or even imagine the amount of labor required to make a home in the frequently hostile wilderness. At the outset a minimum of seven to ten days was needed for a skilled axeman to hack down an acre of forestland to obtain the building logs, caulking and fencing material. The average pioneer could hardly hope to clear and sow ten acres the first year — even if he did nothing else. But he also had to put

Capt. Pliny Miller

Van Buren Miller

Virgil C. Bartlett

Bartlett's on Saranac River near Upper Saranac Lake — Stoddard Photo

151

up a small cabin, fences and a shelter for his stock besides hunting and fishing to feed his family. No time left over for thumb-twiddling in those days.

Furthermore, he and his neighbors had to cut out a rough path or roadway connecting their holdings. If he had no market for his produce there was obviously no point in clearing more land than was necessary for his survival. As a result few settlers ever cleared more than three or four acres a year, which meant that a lifetime of work went into developing a farm of respectable size.

The job of fencing required much labor: wooden rails had be be split or rough boards used to form the barricades. Sometimes stumps were hauled and lined up in a rough manner; occasionally stone walls were build up where plowing was impeded.

The cabin, usually 20' x 40', consisted of round logs chinked with split logs plastered with clay. Split-log floors were put down with flat side up. Doors were thin sections of split logs and the windows were usually holes, unprotected by glass or sash with thin-scraped animal skin or grease-soaked wrapping paper to keep out the weather. A stone fireplace with a chimny of sticks coated with clay provided the hardly convenient and comfortable source of heat and warmth. At one side of the fireplace a crude ladder led to the loft sleeping quarters.

The wife and daughters made clothing from wool, flax and skins. All wore moccasins in Winter and went barefoot in Summer.

In retrospect we tend to idealize the frontier-farmer for his courage, resourcefulness and freedom. They had these qualities of course but self-sufficiency gave them little actual freedom. Understandably nobody could be a competent farmer, carpenter, woodsman, lumberman, toolmaker, cobbler, blacksmith and all-around handyman all at the same time. Just providing food, clothing and shelter meant untold drudgery and poverty. All that kept them going was the hope and expectation of better things to come — if not for them, then for their children....

This pattern of life and living was typical of all frontier settlements and that of course includes Saranac Lake, which was essentially a logging hamlet prior to the Civil War. Actually it had changed very little when Rev. John P. Lundy of Philadelphia, who was convalescing from a breakdown in Saranac Lake in 1877 described it accurately if unsympathetically in the following terms in his generally disparaging book *Saranac Exiles:* "The miserable hamlet of Saranac Lake — its present name twice changed from that of Baker's and Harrietstown[1] as if the people were ashamed of having it long under one appellation — consists of about 50 or 60 log and frame-houses and has a population of three or four hundred souls. It is in a little, deep basin of hills on every side of it, on the branch of the Saranac River, a few miles from its leaving the lower lake of that name and one mile below Martin's [hotel on Ampersand Bay of the Lower Lake]. It is nearly 40 miles distance from the terminus of the branch railroad from Plattsburgh to Ausable and is reached by daily stage. The Montreal Telegraph Co. has a station here from which dispatches can be sent anywhere. It is this sheltered position of the place in Winter, this daily stage and telegraph service that have given Saranac Lake its main attraction to invalids, aside from the pure invigorating mountain air.

"It has two country stores of the usual heterogeneous assortment of coarse dry-goods, boots and shoes, groceries, hardware and quack medicines but no books or magazines. An old rickety saw-mill supplies the place and neighborhood with building materials; and a steam-mill occasionally makes shingles and clapboards. There is also a small gristmill, one

---

1. Not exactly true because the name was never officially changed after the establishment of the post-office in 1854. Baker's and Harrietstown were familiar names long used by old-time residents and referred to parts of the village.

shoemaker and one tailor. The barber of the place is a peripatetic on crutches, going from house to house or from room to room on call, to discharge his tonsorial duties and do the main headwork of the community at the rate of twenty-five cents for each clipping and manipulation....

"To the everlasting honor of Saranac Lake it must be said that it has no lawyers or newspaper editors to do the mischievous and harassing headwork of keeping the community in an uproar of needless excitement and agitation. No newsboys din your ears to deafness or startle your nervous sensibilities by their shrill cries and startling announcements. No lawyers plot for fat fees or manufacture bogus cases; all is peace and quietness. Far-distant (45 miles then), the county -town of Franklin and the residence of lawyer Vice President Wheeler, is rather the place of these tumultuous cries and harassing trials...."

Although by the early 1880s Saranac Lake had ceased to be an important lumbertown and was rapidly becoming a gateway to the famed hunting and fishing areas nearby, it nevertheless was still very much a frontier settlement, mostly composed of a few frame structures on some streets and log cabins of the guides in the outskirts. In the Fall invalids and their families, generally about 75-100 in all, would move in from Paul Smith's and the surrounding region to spend the Winter months. These people were attracted there, as Rev. Lundy stated, by the few conveniences, the protection of the surrounding hills and the presence of Dr. E. L. Trudeau, who had already gained a wide reputation for his skill and manner.

In those days everybody wore black wool boots and rubbers to store and to "meeting" (church) — even Rev. Locke, then rector of St. Luke's Church, founded by Dr. Trudeau. The Methodists had no church or pastor but conducted a Sunday School in the local schoolhouse. There were no other places of worship in the little community. The nearest railroad station was Ausable Forks and the daily mail came in by stagecoach via Bloomingdale. There was no real settlement at Tupper Lake at that time — only a few cabins in perhaps the most remote backwoods clearing in the Adirondacks. The only means of communication from there in Winter was by snowshoes down the Lakes to Saranac village.

There were a few organs but not a piano in the place at that time. The schoolteacher had a violin but couldn't play it well. Ernest Johnson, Tupper Lake resident and later superintendent of the Whitney estate at Little Tupper, was an excellent fiddler who played for the old-time quadrilles and square dances. When sent for he would occasionally snowshoe down to officiate at dances held in a big log dining room on Harrietstown Road, thus breaking the monotony of the seemingly interminable season. [three paragraphs from the recollections of Laura Miller Rice] The late Walter Rice of Saranac Lake, who later became the Hermit of Ampersand Mountain as its fire-tower ranger, in an interview once gave a detailed description of the mail service of the 1860's and contrasted it with that of the present but before the railroads were abandoned in the area. Apparently, up to the late 1960's there were seven incoming and six outgoing mails each day during the Summer season. In 1860 there were two deliveries a week and a clothesbasket served as the post office.

"The first mail carrier I can remember was "Uncle" Peter Carr. Hugh Martin was the first to carry it after the Plank road had been built between Au Sable Forks and Franklin Falls. About 1852, according to A. I. O'Brien, Carr's contract called for mail delivery twice weekly and the carrier was supposed to get through regardless of the weather conditions and for a fee of $400.00. In Summer, the passenger conveyance was a lumberwagon without springs, seats without cushions. In Winter, bobsleds filled with straw so that you could cuddle down in it and shiver yourself warm. Winter, of course, was the most strenuous and difficult period because the roads were utterly impassable for days at a time. Greater snow depths than nowadays. County was very sparsely settled then so nobody cared much about travel conditions. Everybody just plain holed up for the duration of the storms.

"Sometimes it took 10 days for a letter to get to New York City. [Ed. note: not much different from now!]

"The first postmaster was Van Buren Miller and his first post office was his clothes-basket, Mail, of course, was not very voluminous — possibly a half-dozen letters, a few copies of the Essex County *Republican,* Plattsburgh *Sentinel,* Albany *Journal* or *Argus.* These plus one or two issues of Harper's *Weekly,* Frank Leslie's or the N.Y. *Ledger* were dumped into the basket. The residents picked out their own mail from the receptacle. Since Miller's pay was $48.00 a year, not much service was expected from him and there were few complaints. If anyone wanted to write a letter even after the mail had closed, the carrier would wait until you had finished and accept your thanks graciously.

"The next Mailcarrier was "Uncle" Jim Kelly about 1862-1864. Then Jay Miller took over until 1868, when A. F. O'Brien handled it until 1872. At that time the Adirondack Stage Co. came into existence backed by Paul Smith, William Harper and Sons of Wilmington. From then on there was daily mail and new Concord coaches for five months each year.

"Charlie Lyman, whose descendants now live near Whippleville, drove the old mail route between Malone and Au Sable Forks, via the Port Kent and Hopkinton Turnpike, a fifty-mile bi-weekly run through the sixteen-mile woods (now Route 99), a dreary, desolate trip in Winter. Clad in his huge stormcoat, his face beaming with benevolence, he took great pleasure in giving rides to pedestrians. One April morning in 1861 he stopped at Rice's and told them that Ft. Sumter had been fired upon. Harrietstown, Franklin and Brighton responded by sending 175 men — mostly volunteers — to the front out of a total population of a little over a thousand....

"After Van Buren Miller's tenure of office was over, a Miss Morgan became custodian of the clothesbasket. Then followed William F. Martin, Ensine Miller, Orlando Blood and M. B. Miller (15 years), who built the first real post office in Goldsmith's store, now the P. O. Pharmacy. Later postmasters were J. H. Miller, W. F. Roberts, John Harding, Charles Gray and R. H. McIntyre.

"Mail carriers after 1872 were William Harper, Ensine Miller, B. F. Lamson, V. G. Bartlett, J. B. Miller, then Platto & O'Brien until 1892, when the Webb's Golden Chariot Route (later bought by N.Y. Central) extended its track into Saranac Lake and the old mailcoaches passed into history."

Rice's eulogy of the stagecoach era is very eloquent and quotable: "Dear old coach! I can still hear in Memory's ear the rumble of your wheels as you gaily sped along the Old Plank Road, the rhythmic clatter of the horses' feet and the pistol crack of the blacksnake whip wielded by the skillful hands of the genial driver....

"Nowadays with scientific progress anyone who wants to can go on vacation with a combination telephone and Kodak, take pictures and keep in touch with his business at the same time. Perchance some pretty maiden will send a wave laden with coos and kisses to some remote sweetheart while a rival may butt in and go her one better!...."

A hundred years ago the principal means of travel in the Adirondack region were the buckboard and the stagecoach. Actually, from 1855 to 1890 the entire economy depended upon the stagelines because they carried not only passengers but freight, mail and medicines as well. Arrivals and departures of the glamorous old conveyances represented the highlight of the day for all levels of the population. Along the routes the rumble of the

George Meserve, Stage Driver

coaches served as clocks and welcome breaks in the day's routine. Their drivers were important people and they earned the respect and admiration of everyone by their qualities of resourcefulness, endurance and skill in handling four or six-horse teams over bumpy, narrow, pockmarked, boggy or sandy roads, depending upon the season. Their forty-mile runs through all varieties of weather, often in darkness, were every bit as amazing and applicable as the quotation from Herodotus in reference to mail service: "Neither snow nor rain nor heat nor gloom of night shall stay these couriers from the swift completion of their appointed rounds."

Most authorities seem to agree that the two best stagecoach drivers were Alexander Fitch O'Brien and George Meserve. Fitch, as he was usually known, was a Civil War veteran whose early experience was gained on the line between Troy and Greenwich. In 1875 he moved to Saranac Lake, bought the stage-line owned by Ensine Miller, operated it a short time with a man named Platto, then ran it by himself the rest of his career. A small, modest man, the dean of drivers was not talkative unless he wanted to be, but nevertheless he was one of the best-informed people in the region. He could handle one horse or eight with equal ability and, while gentle with them, always managed to cover his run in record time. Undoubtedly, he logged more miles than any other driver in the business.

His first route, after his arrival in Saranac Lake, was from Au Sable Forks to Paul Smith's, Loon Lake and Saranac Lake. Credited with taking the very first coach through the Wilmington Notch he was also the last to drive his Concord coach and four between Saranac Lake and Lake Placid, when in 1893, the D. & H. railroad relegated the stagecoach to the status of museum relic. O'Brien died in 1909, aged 80, in his home at the top of St. Bernard Street hill.

George Meserve, born in Conway, N.H. in 1834, was another wizard with horses. During the Civil War he drove baggage wagons for Generals McClellan, Burnside and Hooker and with Grant at Richmond. After several years on the run between Montpelier and St. Johnsbury, Vt., he came over to the Adirondacks and worked for O'Brien before being hired by Paul Smith to drive the big six-horse coach for a twelve-year period. Following that he closed out his career as coachman for Pres. Grover Cleveland in Washington and at Lakewood, New Jersey. He died at Ticonderoga in 1905.

Other area drivers were William and E. Harper, who owned their own line; Billy

Hinds, George Derby, Dan McKillip, William Burt, Tuffield (Tuffy) Latour, Henry McQuillan, Matt Miller, Phil McManus, Charles Reynolds, Gabriel and Arthur Manning, Fred Cook, Charlie Greenough and Isaiah Vosburgh.

The last-named started driving in 1862, when only seventeen, between Martin's Hotel and Keeseville. After owning French's Hotel in Franklin Falls for a year (1880-81) he returned to his farm in Harrietstown, sold that in 1894 and moved to Saranac Lake where he was active in various businesses. Game Protector from 1896-1910 and president of his village for seven terms beginning in 1908. His home, since razed, was opposite O'Brien's on St. Bernard's Street....

During the course of an interview dated Nov. 31, 1905 with Kenneth Goldthwaite, publisher of the *Adirondack Daily Enterprise* at that time, Milo B. Miller, one of Saranac Lake's most prominent residents, remarked that the greatest boost the village has ever known was the Murray Rush.[1]" Until that time this was a country of extensive lumbering operations. There were great drives of logs down the Saranac River every Spring. The boys and men went away as soon as the ice went out and they followed the drive all the way to Plattsburgh, where they arrived about July 1. C. F. Norton, who lived here for a while as well as in Plattsburgh took out at least 100,000 standards[2] every year. It was logging country all right but there was plenty of game and fine fishing also; often sportsmen came in with packs of hounds.[3]

"Before Murray started them coming, buildings hereabouts were few and far between. There was Blood's Hotel, part of which was inclosed in Riverside Inn (since demolished); the Van Buren Miller residence (later torn down to make way for the LaPan Highway); a small barn on the present site of the Town Hall; a small building where Aaron Goldsmith's store is now (present Western Auto location), and a small house near present location of Methodist Church. These were the features of Main Street.

"River Street didn't have any buildings then and although we had a school the nearest church was in Black Brook, Clinton County.

"There was a stagecoach line from Port Kent via Keeseville and Au Sable Forks and for a number of years they met at noon at Franklin Falls to exchange horses (get fresh teams). Later a switch was made at French's. For a person in good health a trip into the mountains on one of four or six-horse coaches was the thrill of a lifetime, but for one less rugged it was a severe trial from which many died on the way here.

"When Rev. Murray began writing about the woods, lakes, trout and deer and how consumption could be cured by a stay in these mountains, his book started "Murray's fools," as they were called, stampeding in.

"The leading hotel in this locality was Martin's Saranac Lake House, built in 1849, on Ampersand Bay of the Lower Lake, about a mile from the village. Since it was a small set-up we couldn't accommodate even a third of the people who came swarming in. We had to build shacks and put up tents.

"Although many sick people died on the way in and others after their arrival here — people who never should have come in the first place — the country seemed to agree with nearly everyone and the place grew rapidly. It was a boom that never stopped because Dr. Trudeau found a way to treat such folks and cured many of them so I guess the town will never really stop growing....

"In those days I was proprietor of a general store for the New York City market and fur

---

1. Started by W.H.H. Murray's publication of *Adventures in the Wilderness* or *Camp Life in the Adirondacks* in 1869.
2. Saranac standard was a log 13 feet long and 22 inches in diameter.
3. Hounding deer was suspended for five years by a law of 1896; it was permanently abolished in 1901.

The Saranac Stage — Stoddard Photo

Martin's, later Miller's on Lower Saranac Lake — Stoddard Photo

was plentiful too. I bought everything the boys brought me and sold everything I could. Muskrat hides were the most plentiful although there were also mink, fisher, marten, otter, red foxes and bearskins. Deerskins were tanned here and became a feature of the place seldom even thought of nowadays (1905). Deerhides aren't worth much now because there are ten pairs of sheepskin gloves and mittens to every two made of deerskin. Years ago it was just the opposite.

"Keeseville was our nearest express office and we did a big business in venison before railroads got into Michigan and opened up that state for market hunters who supplied New York stores at a considerably lower figure than we could handle. I've known deermeat to drop $.10 a pound in just one day.

"I built the Berkeley House in 1873 and sold it to Streeter Dennison in 1886. In 1880 I got ownership of Martin's on a mortgage foreclosure and ran it until it burned in 1894. After the fire I sold the property to the Ampersand Hotel Co. W. F. Martin then built Edgewood Inn on the hillside overlooking the east side of the Lower Lake but it burned in 1900."

Miller married Katherine Finnegan of Saranac Lake in 1869; she died Dec. 22, 1900. The largest property owner in the village, he also had 400 building lots and 1,000 acres of land around Lake Kiwassa. At one time his holdings extended from the Lower Lake across the hill and as far east as the Saranac River.

The June 31, 1881 issue of the old *Forest and Stream* magazine contained a rather amusing as well as informative article written by someone who called himself a Saranac guide. Whoever he was he turned out an enticing public relations piece plus, in the fable portion, a sound analogy.

"The season has recently opened at the Saranac Lakes and sportsmen are flocking to the forests like doves to their windows. Our woods still abound with game and our streams and lakes are alive with fish. This is the season when they are clamoring to be caught so enthusiastic anglers naturally want to know the best way to reach the Adirondacks. Many, after one trip here — especially if they had good sport and a pleasant time — write articles for the papers and periodicals, describing the route they took as the Adirondacks, thereby not taking into consideration the vast extent of these mountains. Of course there are many ways of entering this region but the experience of 30 years in all parts of the wilderness should give me some knowledge of its ways and byways. To my mind the Lower Saranac combines more advantages than any other place as a departure point for sportsmen or just plain tourists. Moreover, this is getting to be better understood as many parties are proving this season, by coming this way and being met here by guides from St. Regis, Long Lake, Blue Mountain Lake etc. In other words this place is the easiest access for all concerned.

"Naturally, each hotel-keeper thinks and feels that he runs the best place in the woods. In that respect they remind me of the East and West Ponds each inhabited by frogs and separated from each other by a hill. One fine morning one frog from each pond started out on a discovery expedition, each wanting to see how his neighbor's habitat compared with his own. When they reached the crest of the hill, they blinked at each other for a while, then fell into conversation and closed the confab by each accepting the other's invitation to look into his neighbor's pond.

"So each one rose up on his hind legs and, with one foot on the other's shoulder, looked for the respective pond. Now, as we all know, a frog's eyes are on top of his head so each of course looked intently at his own habitat when he thought he was staring at his neighbor's. Thus they were both satisfied, said good-day and retraced their way back home. When they got there they were met by friends who were curious about the trip and who wanted to know

W. H. H. [Adirondack] Murray

Early Saranac Lake from Lake Street Hill, 1880's — Stoddard Photo

how their place stacked up against their neighbor's bailiwick. Both frogs came up with the very same answer: - "Say, I wouldn't give an acre of this water for their whole pond!" And that's just about the attitude that Adirondack hotelmen and natives have toward each other's premises....

"In leaving Lake Champlain at Westport, Port Kent or Plattsburgh you reach Miller's (formerly Martin's) Saranac Lake House an hour or two sooner than you reach any of the other lakes of the chain. The recent thorough renovation of Miller's is about complete from cellar to garret. Guests who have stayed here before and have been satisfied will now be delighted by the improvement.

"I write this for the benefit and information of the uninitiated and not for any pecuniary consideration because Miller is not the man to swap a Summer's board for a literary puff.

"Parties coming into the area are misled in many ways. Some en route for the Saranacs have been taken to Paul Smith's by conniving stage-drivers who use their best influence on behalf of the man who pays them the most. But Charlie Green, the new manager of the line between here and Ausable Forks, can be depended on to carry passengers straight to their chosen destinations without fear or favor. Moreover, he has the best horses ever seen on the route and, having bought out the Harpers of Keeseville, is prepared to transport passengers with both speed and comfort and flatters himself that he can give complete satisfaction to the traveling public." [Ed.'s Note: On second thought the author may quite conceivably have been Charlie G., himself busily blowing his own publicity horn.]

The Trudeau years — from 1884 on, when Little Red was built and the Adirondack Sanitarium got started on its long and glorious era as the outstanding prototype of institutional treatment of Tuberculosis — have been more than adequately narrated by numerous writers so that any further attempt would be repetitious. Moreover, that phase of Saranac history is also very competently covered by Dr. LeRoy Wardner in his excellent chapter on Adirondack Medicine in this same book.

With the closing of the Sanitarium in 1954 and its subsequent purchase by the American Management Assn., the health resort was definitely over. No longer was there any need for the dichotomy of sharing with the more preferable vacation resort image, a far more acceptable turn of events in the opinion of many local residents who resented in varying degrees the fact that the village's economy was actually based on the health industry during most of its history. No longer did far too many tourists drive through town as though it was in permanent quarantine or when an emergency stop had to be made tie handkerchiefs over their faces to avoid the inhalation of viruses. As a matter of health record Saranac Lake, because of strict preventive regulations was much less a contagion area than any large population center in the country.

Although Saranac Lake village is obviously not quite as fashionable or pretentious as Lake Placid's limited shopping center, it nevertheless has natural assets that cannot be matched there or anywhere else in the mountains. Granted, too, that Placid has magnificent mountain vistas and its admittedly alluring lake dominated by Whiteface, but the latter lake is not even in the same league with the incomparable, far more extensive Saranac Chain — Upper, Middle and Lower — and its ever-varying, island-punctuated historic waterways. All the leading writers, artists, photographers and discerning tourists from the 1840s on have used their full arsenal of purple prose in attempts to render literary and artistic justice to Saranac's enticing region.

Best of all, in the considered opinion of most Adirondackers, is the fact that much of the shoreline and the numerous islands are state-owned, thus guaranteeing that this choicest land of lakes will never suffer the fate of so many other scenically endowed areas — Lakes George and Tahoe for example — and the concomitant, usually hideous development and exploitation. In all but a relatively small area of the Upper Lake the presence of quick-buck promoters will never constitute a serious menace to the rest of the region. That, of course, is predicated upon keeping the miniature Ton-de-lays under control.

All in all Saranac and the Saranacs, the village and lakes, have experienced a matchless and often glamorous past and with the impetus of more imaginative and enlightened planning; friendlier, closer cooperation among its several divergent factions and with a deeper, more determined sense of purpose the community should have every reason to look forward confidently to a reasonably rosy future. However bedeviled the area may be — and there's little room for doubt or argument about the region's less than enviable economic situation — these old Adirondacks are still almost as beautiful as ever. All we need are men and women to "match our mountains," as the early Californians so aptly declared. Quite a challenge but one vastly worth the human effort required. After all, as Thomas Paine so convincingly expressed the idea: "The harder the conflict, the more glorious the triumph. What we obtain too cheap we esteem too lightly. It is dearness only that gives everything its value." The burden of proof lies squarely on the minds and shoulders of all who love this lovely northern tier — to prove that we are really worthy of our incomparable natural heritage.

Frederick A. [Adirondack] Hodges

162

Chapter 14

FREDERICK ATHERTON HODGES
Better Known as "Adirondack" Hodges

Although Seneca Ray Stoddard was unquestionably the most proficient of the photographers who glorified the Adirondacks, there were camera artists among his successors who were nearly as competent. One of these was the late Frederick A. Hodges of Utica and Blue Mountain Lake who, over a period of more than forty years and during every season of the year, roamed the mountains recording on film and in his notebook their varying moods and scenes. During that period (1910-1950) his trips took him over most of the central and southern sections and eventually produced more than 8,000 negatives, thus making it the largest such collection in existence.

In addition Fred took twenty-three reels of colored and black and white movie films which in themselves constitute a valuable contribution to photographic art. His still and moving pictures, his tinted photos all form a noteworthy visual record of a lifetime devoted to his profession.

Fred Hodges inherited his love of nature and his flair for photography from his father, Frederick B. Hodges of Rome, New York. Hodges, Sr. was not without local distinction as a camera historian and prolific nature writer. A reserved, dignified man he spent as much time as he possibly could at his favorite photographic sites -- the vast sand plains west of Rome, the old Black River Canal and its combines, the upper reaches of the Mohawk River and storied, meandering Woods Creek, the ancient Indian waterway leading to Oneida Lake and Lake Ontario.

Fred Sr., learned much of his camera skill by watching J. H. Brainerd, a master photographer (of Rome, N.Y.) who advised and encouraged the younger man. Both were thoroughly convinced that picture-taking required just as much artistic ability as did the older media of oils and watercolors. The father's gum prints in particular showed such unusual mastery that they won many honors at big city exhibitions.

Such masterpieces, however, earned far more prestige than dollars. The buyers were unwilling to pay more than token prices and these had to be low to encourage business. A perfectionist who refused to sign his name to any work that did not meet his exacting standards, the elder Hodges discarded many of his prints and thereby pared down his meager profits. Impractical of course but also indicative of his devotion to his art.

The senior Hodges was a true Thoreauvian, an admirer of Bradford Torrey and a discerning lover of all forms of nature and wildlife. He located several species of wildflowers hitherto unknown to that region and was so credited by Homer D. House, the state botanist, author of the classic. *"Wild Flowers of New York."*

Frederick B. Hodges

His reactions to and impressions of the moods and mysteries of nature found eloquent expression in more than 300 articles which appeared regularly in the Rome *Sentinel* and occasionally in the New York *Herald Tribune*. He was also a frequent and featured contributor of articles and pictures to *Photo-Era, American Photography* and *Friends Magazine*.

Therefore, it is quite understandable that the son should show an early aptitude for photography and the desire to express himself in that medium. Very early in life he had also become infatuated with the Adirondacks, whose lower ranges are visible from the hills to the north of Rome. In 1897, when he was nine, he became closer acquainted with those alluring summits. That summer the family spent the first of many such vacations at the Cohasset, on Fourth Lake of the Fulton Chain.

There he met Ed Arnold, best remembered for having been the only boy among 13 children in the Arnold household. The Arnolds had stayed on at Old Forge after the failure of the iron-mining venture, and the tragic suicides of Charles Herreshoff and his own father.

Ed, who was over 70 at the time had just closed out his guiding career and was handyman at the hotel. He was, however, still active and colorful enough to be a fit subject for hero worship. The laconic old woodsman liked the quiet, attentive boy and often took him fishing in his big 18 foot guideboat. Since Ed had already put his walking days well behind him, the lad was never able to persuade the venerable guide to show him his hunting secrets. So Fred had to learn by himself. In fact he learned so fast and so well that during that same season he shot his first deer. That memorable summer was followed by nearly sixty more and all of them were spent in the Raquette Lake — Fulton Chain — Blue Mountain Lake area.

When Fred had finished his schooling at Rome Free Academy and Colgate Preparatory School, he decided to make a career of photography. In order to develop skill as a portrait taker he left his hometown and worked successively for such renowned concerns as Bachrach, Sarony, Morceau and Pierce in Boston, New York and Chicago. While in the employ of H. H. Pierce he was their chief operator and supervisor of a crew of 70. Among his many clients were various Vanderbilts, Goulds, Havemeyers, DuPonts and Morgans.

Even though he had by this time firmly established himself as a superior cameraman, this fourteen-year period, punctuated by too brief Adirondack vacations, convinced Fred that he was not finding adequate self-fulfillment in the cities. In 1923 he returned to Rome; shortly thereafterhe opened a studio in New Hartford and, still later on, moved to Utica.

Ever since he had first gone, as a boy, on one of the Raquette — Blue Mountain Lake excursion trips, he had become strongly attracted by the scenic splendors of that lovely lake and its guardian peak. Right then he made up his mind that someday somehow he would have a place of his own there. That promise to himself became a reality when in the early 1940s the owners of the Hedges gave him permission to put up a camp and have lifetime occupancy. Doing every bit of the job himself he built Meeko (Squirrel) Inn and, on the day when he had finished the work, he felt that he had really come into his own.

That feeling of deep satisfaction provided just the incentive needed to construct another; this one, which he called Partridge Camp, he located on a wooded ridge overlooking North Brookfield, just off the Cherry Valley Turnpike. Finished in 1945 the place provided him with the second escape hatch from the constant pressures generated by trying to wrest a modest living from what is commonly considered to be a precarious, unprofitable profession.

During the war years Fred had a hard time making ends meet. Film was very scarce and he had to improvise ways to use the inferior product that came irregularly from the companies.

To supplement his income from his outdoor photography business, in which sales were mostly seasonal, he also did much indoor work. He had already found out the hard way that very young children especially can be very difficult to capture — literally, as well as on film. "It was," he wrote in his journals, "sometimes a case of practically stalking the child around the room and then snapping the picture when the youngster was either cornered or resting!" He felt that such mutual exertion was just another occupational hazard which he good-naturedly endured. His heart, however, was seldom in this phase of his craft.

Every Summer he used his Blue Mountain Lake camp as his headquarters, and from "Meeko" he regularly made the rounds of the resorts in that region and to the south. At the hotels he would display the photos which he had tinted and processed during the previous Winter and Spring. Sometimes the sales would be brisk; other times disappointingly slow. Although nearly everyone liked the pictures and praised them extravagantly, fiscal extravagance was seldom put into practice when the big decision had to be made.

Usually he sold at least some of his wares but there were many nights when his illustrated lecture made the difference between his eating high or low on the hog. Speaking of eating, sometimes he even had to pay for evening meals at the hotels where he exhibited and entertained. It is characteristic of him that on those occasions he confined his scathing remarks to the privacy of his journals.

By showing several of his repertory of 16mm. color and black and white films which he had taken over the years, he was able to give the guests a more accurate and lasting impression of that great vacation land. The pictures covered a wide range of Adirondack subjects — climbing trips up Marcy and Blue Mountains, feeding deer in winter, wild

St. Louis Point, Little Moose Lake — Hodges Photo

A Back-Country Pond — Hodges Photo

Golden Beach, Raquette Lake — Hodges Photo

Loon Brook near Blue Mountain Lake — Hodges Photo

animals in their own environment and not in cages, wildflowers, the scenic highlights of the mountains, etc.

A jack arangement on his projector enabled him to narate his own films and thus add to their merit as entertainment. When the show was over someone connected with the management passed a hat. The take from this unbusinesslike, informal procedure can be readily reckoned. It ranged from seeming generosity to very slender pickings indeed. For example his carefully noted records show that during one typical season, the highest yield for an evening's work was $62.00, the lowest — less than $12.00. A somewhat unenviable and uncertain way to make a living when one considers that only a small part of it was profit.

The journals which have already been mentioned, as well as his notebooks, provide a fascinating insight into the nature of the man and the era in which he lived. The essays, which say so much about a person who customarily said so little, contribute a great deal to the lore and lure of those bygone years. They deal with accurate recollections of early hotels and steamboats and excursion trips on those long-departed craft; Adirondack guideboats — who made them and how they were made; impressions of such colorful characters as Ed Arnold, Bill Dart, and French Louie Seymour, and the Bennetts. Outstanding are his narratives of his first camping trip to Limekiln Lake; his successful, eventful boyhood hunting trip to the Moose River Plains.

These stories are told simply and directly, with sincerity and authority.

Besides being a photographer, sportsman and writer Fred was also a collector and dealer in antique firearms. Not having anywhere near the financial solvency needed to pursue this sideline as far as he wanted to, he nevertheless by shrewd swapping and trading tactics was able to accumulate an impressive array of those expensive relics. He had contacts all over the nation and often stretched his slender resources to the utmost in order to acquire a prize item.

Hodges was also a crack shot with both the pistol and the rifle, and did not hesitate to share this skill with others. For many years he was the firearms instructor for the Utica Auxiliary Police, the DeMolay rifle team and the Junior Hunter Safety Program sponsored by the New York State Conservation Department. A member of the National Rifle Association he was considered to be one of its most respected and effective instructors.

Winter was his favorite season in the mountains. "Everything in the woods and about the woods satisfies me. Space, quiet, no need to lock your doors, lots of sky and weather — just all kinds of weather a man could ask for and all of it just right. As for being lonely in the woods that's something I can't understand. It's in the city that a man's lonely, to my way of thinking."

Since my personal knowledge of Fred Hodges is admittedly sketchy, it is only logical that those who knew him far better should help fill in the informational gaps. Out of a list of many three were contacted and each one was anything but lukewarm in his evaluation.

The first, probably Fred's best friend in the mountains and one who shared his passion for old guns, was E. H. Griffin of Deerland. This man and his late wife liked Fred and were willing, sympathetic listeners whenever the latter felt impelled to air his worries and problems. They often invited him for meals and from them came the statement that Fred had been there the day before he died and that he seemed to sense that death was near. Having had a heart condition for several years he knew that he was nearing the end of his mortal trail. The last afternoon he had spent under the big pines and beside the rushing waters of nearby Buttermilk Falls (Murray's Phantom Falls) on the Raquette River.

He probably felt the same way about that beautiful place as Dr. Noah Porter had felt about Upper Ausable Lake. Donaldson recorded that when that distinguished man realized that he had not much longer to live, he requested that his guide take him on a farewell tour of his beloved lake. Tears welling from his eyes, he looked for the last time at those familiar scenes. Later, the guide remarked that this had been one of the most touching moments of his (the guide's) life.

Another testimonial came from Blair Kenney of Cedar City, Utah; he, a companion named John Tanner and Fred had climbed Marcy in the summer of 1949. Quote: "It is hard to put into words the respect I had for Fred, but I think it can best be summed up by saying that he was a man of great depth. He was always four or five times the man he appeared to be. He never tried to put on a show or make people feel that he was important or wise. But he was very wise and could have been very important if he had wanted to be... He was very quick to grasp new ideas and his mind was never clouded with prejudices. He was always true to his convictions...

"Another thing I remember about him was that you could never guess what he was thinking about or what he would do next. Very quiet but always thinking while he was quiet, because when he did speak he was well worth listening to. He had a large Bible in his home and in each of his camps — and these were not there for decorative purposes only. They were read, studied and their precepts constantly put into daily practice."

From the third man, Stan Countryman of Whitesboro, New York, who had hunted with Fred for 17 years, came the following observations and impressions: "He often hunted in gray wool clothing and Cree Indian moosehide moccasins which of course, though soundless, wet through almost immediately. His knowledge of the Loon Brook-Big Bend country and thereabouts was like the average person's familiarity with his own living room. He never talked unnecessarily at any time, except possibly when discussing guns, and in the woods he made no sound. His voice was very soft and he was quite undemonstrative. His walk in the woods never appeared to be hurried or fast but he covered ground much faster than the average person — I well know this because of my trying to keep up with him. His reflexes were lightning fast which of course came from 50 years of hunting and target shooting.

"The fun all ends in deer hunting when the deer is shot. Of late years Fred and I have enjoyed partridge hunting better."

These same eulogistic remarks could have been augmented or repeated by others such as the Glade brothers of North Brookfield; Col. Cronk of Hempstead, New York or the late Judge Ezra Hannigan or Dr. Cole of Utica, but the point has already been made: Hodges was quite a hunter and gunner.

My only outdoor experience with him was limited to one brief afternoon of trout fishing near Partridge Camp at North Brookfield. We had separated to give each other sufficient fishing room. I had located a likely hole in a dense alder thicket and was concentrating on trying to extract something sizeable from under a big log close to an undercut bank. Suddenly from just behind me came the question, "How are you doing? Looks like a good one you have on!" To this day I don't know how he was able to get that near me without making enough noise to attract my attention. Just another proof of his woodsmanship.

This is a long-overdue tribute by his son-in-law to the memory of a man who, while he was still alive and could enjoy it in his own modest way, should have received far more recognition and compensation (other than artistic satisfaction). These he was never adequately accorded. So since that form of fame is now impossible, this belated effort will have to suffice.

"French Louie" Seymour — Hodges Photo

Buttermilk Falls near Deerland — Stoddard Photo

It is in a sense the keeping of my part of a promise. Just a few days before he died we had talked over the possibility of our collaborating on a book about him and his work. He seemed interested and said that he had been thinking about getting around to just such a venture.

Later on, after his death, when I asked for and was given his journals and most of his notebooks by his widow, I found that he had been readying his material right up until the week of his demise. He was, therefore, certainly carrying out his end of the tacit agreement and his providence has made my part of it infinitely easier and far more authentic.

For the sake of the record it should be stated that Fred Hodges was by his very nature a person whom very few people knew well. Of course he had a wide circle of acquaintances and hunting and shooting companions; but there were only two or three men in whom he ever felt that he could confide. This was not because he was distant, disinterested or distrustful but rather because he was inherently shy, unaggressive, undemonstrative. He was soft-spoken, unassuming and often unbusinesslike and impractical when judged by the usual standards and ethics. Yet these same seeming shortcomings were in fact the very reason why those who knew him placed a high value on his friendship.

He was the kind of man who seldom complained when he felt that he had been victimized or when his actions and motives had been misinterpreted or misunderstood. He

disliked intensely any emotional outburst or involvement and nearly always either gave in or got out rather than precipitate, participate in or prolong an incipient argument.

Obviously, he had marketable talents, especially his skill with a camera. Proof of this was the inclusion of some of his photographs as illustrations for *"Township 34"* and *"Adirondack French Louie"*, but he could never have gained any appreciable degree of inward peace and self-satisfaction from following the usual photographic routine. Family portraits or pictures of smirking children, although they provided needed income, never had much appeal for him.

Only when he was in the dense forest, on a lonely mountaintop, in a canoe or skiff on an Adirondack lake did he feel that he was where he really belonged, that he was in his own special element, and that he was an important part of God's great natural scheme. His films and photos, his journals and his notebooks furnish the missing details which round out the picture of the man.

I greatly regret that I was not one of those who was closest to him. Even though I had married his daughter by his first marriage, I hardly knew him. In fact I was with him only five times and for short periods even then, because circumstances seemingly beyond our control made further acquaintance impossible and somewhat unpleasant for him..

With the passing of the years since his death at Blue Mountain Lake on August 15, 1959, I have become more convinced than ever that Frederick A. Hodges — Adirondack Hodges — was quite a man. Proof that I was not the only one who held this opinion can be found in the closing paragraph of a lengthy interview which appeared in the "People Worth Knowing" section of the *Sunday Observer Dispatch* (Utica, New York) on April 20, 1941.

Quote: "Hodges waits, camera set for action, hour after hour for a certain change in cloud formation, for the right light on a stream, for deer to cross a sunflecked trail. And calls the waiting good, exciting and worthwhile. Not for nothing did the North Country folks long ago nickname him "Adirondack!"

Ed Arnold, Fulton Chain Guide
— Hodges Photo

Chapter 15

ED ARNOLD, OLDTIME ADIRONDACK GUIDE
From the Notebooks of the Late Fred (Adirondack) Hodges
(Edited by His Son-in-Law, Maitland C. De Sormo)

Back in 1897, when I was nine years old, my family spent the first of many vacations at the Cohasset, located on Fourth Lake of the Fulton Chain. In those days there were no automobiles nor good roads in that section of the Adirondacks, so we got there by railroad and steamboat. At the old New York Central station in Rome we got on the train for Utica. There we changed to the Mohawk and Malone division, destination Thendara, where we again changed cars, this time for Old Forge. From there we walked to the dock and boarded the steamer "Fulton" for the last leg of the trip. Other boats making the same run during that time were the "C. L. Stowell" and the "Zip."

The Cohasset was owned and operated by Josiah Wood and his wife. Josiah, better known as Si, had bought the land from Ed Arnold and had built the hotel only a short time

Cohasset, Fourth Lake, Fulton Chain — Stoddard Photo

before. Si's father, Alonzo (Lon) Wood, had been one of the pioneer guides of the region. Work on the hotel had not yet been completed. It still had the yellow priming coat of paint, the porches had no railings and the rear of the place was still unfinished.

Even though it was late May when we got there, the main house was already full, so we were assigned rooms in the "old house", a somewhat ramshackle log building that stood in front and slightly downlake from the new hotel. The place where we stayed was a delightful spot, shaded by huge pines and hemlocks, and had a pair of hoot owls to lull us to sleep.

Ed Arnold, who had sold Cohasset Point to Si Wood, was the only son among the ten children in the Arnold family who had stayed on at Old Forge after the suicide of the owner, Charles Herreshoff. Ed had been a well-known guide in his day but, being then well over 70, had given it up for good and was working as a handyman at the hotel.

He was a rather portly old fellow with grizzled whiskers and a stubby pipe. He usually wore a felt hat, a blue flannel shirt, a pair of pepper and salt wool pants and lumbermen's boots. On colder days a wool mackinaw completed the outfit.

I well remember the color and texture of his skin. His face was blotched with pink and brown. It was as weatherbeaten as the backs of his hands from constant exposure to sun and wind.

The pipe Ed smoked was the very best brier. I know because I gave him many of them. He would accept the gift with a "Thank you, Bub" and stow it away in his pants pocket. I wouldn't see it for a while, then when I did there was always something different about it. It was the new one, all right, but altered in appearance. What he had done was cut a section of witchhopple branch of the right diameter, push out the pith and then shape the outside to fit the pipebowl. Those homemade stems he would use until the bowl would be about all burned away or badly chipped from knocking out the ashes. When that happened I would see one of the new bowls come to light.

He, like all the other guides and woodsmen, liked Warnick and Brown tobacco and wouldn't smoke any other brand. Said that it was the only kind that would stay in his pipe. It was stringy and spongy but once stuffed in it would burn to a fine ash. Its distinctive sweet fragrance could not be mistaken for any other weed.

The old guide spent most of his time in his boat, an 18-footer built at Old Forge by Parsons and Roberts. It was painted dark blue outside, brick-red inside and had black decks and trimming. Being well along in years, the old fellow liked his boat to be comfortable too. Therefore, in place of the usual center seat found in guideboats, he had made one of his own by removing the legs from an old armchair of the type usually found in saloons or poolrooms. Well padded with an old cushion and burlap bags, it made a fine seat.

Many the ride I had in that famous old boat, which could be recognized as far as it could be seen. Every morning, long before the older folks were up, I would go down to the dock and watch Ed get ready to go fishing — hoping that he would ask me to go along with him. This he sometimes did, but even when he didn't invite me I still liked to see the preparations. On the lucky days he would stop just long enough to take out his pipe, look up and say, "Better get in, Freddie."

His first project was to haul up his minnow trap, which he had baited with pancakes and set in fairly deep water the night before. Then he would dump the flopping fish into the boat and cut them up into small pieces with a thick black jacknife. These chunks he would throw into a pail which was stowed into the boat with his tackle.

The tackle was not very elaborate but it certainly was effective. It consisted of wooden bobbins about a foot long, made from a piece of flat board hollowed out at each end. On these he wound a heavy linen line rigged with a big lead sinker and a large-ringed hook. Two or three of these ready-rigged bobbins were always stuck under the cleats which held the center seat.

Another piece of equipment which he carried was his "priest." This was a short, thick club which he used to persuade the fish to stop flopping around in the bottom of the boat. It seldom took more than one well-aimed blow to make even the largest lakers quiver for a few seconds then stop moving for good.

With his pipe freshly lit, his gear stowed in the boat and me ensconced in the stern seat, he would push away from the dock with one oar and we were off for another day of adventure for me but just another day's fishing for him. Ed always had several favorite fishing spots — usually in 45-60 feet of water — marked by buoys of his own making. These were straight, slim spruce poles about twelve feet long and tied securely to the anchor ropes. As the ropes shrank, the poles would stand upright in the water and could thus be seen from some distance. He baited these buoys regularly the last thing each day. Baiting consisted of scattering a large quantity of cut-up fish in the vicinity of each marker.

Upon our arrival at one of these locations, the old man would tie the boat's painter to the buoy and we would then drift around with the wind. Ed would bait the hooks with chunks of bait, and with a bobbin in each hand, he would lower the lines over both sides of the boat. When the sinkers hit bottom he would raise them a foot or so. Every now and then he would raise the lines a few feet and then lower them again. Usually he would let me fish too, but sometimes I just sat there hour after hour without either of us ever saying a word.

I can still remember the charm of the sky and water, the lapping waves and the breeze blowing by. Some days the clouds would be scudding along in layers and the water would be a grayish blue. Other times the clouds would be white and feathery with the blue of the sky filtering through. Other days the sky would be clear deep blue and the water of the lake would seem the same color. At such times I would wonder how far down I could see into the depths, how far down the bait was and how far it was from the wary trout.

Sometimes, when I was deepest in thought, there would be a sharp tug which would shake the boat, and old Ed would start hauling in his line hand over hand. Usually there would be a surface splash and then a sizeable trout would flash over the side of the skiff. The fish would manage to get in just one good flop before the priest did its deadly work. On one memorable day a 9 lb. rainbow trout, the only known one of that breed ever caught on Fourth Lake up to that time, was among the big lakers taken.

Ed was a good fisherman — he sure got 'em. I well remember how folks from all around the Lake would come to buy or see his catch. Invariably they would ask him how he got 'em and generally Ed would just grin. Occasionally, though, if he was in a rare talkative mood, he would tell them how it was done. Usually, however, he had very little to say. In fact, it was almost impossible to get him to talk about his fishing and hunting experiences.

How well I recall those trips with Ed which seemed all too short. There were days, though, when the fishing was slow and the silence seemed so endless that I wondered if he would ever give up and go home so that I could get back on land again and do something besides sit.

Ed taught me how to use a flyrod. "Throw a fly," he called it. He also showed me how to tie them on a leader and how to manage them in the water. His favorites were a Scarlet Ibis for the tail fly, a Grizzly King in the middle and a Brown Hackle for the dropper. Another set had the Montreal, Cowdung and Black Gnat in the same order as the other cast. A Yellow Sally took many trout for us.

Flyfishing was royal sport for me and, because of the constant action, it was a lot more fun than just sitting in a boat by the hour.

Ed would row into the bays and I would cast toward the edge of the lily-pads or toward the mouth of the small brooks that emptied into the lake. There were times when we had two on a line at once. I recall one evening when we were working along a narrow inlet I was having a hard time getting my flies to land where I wanted them to. I was casting right handed and the boat was not headed so I could use that hand well. Old Ed, seeing what was happening, said, "Use your other hand, Freddie."

"I can't," I replied.

"Oh yes you can!" was his answer.

So I tried it and found out that he was right and soon, much to my surprise, I was using either hand almost equally well.

I never could get "Uncle Ed" to go into the woods with me. Walking very far was too much for him as he was well into his 70's. He would work hard in the garden or at the woodpile, or stand waist deep in the cold water building a dock or a breakwater, but when Winter came he went to Utica and stayed with his sister. 'I'm gettin' too old to waller around in the snow," he would say.

Although he already had a great deal of respect for axes, one day he got careless. While splitting wood with a double-bitted axe, he had somehow tangled with a low-hanging clothesline which swung the axe back into his face and made a nasty cut which ran from the inner corner of his eye, just missed his nose and on down to his jaw. The gash should have been sewed up by a doctor, but he nursed it with home remedies and in a short time it had healed into a red blob and eventually a long permanent scar.

Later on I found out that there were two main types of Adirondack guides. One kind was full of all sorts of remarkable stories and experiences. He had seen the largest trees, knew where the choicest berries grew, had caught the most and biggest trout, had been chased by wildcats, bears and wounded deer. But strangely enough he had always come out on top. He and other chaps had cut the most wood and in the shortest time. Whenever he carried a boat he never had to rest even on the longest portages. He knew the names of all the trees, birds and flowers and whenever he didn't really know, tried to make you think that he did.

The other type of guide said little and made that little go a long way. He was courteous and efficient. He did not brag about his ability and his exploits with rod, gun, axe and guideboat. He was always inclined to underestimate the number of deer and bear he killed or trout he had caught, and their sizes. Whenever he didn't know the answer to a question, he readily admitted that he didn't know and didn't feel that he had lost face by doing so. Whenever these men talked, you sat there and really listened.

Ed Arnold was one of the second kind of guides. Like them, he never felt he had to fill the city sports full of bunk. Moreover, he never drank and that was a distinction in itself. He was a genuine Adirondack native, a true woodsman, a great guide and a good friend.

176

Chapter 16

EARLY STEAMBOATS ON THE FULTON CHAIN
From the Notebooks of Fred (Adirondack) Hodges
(Edited by his Son-in-law, Maitland C. DeSormo)

When my parents first started vacationing at Fourth Lake in the Adirondacks, back in 1897, even though I was a young boy at the time, I can still remember the steamboats that served the Fulton Chain.

One of them was the *Zip*, a comparatively small boat with open sides and a roof over all but a few feet of the deck. The small pilot house had the usual window and was protected from the weather for a short distance on either side. The steam boiler was located amidships; a rotary valve engine turned the single screw.

The engine had been made and patented by a man named Walker, who lived in Rome, my hometown. He had manufactured several of these engines, but somehow had not been able to sell many, even though they were very efficient.

The *Zip*, a trim little craft with a bowsprit like a yacht's, cut through the water at a lively pace. For many years it was a familiar sight on the Chain because it was the mailboat. Its cargo of mail pouches was frequently tossed onto hotel and camp docks while the boat was still in motion.

One day, while crossing Second Lake, this craft collided with the larger *C. L. Stowell* and was nearly cut in half. Although the *Zip* sank almost immediately, the two men aboard were able to scramble to shore. Raised soon afterward, fitted with a small cabin aft for the mail clerk, and renamed the Old Forge, the tough little steamer stayed on the mail run for many more seasons.

Another steamer of that era was aptly named the *Fulton*. A combination passenger and freight carrier, this craft was larger than the *Zip* and had a cabin in the rear section. The front section had a closed-in pilot house. Whenever there were more passengers than the cabin would accommodate, some of the hardier souls rode in deck chairs.

The *Fulton*, a single-screw vessel, was used as the regular general duty boat for many seasons. Eventually it was rebuilt, enlarged, refurbished and renamed the *Mohegan*. Though used as an extra during the summer, she saw much more service, because of her shallow draft, in the Fall and whenever the water was low.

One Summer, upon our arrival at Old Forge, we were met by an even larger steamer, the *C. L. Stowell*, the same boat that later sent the *Zip* to her temporary watery grave. This steamboat had two decks with the cabin on the main one. The upper deck was open behind the pilot house. This boat, with its black hull and white superstructure, gave the passengers a feeling of greater pleasure and security.

Not long after the ramming incident, it was revamped and renamed the *Nehasane*. It

Killoquah 1, at Foot of Raquette Lake — Stoddard Photo

was the main means of transportation until increased demands for transportation on the great waterway made necessary the addition of other steamboats.

One of these, owned by the Webb lumbering interests, was the *W. S. Webb*. Like many of the others, this was a single-screw, single-decker with cabin and pilot house. It was seldom, if ever, used for commercial purposes until it was bought by the Raquette Lake Transportation Company. Then it was enlarged and converted into a double-deck, double-screw craft and renamed the *Uncas*. This boat always seemed top-heavy. It was used mainly to make extra runs or to carry the overflow passengers when there were large crowds of travelers.

The *Caprice*, another Webb boat, was small — about the size of the *Zip*. It served mainly in towing log booms. One windy day it capsized and sank off Cedar Island. It was eventually salvaged by Hy Bowman, who for some reason never put it to use again. It rotted away at his dock.

One day while we were staying at the Cohasset, we noticed signs of much activity over at Lon Wood's place. The unusual activity turned out to be the building of two steamboats subsequently named the *Clearwater* and the *Tuscarora*.[1]

The *Clearwater* became the main steamer on the Fulton Chain until such service was discontinued entirely. It was a beautiful boat — a twin-screw, double-decker with closed cabin on the main deck, an open top deck and closed-in pilot house. Though originally painted all white, its hull was later black.

I can still remember the maiden voyage of the *Clearwater* around Fourth Lake. She blew her whistle in answer to anyone who in any fashion saluted her. Although there were far fewer camps then, the whistle sounds echoed and re-echoed for a long time. How proud

---

[1] Hodges may have been mistaken because *Township 34's* author — Harold K. Hochschild — stated that the *Tuscarora* was built in Tottenville, Staten Island.

Tuscarora, Beached in 1929. Owner Mrs. Robert Graham

Clearwater, Hollywood Hills

Terminus of Marion River R.R. — Stoddard Photo

Marion River Railroad — Stoddard Photo

we were of her; how steady and fast she was! Even the stiffest breezes and the biggest waves never seemed to bother her in the least.

Summer after Summer she sailed her course from the station at Old Forge up through the channel to First Lake, around the points into Second and Third Lakes, and sometimes bumped along through the shallow water of the Narrows into Fourth Lake. She would stop from time to time to unload passengers and baggage all along the route.

For many years her pilot was Verne Irwin, who always took her through safely. As a boy I came to know Vernie well; he let me ride in the pilot house and had a way of making me feel at home there. Whenever the *Clearwater* was due at the Cohasset, I would be waiting on the bluff. As she came into view, I would fire three blanks from my .38 revolver, and Vernie would reply with three short blasts of the whistle.

Prospect House, Blue Mountain Lake — Stoddard Photo

Prospect House Landing — Stoddard Photo

This boat was used also to start the excursion trip to Blue Mountain Lake. By 8:30 in the morning on those red-letter days, the people would have gathered on the docks along the Lake. The *Clearwater* would pick them up and take them as far as Eagle Bay. There they would board the train for the ten-mile trip to Raquette Lake, where other steamers waited for them. Then came the trip across Raquette Lake, up the Marion River and its hairpin curves to the Carry. Here they would climb into the old Brooklyn open trolley cars and be drawn by the dinky locomotive the half-mile distance to the foot of Utowana Lake.

At that point the *Tuscarora*, the *Clearwater's* twin, would take them through that lake and Eagle and past the swinging bridge at the entrance to Blue Mountain Lake. This passage was not much wider than the steamer itself, but it always managed to get through safely. Then came the unforgettable and all-too-short trip across that lake to the steamboat landing. Here the boat tied up, and the passengers who were interested in doing so climbed Blue Mountain.

The return trip started at 5 p.m. Then over the same course in reverse and back to the Cohasset by 9:30 or 10:00 p.m.

Later on, when steamboat service was discontinued on the Fulton Chain, because such business was no longer required nor profitable, the *Clearwater* was towed to First Lake and grounded there. She was finally destroyed by fire.

Another steamer built on Fourth Lake was the *Adirondack,* a two-decker like the *Clearwater*, but not so sturdy or trim-looking. Although this boat had many fancy decorations, she was not in the same league, as far as speed was concerned, with the *Nehasane* or the *Clearwater*. Shortly after she was built, she was sold to the Raquette Lake Transportation Company and taken to Raquette Lake to help handle the excursion trade.

Another craft which was important to the Summer people was the grocery boat. This was a small, closed-in, single-decker powered by a small engine. The interior was fitted out like a grocery store. It made a daily run from Old Forge to Inlet and stopped at the camps and hotels on the lakes.

The distinguishing feature of this stubby boat was the barrel of pickles carried on the rear deck. The young people used to look forward to the arrival of this boat as the highlight of the day — next to the mail boat's visit. A popular girl at the Cohasset one day gave it its nickname — the pickle boat. From then on, Charley Wilcox, its operator, was known as the engineer of the pickle boat.

Finally, as roads were built across that picturesque part of the Adirondacks and automobiles became far more numerous, the steamboats became obsolete. But there are still some people who remember with deep pleasure those craft, their pilots, and the heyday of the Fulton Chain.

The Pickle Boat,
Raquette Lake

Chapter 17

ADIRONDACK MEDICINE
A Historical Outline [1]
LeRoy H. Wardner, M.D., formerly of Saranac Lake, New York

Outstanding pioneers of Adirondack medicine from René Goupil in 1642 to the elder Trudeau in 1873 came to the mountain region through the influence of ill health. They met there the characteristic hardships of the frontier. The health-giving benefits of its climate gained wide recognition in Trudeau's time and spurred the medical advances in the treatment of chest diseases for which the region is noted.

The Adirondacks are a group of mountains in northeastern New York, the most prominent feature of a region long unsurveyed and unmapped formerly known as "The Wilderness" or "Great North Woods." Their name was first loosely applied to the entire region until the State set definite boundaries to it in establishing the Adirondack Park. In it are contained all or a portion of ten counties of the State comprising a total area somewhat larger than the State of Connecticut. It was the State's last frontier and the story of its medicine should consequently be of interest.

Ill health has powerfully influenced the lives of outstanding physicians in the history of the Adirondack region. Early in the fifteenth century it prevented René Goupil from taking the vows of the French Jesuit Order. He was able to study the medical art, however, and his religious ardor brought him to New France as a Jesuit lay brother, perhaps a counterpart of the modern medical missionary. In August, 1642, he set out in a party with Father Jogues to travel up the St. Lawrence from Quebec on a mission to the Huron Indians of the Great Lakes. They were ambushed by hostile bands of Iroquois just above what is now Three Rivers, Quebec; both Jogues and Goupil were captured along with a number of friendly Hurons. Their captors then set out with them to the Iroquois country through the watercourses of the Richelieu River and the Champlain Valley.

Torture was immediately their lot. They were beaten, their finger nails were torn off, and the savages chewed the raw quick with their teeth. Goupil retained composure through it all, ministering to the wounds of the other captives as best he could and even opening a vein for a sick Iroquois on the journey. Father Jogues related that he bore himself with great humility and obedience, even to helping to paddle the canoe for his captors. Their route carried them by water through Lake Champlain and into Lake George, skirting the boundaries of the present Adirondack Park. From Lake George their party followed an old trail near Saratoga to the Iroquois villages near the present site of Auriesville, near Johnstown on the Mohawk River. Then the ordeal of torture increased. For six days they were

[1] Read at the annual Meeting of the Medical Society of the State of New York, Buffalo, New York, April 30, 1941.
Reprinted from NEW YORK STATE JOURNAL OF MEDICINE, Vol. 42, No. 8, Apr. 15, 1942

Father Isaac Jogues left, Dr. Francis D'Avignon right

exposed to the cruelty of all the village. After six weeks Goupil was dispatched by a blow on the head, thus gaining a martyr's death for the first physician to set foot within the Adirondacks. Father Jogues was spared and later escaped to France with aid from the friendly Dutch at Fort Orange. His letters recording the martyrdom of Goupil are preserved in a volume of the *Jesuit Relations*.

History of the next century and a half leaves the Adirondack region relatively untouched. As the "dark and bloody ground," it was the private hunting preserve of the Iroquois, traversed only by occasional parties engaged in hunting or war. The Champlain Valley to the east saw the ebb and flow of Indian, French, and British fortunes through the Colonial wars and the Revolution, but the medical men of these armies came no nearer to the mountains than Goupil and they lacked such historians as Father Joques.

After the Revolution, as the urge for westward colonization became stronger, two adventurous spirits from the little Vermont community of Panton crossed Lake Champlain on the ice and discovered by chance the natural beauties and agricultural promise of the valley of the Bouquet River. This was 10 miles inland from the lake extending in a southerly direction from the present site of Elizabethtown, in Essex County, New York. Their enthusiasm inspired a small migration across the lake the following Winter of 1792 to this "Pleasant Valley." They struggled inland over a narrow trail through deep snow without benefit of even a road for sleighs. They harvested a good yield of maple sugar, however, and prospered sufficiently through the year so that they were able to persuade their former physician in Panton to cast his lot with them. He was Asa Post, then a young man of 27, who is reported to have come to Panton from Saybrook, Connecticut, for the "cure of consumption." Post served the young community with satisfaction until 1800, when the arrival of a colleague in the person of Dr. Alexander Morse enabled him to retire to a farm in the valley, where he died at the age of 92. He was the first physician to settle in the mountains.

Alexander Morse, who followed him in Pleasant Valley, served the mountain community for half a century. His saddlebags and blood-letting lance are preserved as mute witnesses of the rigors of early medicine there. In 1809 he was a delegate to the State Medical Society, where he presented a paper on the "Effects of the High Altitude of Essex of Certain of the More Common Diseases." Hence, the mountain physicians lost little time presenting the advantages of climate and altitude in disease therapy.

A fringe of small communities grew up in the valleys of the northern and eastern

184

Adirondacks in the fifty years after the coming of Dr. Post. Lumbering, iron mining, charcoal making, hunting, fishing, trapping, and farming occupied their rugged citizens. Gradually, medical pioneers moved in to make a hard life more bearable. Outstanding was F. J. d'Avignon, the second, who escaped to Au Sable Forks in 1837 under sentence of death for activities in inciting the Papineau Rebellion in Lower Canada. F. J., the first, had come from Avignon in France to practice in Lower Canada. His son's adventurous spirit could not be held there, however. F. J., the second, found in the Adirondacks freedom and the opportunity to practice a brilliant and enterprising type of medicine and surgery in which he readily excelled. His Gallic mannerisms and wit lent him an almost legendary character, and his ability soon made him in demand far outside the confines of the Au Sable Valley. He traveled on horseback prepared to do his operating by lamplight on any kitchen table. County historians mention his outstanding work as regimental surgeon in the Civil War and, then, begin to speak of F. J. d'Avignon, the third, who became as able and equally in demand. His team of spanking blacks and the improving roads connecting mountain communities enabled him to range over an even wider area than had his father. The dynasty continued with F. J., the fourth, who maintained the colorful traditions of his family in his practice at Lake Placid.

But more isolated communities were late in securing their own physicians and were long dependent upon doctors miles away, or lucky to have the incidental advice of medical men who came to hunt or fish in their vicinity. When the invalid Trudeau decided to spend the winter of 1876 and 1877 in the "miserable hamlet" of Saranac Lake, he became its first resident physician. In 1880 a contemporary historian recorded that the 11 families in the Tupper Lake region were dependent for medical care upon doctors 30 miles away. Under such conditions, the layman's knowledge of medicine often reached high standards of practical application.

W. F. Martin, pioneer resort hotel proprietor of Saranac Lake, was for many years on call to the sickbeds of the community. The winter of 1862 was unusually severe. His only daughter became seriously ill in March. A blizzard was raging and roads were practically impassable. The nearest doctor was 45 miles away at Keeseville, but as the child became worse Martin determined he must be obtained. He chose his most powerful horse and hitched him to a "pung" — a handmade, woodshod, low box sleigh. He put in an ax and a shovel and started to dig and plow himself through heartless miles of drifted snow where drifts were 10 to 12 feet high in narrow places. As he came to houses he made his errand known, and all the men turned out to help him dig, often going a mile or more until fresh help was volunteered. In this way he reached his destination with his powerful horse exhausted and unfit for the return trip. Without resting himself, he secured a fresh horse and started back with the doctor. The return journey was comparatively easy and swift, but the great effort was in vain as the child died just fifteen minutes before the doctor reached her bedside. The Adirondack historian Donaldson termed the effort, "an Erlking ride of the North Woods — one of those tragedies of distance that bring home to us the epic hardships of the pioneers."

After the death of his little daughter, Martin was deeply impressed by the fact that it was largely due to the remoteness of the nearest physician. Hoping to save himself or others from similar tragedy, he began reading medical books and seeking from medical men who stopped at his hotel fundamental instruction in the treatment of the most common diseases. The members of the profession were coming to the Adirondacks in increasing numbers for sport and recreation, and they recognized Martin's ability and the wisdom of his effort. Dr. J. Savage Delavan, of Albany, was his chief mentor of his Spring and Fall visits, but all gave him suggestions freely and furnished him with authoritative books, pamphlets, and even medicines. His fame as an amateur doctor quickly spread in a community where there was no regular one, and he was called to sickbeds over a radius of 10 miles about Saranac Lake until regular practitioners arrived in the early eighties.

Writers began early to attribute healing powers to the Adirondack climate. Dr. Morse's paper of 1809 has been mentioned previously. In 1857 Hammond's *Wild Northern Scenes*, a chronicle of a decade of mountain vacations, paid tribute to the tonic effect of the region. In 1869 a Boston clergyman, better known as "Adirondack Murray" for his *Adventures in the Wilderness or Camp Life in the Adirondacks*, was widely criticized for his account of the tuberculous invalid who was brought into the mountains on a stretcher and improved sufficiently to walk six months later. Many invalids jumped at the unwarranted conclusion that Murray had said the Adirondacks would infallibly restore health in any stage of tuberculosis. Consequently, without an investigation or reasonable preparation they started for the wilderness and some of them died there. Winslow C. Watson, in his *History of Essex County* published in the same year, stated: "I have met with instances of individuals who had reached their forest homes in advanced stages of pulmonary affection, in whom the disease had been arrested, and the sufferer restored to comparative health."

The medical profession began to appreciate the advantages of climatic treatment in the next decade. In 1879 the well-known New York internist, Alfred L. Loomis, was able to address the annual meeting of the New York State Medical Society on "The Adirondack Region as a Therapeutical Agent in the Treatment of Pulmonary Phthisis." He recorded 20 tuberculous case histories of whom 10 had recovered, 6 were improved, and 4 were failures. One of these was the case of Dr. Edward L. Trudeau, whose enthusiastic and logically written letters setting forth the values of the 'salubrious" climate were fully reproduced. "Not only in New York but all over the country, the doctors evinced a sudden enthusiasm respecting the Adirondacks that was obviously kindled by Dr. Loomis's torch," so wrote Marc Cook in his *Wilderness Cure*, published in 1880. His was the first guidebook and curing manual for the tuberculous patient, and Cook freely admitted that the interest arising from Loomis's paper was the excuse for his book. By 1886 the concept of the mountain cure for chest diseases had so developed that Dr. Joseph W. Stickler, of Orange, New Jersey, wrote a book called *The Adirondacks as a Health Resort,* containing numerous testimonials of doctors and patients on experiences concerning the Adirondacks. These form an authoritative record of early health-seekers, most of whose experiences were prior to 1880 and many to 1870.

Clearly the idea of the climatic treatment of tuberculosis in the Adirondacks did not arise with Dr. Trudeau, but it was he who demonstrated its effectiveness and, by controlled study, placed it on a rational basis. When he developed the disease at the outset of a promising New York City practice in 1871, he was sent to the South for treatment. Later, as the disease progressed, he remembered good times on earlier hunting and fishing expeditions at Paul Smith's and asked to be taken there. He was quite literally brought in on a stretcher in the Summer of 1873. He improved surprisingly in that Summer, but left the mountains in the Winter only to return in much poorer condition in the Spring. In the Fall of 1874 he had improved so greatly that he determined to remain for the Winter. The venture succeeded and he improved steadily all through that Winter and the following Summer. In the Autumn of 1876 he moved to Saranac Lake for the Winter, thus beginning a custom of forty years. In the joy of returning health and vigor his old love of hunting and fishing asserted itself and the guides were quick to learn his excellence. While he made no

William F. Martin

Dr. Edward Livingston Trudeau

Dr. Trudeau and Fred Martin, his guide

Trudeau Sanitarium 1900 — Stoddard Photo

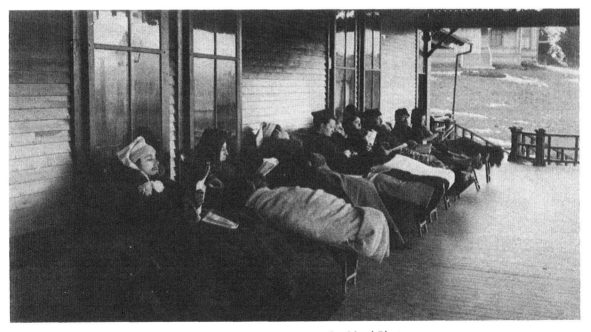

Trudeau Patients — 1900 — Stoddard Photo

effort to practice medicine actively, his services were often in demand and he gave of them freely to all.

A handful of invalids had preceded Dr. Trudeau at Saranac Lake, led no doubt by the obvious advantages of a post office and telegraph station in the midst of the wilderness. His first five Winters there brought him continued good health, and the publications of Dr. Loomis and Marc Cook widened its fame as a health resort. The increasing number of patient-arrivals began to tax the village capacities, and the good doctor pondered the problem of care for those unfortunates who came with high hopes but inadequate means. His renewed interest in medical literature brought him by chance upon the theories of the German physician, Brehmer, who tentatively advocated the outdoor and institutional treatment of tuberculosis. Then, in 1882 Koch's epoch-making discovery of the tubercle bacillus fired him with great enthusiasm. He began at once fundamental experiments with the bacillus and, working in a laboratory heated by wood and lighted by kerosene, he succeeded in growing tubercle bacilli in a homemade thermostat for only the second time in this country. In 1884 wealthy friends supplied the capital and his guide friends bought land to make possible the humble beginnings of his inspiration, which has become the Trudeau Sanatorium of today.

The next decade saw almost unceasing labor accomplish great strides. A surprising number of scientific papers based on his laboratory studies came from his pen as he struggled to care for the ever-increasing load of private patients, to supervise the administrative and medical problems of the growing sanatorium, and to solicit funds to make up the yearly deficits of the sanatorium and laboratory. The sanatorium treatment of tuberculosis proved successful and gained wide acceptance. This experience was plainly the inspiration for companion sanatoria of the region — Gabriels, Stony Wold, Ray Brook, and Sunmount. Through it all shone the lovable and sympathetic quality of his physicianship best exemplified by the maxim of which he was so fond: "To heal sometimes, to relieve often, to console always."

To quote Donaldson: "Trudeau's was the first laboratory in this country devoted to original research in tuberculosis, and from it the doctor began to turn out work that was soon attracting attention all over the world. The experiments made and the papers written in Saranac Lake became the last word in tuberculosis. Gradually, the doctor gathered around him a growing group of younger men, imbued with his ideals and trained to his high standards of research and experimentation. Under his guidance and inspiration they have done yeoman service in the great battle and achieved results that no man could have compassed singlehanded." Dean of the surviving group is Dr. Edward R. Baldwin, who came to Dr. Trudeau in 1892 to say that he had contracted tuberculosis and that he wished to come to the Sanatorium for cure and to study with him. When asked how he knew he had tuberculosis, he said he had used his microscope. Trudeau's *An Autobiography* remarks of this: "Truly Koch's teaching was beginning to bring practical results."

By 1900 both the Sanatorium and the Laboratory were well established, and the good doctor delegated almost all the active duties to his assistants, although he continued his efforts to raise funds for their support until the last. He had frequent relapses of his old disease in his later years, but again and again he rose from his sickbed to continue. In 1910 he addressed the Congress of Physicians and Surgeons on "The Value of Optimism in Medicine." His paper quickly revealed itself as autobiographic and awakened wide attention. It was then learned that he had written it during a period of relapse when he awoke in the small hours each morning and needed some activity to relieve his mind from his own suffering.

Dr. Trudeau died in 1915 in his sixty-seventh year. His friends and colleagues took immediate steps to preserve and expand the gains of his lifetime by forming the Trudeau Foundation. This serves as a governing and planning body for both the Saranac Laboratory and Trudeau Sanatorium. To these were shortly added a third project, the Trudeau School for Graduate Teaching in Tuberculosis, so that yearly several score of disciples of the "Beloved Physician" go forth to practice his teachings and humanity in all corners of the earth. His life had spanned an era in Adirondack medicine from backwoods practices to advances that won the continued admiration and attention of all in the field of tuberculosis. And with the passing of its greatest character this outline is properly closed.

Chapter 18

The River-Driving Days — Part 1

From time immemorial, forests have been considered to be both friend and enemy. They have of course been the main suppliers of building materials for houses, ships and fuel but, at the same time, they provided protection for wild beasts, marauding savages and engendered an aura of mystery and even fear. Woodlands also kept the soil damp — ground that required sunlight in order to grow the grains that helped feed the settlers — the basic priority in the minds of all the newcomers. Clearing and planting the crops and building homes therefore accounted for most of their time and efforts. For those reasons it is easy to understand why early sawmill and gristmill owners were looked upon as local benefactors and public heroes. Letting more and more daylight into the swamps and woodlands was both a stupendous chore and a constant challenge.

Up to now, no chronicler has apparently been able to pin down the date when the first logger or lumberjack, as they are known today, arrived on the scene. The very earliest sawyers and timber hewers were all called lumberers regardless of whether they worked in the mills or in the woods — and most of them did both. Summers were spent sawing into deals or boards the logs which had been cut the previous Winter, so for many lumbering became a year-round occupation.

E. A. Kendall, an eminent English tourist, in 1801 described the professional loggers whom he observed in action: "Their habits in the forest and on the voyage [the river drive] all break up the system of persevering industry and substitute one of alternate toil and indolence, hardship and debauch; and in the alternation indolence and debauch will inevitably be indulged in the greatest possible proportion." Quite an indictment!

A half-century later another discerning author — Charles L. Lanman — found Maine loggers "to be mostly young, generally unmarried, rude in manner, quite intelligent, but also intemperate. They seemed to have a passion for their wild and toilsome life and a fine eye for the fantastic in dress — even wearing two red flannel shirts at the same time!"

Until recent years the word forest was seldom heard except as used rhetorically. It belonged to poetry and literature. People lived in the backwoods, traveled in the woods, went into the woods, came out of the woods or were lost in the woods — never in the forest. People spoke of the North Woods, the South Woods, the Nine-Mile woods and the Shattagee (Chateaugay Woods.)

Although both descriptions contain more than a modicum of truth, anyone who knows first hand the difficulties and complexities of the lumber business can easily understand that this special breed of men, risking death daily, and the certainty of future crippling by rheumatism would not be satisfied with the usual humdrum, run-of-the-mill varieties of pleasure and recreation. From my own admittedly brief experience in the pulpwoods, I developed a healthy respect and appreciation for the men — mostly Scots and French-Canadian (like myself) — and for the very dangerous, ever-varying life they led. Unquestionably, this type of existence demands far more strength, endurance and just plain know-how than any other business known to man.

Moreover, since weather plays such a dominant role in any outdoor labor, the range of exasperations and frustrations are enough in themselves to make many of those so precariously occupied seek strenuous outlets for their long pent-up emotional urges. For woodsmen the natural pattern ran the full gamut between deep snow and no snow; high water, low water and occasionally no water; wind, fire and the predictably unpredictable natures of the men themselves — all too often the here-today-but-gone-tomorrow-morning type of rugged, mercurial, characteristically independent characters.

According to certain knowledgeable participants and interested lookers-on, it was virtually true that by-gone loggers would enthusiastically eat marsh hay if it was sprinkled with whiskey and that they habitually lived in trees. When you consider that most of their time was spent felling trees all day and then being cooped up at night in crude, overheated but underventilated, foul-smelling shanties or shacks, small wonder that many felt impelled to cut loose completely whenever they tasted the so-called freedom of the river towns. Their appetites — sexual and gastronomical — were immense, but the brothel and tavern owners were ready, willing and able to stoke the inner fires. Moreover, their living conditions were incredibly primitive. The earliest shanties had bark or bough roofs, later replaced by hand-made cedar shakes or shingles, then still later by poles covered with layers of tarpaper. The first floors were packed dirt, then corduroy (poles placed side by side) and finally planking.

The bunks were called muzzle-loaders because the men crawled into them over the foot. These were either double or triple-deckers with heavy wool and shoddy blankets spread over hay or balsam-boughs. The celebrated deacon seat, the featured fixture of the modern lean-to or open camp, was made from a split half-log, supported by legs with the smoothed, flattened side up, and ran the length of the room along both sides. In the center of this single room was an open fire set in sand and stones and located — hopefully — directly under a hole cut in the roof. By the expedient of swinging cranes the cook did his culinary chores and around this same source of heat the lumberjacks either sat or knelt as they drank their tea and helped themselves from the bean pot. The ubiquitous grindstone was usually the only other object in the room.

No wonder then that the men who worked in the prototype Adirondack lumbercamps were reportedly treated with less consideration than the oxen and horses, which at least had clean straw and suitable food.

Not long afterward a major concession was made to the all-important cook — he got a separate kitchen-dining room and better equipment, a cast-iron range. The food also improved in quality and quantity even though much of the meat was still salted-pork, corned beef, salted codfish, beans, johnnycake and bread, molasses as the sweetener and the inevitable tea, usually potent enough to curl one's eyebrows and float a double-bitted axe. The cook personage ran the entire indoors operation and always insisted upon — and got — table silence. Conversation-less meals not only got the meal out of sight and out of the way faster, but it also prevented discussions, which might lead to arguments, which in turn might erupt into quarrels — which were usually settled by sending the proponents packing.

The standard of living of lumber company employees during the early years was

An Adirondack Lumber Camp — Rison Photo

Working Hours, The Bunk Room — Rison Photo

193

enough to make a union organizer twitch with eager anticipation. Wages in the woods were $13.00 per month and board (which cost $.23 per day) for most of the help. In the mills the pay was from $.50 - $.75 a day up to $1.00 - $1.25 depending upon experience and the degree of responsibility of the job. The foreman, sawyer and filer drew more. Those days were nostalgically called the 10-cent era because butter, all cuts of meats and eggs all cost a dime a pound or dozen. Other foods were proportionately priced. The millhands were charged $5.00 a month rent for their plain out-of-the-same cookie-cutter company homes. By way of contrast, in 1919 the men were making $60.00 - $100.00 a month and board, but of course the cost of living had also gone up appreciably and accordingly. [In 1948 lumberjack wages on the Upper Hudson were $1.00 an hour, without board, a noticeable drop due mostly to a glutted labor market.]

Still later on, in 1927, the Adirondack timber barons were complaining that it was almost impossible to hire enough lumberjacks to fill the camps and handle the logging operations. Many who used to work in the woods each winter would no longer go into camp. They had learned that easier work and better pay were to be had elsewhere — on the railroads, in the mills or even in the company offices. While there was no question that the jobs were still hard, despite the use of tractors and other devices, oldtimers maintained that the work was far harder back then. They told of going to work at 2 or 3 o'clock on bitter cold mornings, the first hours of back-wrenching toil illuminated by pine torches thrust into the snow. And the veterans also insisted that food and working conditions were far inferior to what they are today. It would appear that the old-time lumberjacks were a much sturdier breed than today's knights of the cross-cut saw and double-bitted axe — and eventually those workers of the chain saw period.

The French-Canadians, who numbered nearly three-fourths of the early loggers, were among the first to abandon the woodswork. They, along with Scots-Canadians were the hardest working, most obedient and dependable, willing and expert of them all.[1] The Scots in particular, were outstanding workers, many of them six feet plus and weighing from 180-220 pounds — a powerful, intelligent and thrifty crew. Gradually these men found better jobs and were replaced by Hungarians, Poles and Austrians, none of whom was as skillful with the canthook or peavy,[2] or ax and saw as the picturesque, venturesome colorful Canucks.

Very little so far on the most spectacular phase of the entire logging operation — the river drives — but the background material was felt essential to setting the stage for the main event.

Anyone who wants the best comprehensive coverage ever done on lumbering in general should know about Col. William F. Fox's masterpiece, entitled "History of Lumbering in New York State," which was published in the 1900 Annual Report of the New York State Forest, Fish and Game Commission. Seventy pages of readable and instructive material which has never been surpassed. Although by no means limited to the Adirondacks, (in fact only a small section is) his generalizations and comments are relevant to any heavily-forested region.

---

[1] The same combination was also primarily responsible for the success of the Canadian fur trade, mostly beaver, in the days of fierce rivalry between the Northwest and Hudson's Bay Cos. Their prowess as canoe and packmen was almost incredibly formidable. Washington Irving, for one, stated that the best of them all — a bandy-legged French-Canadian — toted loads of pelts weighing 480 pounds across a half-mile portage without once stopping to rest. 300 pound loads were considered ordinary. Small wonder that their main occupational hazard was strangulated double hernias.

[1] A Maine blacksmith, Joe Peavey, invented the improved cant dog that bears his name. He also invented the Peavey hoist used for raising dam gates; the hay press was another of his innovations. This very useful gadget squeezed loose hay into small, tight bales for easy hauling to the logging camps.

Log Jam On Lower Raquette — Stoddard Photo

For a great many years the trees were cut only in Winter. The only departure from that routine came much later when it was considered more sensible to cut evergreens for pulp during the Summer months when the sap made it easier to ross or debark the trunks. Another logical reason for Winter work in the woods was the fact that, since most of the men were also farmers, they had to take care of their crops first and then became lumberjacks during the slack season. Since these men were also the guides, fishing and hunting seasons saw them busy elsewhere.

Log driving and marking, according to Donaldson, probably started in the Adirondacks, although the marking hammer itself originated in Maine. This device served the same purpose as the Western cattleman's branding iron: ownership identification.

In 1851 a law was passed requiring the registration of all log marks in use on the Raquette River. By 1900 these totaled 102, which gives a good idea of what was going on in the tall shrubbery of the People's Park.

Because hardwoods won't float, only conifers, such as the big white pines and spruces were used for lumber at first. After they had been cut down and sawed into logs they were skidded to form piles and then hauled by horses or oxen to banking grounds, or else stacked on the ice of the larger lakes and rivers to await the Spring freshets. Farther upstream on every stream of any appreciable size, head or splash dams — sometimes as many as four or five — were built to impound the water for release at the most strategic time.

When the ice broke up, the logs ranked on the river banks were shoved into the water, the splash dams were consecutively opened and the resulting rush of water sent the log avalanches roaring down on their long trip to the sawmills. A writer of 1872 vintage, an

195

Camp of Adirondack River Drivers. Travelling Kitchen, or Cook-Shanty in Background — F.A. Van Sant Photo

Adirondack Log Drivers. The Halt at Noon, Coffee and Baked Beans — F.A. Van Sant Photo

early forever-wilder, gave the following vivid description of a Hudson River drive: "The river was full of rolling logs, rumbling and tumbling promiscuously together, some in a desperate hurry to reach Glens Falls, their destination, though stopping at many stations en route. Others found or foundered on the rocks. They all tell a tale of devastation — how the mighty are fallen! — and prompt the inquiry: shall the axe devour forever? This may be viewing the matter in a totally utilitarian manner, but it is a viewpoint nevertheless. Going, going, gone! as the auctioneer exclaims; fair warning that unless arrest sets in, all will yet be gone. It was computed last Summer that on July 30, 1872, 100,000 logs passed a given point in a single day. It is said also that 1872 was the biggest year ever for log drivers on the Hudson, with well over two million pine and spruce logs floating down to the Big Boom above Glens Falls.

"I saw a man on a height, with a long pole, apparently seeking to bring two large logs ashore. In a moment he had disappeared, but soon was seen again taking passage on those logs on down the stream. By keeping those two logs as one, close together, their rolling is prevented and skillful men with iron spikes [caulks] in their shoe soles may thus navigate in comparative safety.

"I saw another man, however, on another log just before I saw him struggling in the water at Pottersville...I pushed my way against headwinds. I saw the Schroon River, but the sight was forbidding and the sound terrifying so I turned my back on it..." Somewhat fanciful but provocative nevertheless.

The river-driver's job was strenuous as well as dangerous. It meant almost constant exposure, not only to wind and weather, but to ice-cold water for as long as 90 days at a time. It provided numerous opportunities for great skill and daring and many of the men became famous for both. All of them had to be able to ride a bucking log, balancing themselves with their pike poles as a tight-rope walker teeters on a high wire. Some of the more adept could do a jig on one while birling (revolving) it with their feet. The real daredevils, the cattiest-footed, could even do a somersault on a big log. These show-offs were usually the French-Canadians, reputedly the best and most cunning drivers of them all.

Although the rafting of logs and floating them down the bigger rivers was a common custom from the earliest days of the settlements, the method of sending separate logs down narrow, rock-infested streams was first tried in 1813 by Norman and Alanson Fox on the Schroon River tributary of the Upper Hudson. At that time they were lumbering the Brant Lake Tract, west of Schroon Lake and partly within what later was designated as the well-known "blue line." It soon became the standard procedure and made it both possible and profitable to remove timber from the remotest sections of the mountains.

In the Adirondack woods all logs with very few exceptions were cut 13 feet long and for a reason not known now. So for nearly a century the lumbermen cut 13 foot lumber for the Albany and New York markets, although elsewhere in the United States the lengths are 16 feet or some other even number.

This use of rivers caused a great deal of damage and annoyance to shore owners and led to early legislation, dominated and promulgated by influential lumbermen, which designated certain rivers as public highways. The first of these was the Salmon, north of Malone, in 1806. The next was the Raquette from its mouth at the St. Lawrence to the first falls in 1810. It was not until 1846 that the Raquette and the Saranac were labeled public highways along their entire lengths — thereby opening up huge interior Adirondack tracts.[1]

It is noteworthy that the few restrictions specified in the enabling acts were never parti-

[1] Holbrook, Stuart; *Yankee Loggers*. International Paper Co. 1961.

Drowned Lands on the Raquette River near Tupper Lake — Stoddard Photo

cularly drastic or burdensome for the lumbermen, aided and abetted by the smartest legislators that money could buy. Moreover, more than a few of the persuasion — like Sen. C. F. Norton — got themselves elected and went to Albany to take personal charge of their own best interests, which were not often those of their constituents. Talk about present-day conflicts of interests!

Just to give an idea of how much clout the lumbering interests had, as early as 1804 the Legislature passed a law, Chapter 103, to punish anyone who stole timber or lumber that was floating down the river or lying on the shore. This act refers to "any timber, hewed, sawed or riven," terms which do not seem to include saw-logs, and which indicate that only long timber, spars and masts were floated at that time. Section 2 of this law provides a severe penalty for persons who shall "deface or alter any mark, or put a false mark on any such timber," from which it appears that log marks were in use then, even if short logs were not being driven. In 1825 a similar act protected log marks on the Au Sable River.

As Col. Fox pointed out, the progress of the logging operations started on the fringe areas as early as 1813, but they did not penetrate the heart of the wilderness until about 1850. Like everyone else during that pioneer period they squandered this particular priceless natural resource as though the supply were limitless. They operated heedlessly and carelessly and their slogan seemed to be "chop 'em down and chop 'em up — and then move on into the next township." Since survey lines were still notoriously inaccurate and almost universally ignored, literally hundreds of thousands of state-owned trees were easily stolen by greedy local opportunists — often with the connivance of area and State officials themselves. And even when the timber thieves were caught red-handed the cases were almost invariably dropped for lack of sufficient evidence. In that connection the minutes of the Conservation Department for 1900-1915 make very interesting and eyebrow-raising reading.

Col. Fox also explained that lumbermen did not build the dams, such as those at Setting Pole Rapids below Tupper Lake, which caused so much damage during the 1870's both upstream and down in flood-time. Loggers' splash dams were soon reopened and the impounded water did not create environmental problems. "There was no backflow during the period of vegetation and temporary flooding of the tree roots does not kill the timber. Trees are killed by water only where it is allowed to cover the ground for two or more successive Summers... In nearly every instance the dead timber in the flowed lands of the Adirondacks is the result of some dam or reservoir built in the interest of State canals, local steamboat lines or manufacturing concerns on the lower water. The lumbermen had little or nothing to do with them....

Potsdam lumber interests had experienced considerable difficulty in making clean runs of their logs and were also inconvenienced by low water in operating their mills. As early as 1850 the State appropriated $10,000 to improve the upper Raquette for their benefit, and part of this sum went into the building of a small dam at Setting Pole Rapids. It apparently didn't do the job intended so the downstream lumbermen wasted no time in promoting a "real dam" to hold back a huge head of water that would later insure proper sluicing of their timber. The fact that it would ruin thousands of acres of valuable forest-land and convert some of the most beautiful country in the State into a malodorous eyesore didn't seem to have bothered the industrialists unduly....The dam broke in May, 1871 and the flood took 36 hours to reach Potsdam, where it caused great havoc.

The dam was repaired in 1872 but certain Moody natives, angered because they claimed that the fishing had been ruined and meadowland flooded, sawed off the top ten feet of the barrier and then dynamited it even lower.

Maintenance of this and subsequent dams at the same site have caused recurring headaches and much outlay of money even to this day.

As Tupper Lake became more settled the gaunt trees and stumps were cut by residents for fuel and more of it was removed by lumber companies in order to improve navigation for their steamboats and scows. The rest of the mess was taken care of by C.C.C. (Civilian Conservation Corps.) crews during the Great Depression, so nowadays the drowned lands of the Raquette create comparatively little visual pollution...

A century ago there was no Spring until the drive had come and gone. Although the three biggest drives were in the three longest rivers and not in this order — the Raquette, Saranac and the Hudson — there was also plenty of action on the Schroon, both branches of the AuSable, the Boquet, Moose, Black, Indian and Beaver; the Sacandaga, the West Canada (the Big West), the Grasse, the Oswegatchie and all three branches of the St. Regis, but to a lesser extent. The list is lengthy and the names themselves offer fascinating research.

For decades one of the great centers for milling long logs — up to 16 footers although 13 was the Saranac standard — was Tupper Lake. Activity began there in the 1880's when John Hurd, a Connecticut Yankee, bought 60,000 acres of timber, laid out the Northern Adirondack R. R. and later established a ten-band sawmill for the Santa Clara Lumber Co. Other outfits which followed suit were the St. Regis, the International Paper Co., Emporium, the Norwood Manufacturing, the A. Sherman Lumber Co., and others.

Quoting again from Stuart Holbrook's fine book — *Yankee Loggers:* "Not before or since has such an industrial boom hit the Adirondack country. By railroad and by a complex of connected streams, rivers, ponds and lakes, logs were landed at the plants around Tupper Lake, where a vast sorting-gap [similar to the Big Boom above Glens Falls] and booming grounds segregated them. Then a fleet of tugboats put them within reach of the bull chains of the mills. At one time there were fifty-odd camps cutting stuff on Tupper waters.

"One big drive started at Ampersand Brook, from there the logs went into Calkins Creek, then into Cold River which took them into the Raquette and down to Raquette Pond, just below Big Tupper. These logs were 12 and 16 footers.

"No saws were used for felling trees — it was all chopping work. All hands on the drive used calked shoes made by the Croghan Co. at Croghan, N.Y. 'The biggest improvement on the drive in my time,' George Bundey told Holbrook, 'was the use of telephones to tell the head-dam crews when to open or close the gates. Before then we were forever having trouble because of no water or too much water.'

"Tupper village in those days had practically unlimited possibilities for entertaining the 500-700 revved-up lumberjacks who hit the village all at once and gave the local gendarmes all the exercise they ever wanted. The invaders provided hotels, saloons and bordellos with fast-disappearing payroll money — many months' wages blown in one wild spree. Hard come, easy go for too many of the jacks....

"One of the biggest drives in the history of the North Woods went down the Big West [West Canada Creek] in the Spring of 1895. By exact count 20, 194, 156 board feet of spruce with a few sticks of hemlock. All saw-logs and no pulp. And that was the year of the big jam — below Outlet Brook, one that had to be dynamited. The flood had hit the upper end of the jam and the men had to scramble to safety. By looking upstream one could see the lower half of the great mass of logs. A low, muffled, grinding, ripping sound could be heard and far up the Creek the water cascaded down over the top of the jackstrawed logs, piling them up until they were 20 feet above the shoreline, but still the jam wouldn't budge. The men kept working on the monumental mess, but accomplished practically nothing. Again the men saw the tail end raise, saw the rear end coming toward them and piling up fast. They ran about looking for a place to get off. Just then the jam started to haul.

"One of the lumberjacks finally found a spot from which he could jump into a big birch on the bank. He leaped, caught hold and clambered out on a limb. Just as the jam uprooted the tree, he dropped to the ground. Other men were clutching trees as the jam went roaring past, hoping their anchors would hold. Other trees — some of them two feet thick — along the banks were being mowed down or uprooted.

"The water, logs and accumulation of debris tore down over the jam once more. The whole jam was hauling them, but when the flood went past, the logs were still as badly plugged as before. The crew called it quits for the day....

"Early the next morning the men were back on the job, picking at the pile to find the cork logs. The water was low and everything was peaceful. No confusion although the face of the jam was like a fortress. Why hurry? They still had an hour left.

"'What's that noise?' one man asked.

"'Wind. Sounds like wind in the pines.'

"'Listen! Fellas, that ain't no wind!'

"'Water!'

"'It can't be. We got an hour yet!'

"'It's water! She's hit! Get off!'

"It was upon them before they knew it. Sandy Flanagan just barely made shore. Ab Carnahan and Dan Kennedy were on the same log as it swung out into the current below the jam.

"'Jump! Grab a bush!' Ab yelled, but Dan had already made his move. The water caught him, but he had hold of a branch and was able to pull himself to safety. The log with Ab on it shot away like an arrow. Ab tried to ride it down and for a moment it looked as though he might do the impossible. The mass of the jam was now right behind him, plunging, tearing and grinding. The men on the shore watched him go. They saw the log toss Ab nearly ten feet up into the air. One instant he was there and the next — nothing to be seen but logs, end over end, standing upright or nosing under. The great turmoil of spruce logs swept over the place where Ab had disappeared. He never had a ghost of a chance....

"The men worked their way along the shore. Shortly afterward they pried him loose from under a corner jam at the head of an island about a third of a mile below, a mutilated body with a broken neck....

"For a while there was surly grumbling in the camps when the men found out that, down at the big boom before the flood, they had sent their woods boss up the Creek. He had gone by saddle horse to all the dams and had given his orders. Consequently, the dams were opened an hour earlier than Sol had told them. The floodwaters had hit the jam at 9 o'clock instead of 10."[1]

This incident, taken from Harvey L. Dunham's great regional classic — *Adirondack French Louie*[2] — epitomizes the excitement, peril and tragedy that were concomitant factors of every river drive. Another true account, a hair-raiser with a happy outcome, was the experience of Leonard Collins as he told it to John B. Burnham. "Talking about premonitions," said Collins, "my wife had one nine years ago that came very close to being the real goods. I was going on the drive down the Middle branch of the Grasse that Spring, and I had bought my shoes — I generally wore a new pair a couple weeks or so to get used to them. My wife remarked when she saw the shoes, 'I wish you'd give up river driving, Len. I have a feeling that if you go this time you'll be killed.' I just laughed at her and told her that no man died till his time came — and that mine hadn't come yet. You know, a man that's engaged in dangerous business always feels that way, so I didn't let her remark worry me any, beyond the effect it had on her.

"When I got over on the drive they had a jam two miles long in the rock-cut just above Ore Bed Falls. They call them Collins Falls now on the map, after me, just as they have named half a dozen other falls on these rivers after men that had drowned in them.

"Spear was there himself looking after the drive. I had worked for him a long while so he knew that I was a capable hand.

"'I'm glad you come, Leonard,' says he, "because we're in a devil of a fix with this jam! 70 men running up their time on the payroll and no man jack among them understands his business well enough to break it. Len, I think you can do the trick!'"

"Well now, I knew that he had good men on the job more experienced than I was and told him so but, as he still wanted me to try it, I put on my togs and started in. Now, you see, they were driving with a flood — that is, they had a trip [splash or head] dam further up the river where they backed up water and then let it go at regular spells to boost the logs along. We got the jam leveled off that morning so when the flood came the jam started to move. I thought it was all going to go out, but on the tail end about 500 pieces, as near as I could estimate, got hung up again and in the same place.

"Most of the other men went down to the stillwater and I set about busting this little

---

[1] The most dangerous work was done by volunteers and, if all the anecdotes of the veteran drivers could be collected, they would reveal accounts of unrecorded heroism every bit as splendid as anything which ever occurred in fire and flood and battlefield.

[2] Dunham, Harvey L., Adirondack French Louie, Utica, 1952. Reprinted by North Country Books, Saranac Lake, N.Y. 1970...By permission of his daughter, Mrs. J. Beardsley Keck.

jam with four helpers. We rolled the logs off and leveled it down. I found the key log and then looked around for a good spot on the bank where I could jump to if necessary. Then I sank my canthook into the log as it stood up in the jam and gave it a twirl. The jam started. I got ashore all right, but the jam hung up again and I had to get it started once more. Straightening things out a little I found that the culprit was the same log as before, so I set my hook into it a little savage-like. But I never lost my cautiousness, got my escape route figured out, then gave the pesky log a hard twist — and this time the jam broke up but fast.

"I only had about two rods to go to reach solid footing — but I never got there. The logs took off fast and halfway to shore one of them swung around on a pivot, like an alligator striking with his tail, and caught me on the ankle. It whipped me around so that I was heading straight downstream instead of up and into the cut. Ahead of me the walls were like the sheer sides of a house that nobody could possibly climb. So there I was — trapped and as you might say, face to face with Death in an ugly form. I rode the logs for a second or two but then something struck me and I pitched head-first into and under the logs. For the rest of the time I was just a part of the drive and just as much a log as any of the other 500 or so pieces that was going over the Falls.

"I kept my eyes open so I could see the bottom where they had blasted the points off the rocks. Then the logs opened up at the foot of a pitch and I shot up same as any other log and landed on top of the pile. I knew than that if I could reach the stillwater below the rapids half a mile away there would be lots of men to pick me out. Naturally I did all I could to stay on top.

"I rode about 40 rods and was then thrown off, but I managed to keep my arms out and my head above the logs. But just then the logs started jamming again. There was a big rock there that held them. After the pieces that I was among stopped, the others behind began diving under. I was vertical so my legs had to take the punishment. After they finally hauled me out I found that the calves of my legs was turned around on the front side and the lower half of my body was not the same way God intended it to be.

"That's all there is to the story. I went over the Falls and when the logs jammed again they pulled me out. But your talking about premonitions made me think of it. All the time I was in the water I kept thinking about what my wife had said and then I thought about what I'd said and I knew my time hadn't come. And sure enough it hadn't!"

There's still another log jam story, this one by an E. C. Baker, which was in the Plattsburgh *Sentinel* dated May 30, 1907.

"One Spring we got caught in a jam on the Saranac River. A huge log had swung sidewise across the very edge of the last precipice at High Falls [Moffitsville] and soon over 40,000 pieces massed solidly in the narrow gorge. Since we didn't use dynamite those days, nothing could be done except cut out the key log. [the cork of the bottleneck]

"A volunteer was called for and Henry Martin [Paul Smith's brother-in-law] was the only one who stepped out. A long rope was thrown across the river and held at each end by the other men. Martin lashed himself to the rope and, with ax in hand, was hauled to the center of the gorge and then lowered to the pile-up. He chopped away for two hours while the rest of us just waited in terrible suspense. Finally the key log snapped apart and immediately thousands of pieces were released and, pushed by the great accumulation of water, went tumbling, thundering and groaning like a huge avalanche slithering over a precipice.

"Just as the log snapped Martin signaled us and the rope was pulled taut by the watchful men on the river banks. The logger hung there, poised in mid-air momentarily, then was pulled ashore amidst the welcome cheers of his comrades...."

202

Chapter 19

The River-Driving Days — Part 2

The Plateau lying along the west shore of Lake Champlain and reaching as far back as the Adirondack foothills and mountain ranges was originally covered with a massive growth of snagbark or first-growth white pines, the big whites, the monarchs of the forest. These stands were rapidly cut over by the early settlers, hewed into square timbers and rafted via the Richelieu River (the outlet of Champlain's Lake) into the St. Lawrence to be sold in the Quebec market at a price scarcely equal to the labor cost entailed — to say nothing of its stumpage value and the hazards of the woods, floods, custom house inspection and the constantly fluctuating market. Old-timers reported that after their rafts had been sold and their expenses paid, they had enough to get home provided they didn't drink or smoke and could walk fast.

The first sawmill on the Saranac was built by Count Charles de Fredenburgh at Fredenberg Falls about 1767. This was the prototype of a long succession of mills that included in their development the employment of choppers, teamsters, sawyers, blacksmiths, carpenters, shoemakers, tailors, spinners, weavers, farmers and merchants. To serve them along came the schools, hotels, churches and the combination courthouse-jail. As the late Marjorie L. Porter pointed out, just as far as the woodsman's axe and the sawmill penetrated the forest, not far in their wake came the other satellite industries and services. In fact the lumbermen were the real pioneers and to them belongs much of the credit for clearing, developing — and devastating this North Country.

One of the most prominent of the early lumbermen, a man who later became King of the Hudson, was Orson Richards, who did an extensive business rafting logs down Lake Champlain and who also obtained a great amount of timber from the lower Saranac Valley. In 1847 Richards bought Township 24, which surrounds Lower Saranac Lake. The run consisted of 50,000 markets, or ten million board feet of lumber. This triggered an era of extensive logging in the very heart of the Adirondacks and it continued for over forty years.

A little later the Maine Company, a Boston group, purchased Township 20, which encircles the northern half of Upper Saranac Lake at the head of the Lake. Where the defunct Saranac Inn now stands vacant, the firm built a large mill and headquarters set-up.

In 1864 Township 21 was also acquired and the trees came tumbling down in that area as well. By then the entire Saranac Lakes region was being systematically exploited.

The best-known lumber firms which operated along the valley of the Saranac were the

Hon. C.F. Norton, left; Col. Milote Baker, right

Maine Co., H. & O. A. Tefft, J. H. & E. C. Baker, Thomas & Hammond, Loren Ellis and Christopher F. Norton, who later earned the title King of the River but, still later, became a virtual bankrupt.

Norton was born in Fredonia, N.Y. in 1821. His father, John, had emigrated from Connecticut and engaged in the wool business. In 1845 C. F. went into the lumber business in Erie, Pa., and amassed a small fortune before moving to Plattsburgh in 1886. A man of impressive physique and appearance, dynamic and ingratiating he had an encyclopedic memory and a remarkable talent for administrative details and handling men. A big man in every respect with a giant-size ambition to match. He was always as well dressed as his lumber. His rise to dominance was fast and his financial collapse was equally speedy — too many irons in the fire. The precipitating factor was not lumber but sour investments in properties and iron in 1877 cost him more than $100,000.

It was believed that had he been able to raise sufficient capital to tide him over a six-month period, he might conceivably have recouped his money because both the iron market and the real estate situation staged a fast switcheroo at that time — too late of course to be of benefit to him.

Like many other successful industrialists Norton was thoroughly aware that most of the action affecting his varied interests was taking place in Albany so, when asked to consider a nomination as State Senator on the Democratic ticket in a notoriously Republican district, he readily consented and was elected in 1869 by the voters of Warren, Essex and Clinton Counties.

But, like too many other politicians who never could conceivably be classified as statesmen, the Colonel got himself entangled in a very obvious personal power play in which he gave his own self-interest priority over those of his constituents. The following letter, signed Cob, which appeared in the Plattsburgh *Sentinel* on Feb. 23, 1871 tells the sordid story. "Mr. Editor: My attention has been called to a bill introduced in the Senate by Sen. C. F. Norton which, if it passes, will practically place the entire Saranac River in the hands of a corporation (C.F. Norton & Co.) and will deprive others of its use, subjecting them to the corporation's dedication and preventing their using the river if the Norton Company so chooses...

"Among its provisions the Norton Co., would be given the privilege of driving other owners' logs — whether they wish to employ the company or not — for one-half cent a log per mile. This would deny them the right of doing their own driving. Now this may look like a small price to pay but I have been informed by a man who had charge of the finances of drives that the average cost per standard (log) for driving logs the whole distance from Saranac Lake to Plattsburgh was only $.17 apiece. By the terms of this proposed bill it would cost nearly three times as much as that.

"Another stipulation in the Norton Bill is the "hydraulic" clause which would enable him and his three associates (John Merrill, L.L. Smith and J.K. McKillip) to build more dams and reservoirs to impound water and in doing so to take over people's property whether or not they wish to sell. Also included is the privilege of withholding when wanted for other uses by other people and then releasing it in such quantities as they wish for driving the logs — and then shutting it off completely without giving downstream businesses a sufficient flow of water for any use whatsoever.

"Forge and mill-owners, how does that suit you?

"Another point : Norton's Company will also have the right to 'improve' the North branch of the Saranac at the 'Thousand Islands' below Hunter's Home — thus giving them another monopoly.

"These are just some of the provisions of the Senator's bill which require looking into by everyone with riverbank property. It has been generally assumed that the 1847 law making the Saranac public highway was very liberal in its coverage and permitted everyone concerned to enjoy its benefits.

"The question now is: was Christopher F. Norton elected to represent the best interests of his constituency or is he there to subvert their interests to his own?"[1]

Col. Norton moved to Perry's Park, Colo. in 1877 and was active in the lumber business. He died there in 1890. His wife, Charlotte Moore, a member of one of the oldest Plattsburgh families, studied medicine after her husband's death and went into practice in the West.

E. C. Baker, one of the most prominent Saranac Valley lumbermen, wrote up his experiences. One of the most relevant he told in this manner: "In the Spring of 1861 I asked for authorization to go up the river with the drivers and come down with them and the logs. Frankly, I little knew what I was undertaking. We started on foot and late in the night of the second day arrived at what is now Saranac Lake village but then a place of three houses — Col. Milote Baker's (now the R. L. Stevenson cottage), an unfinished house called Blood's Hotel (later the woodshed and kitchen of the Riverside Inn) and Capt. Miller's little home on the bank of the river. Finding no accommodations there we went on to the partly-finished house of Bill Martin on the Lower Lake (Ampersand Bay). The next morning we took boats to go through the lakes to Floodwood at the upper end of Upper Saranac Lake. We broke ice a good deal of the way and landed at our journey's end the second night . . .

"Our logs were surrounded with a boom covering about 20 acres. Upon the front end we erected a windlass and paid out our anchor and turned around and around until we had wound up the warp and drawn the raft presumably the length of the rope . . . Our work was mostly at night and frequently we were driven back by the winds of the day fully as far as we had progressed the night before. This being April the weather was very cold with

---

[1]Such frustrated concern is perfectly understandable since it has been symptomatic of all the smaller people - average cloutless individuals - all through history and in all nations of the world. It helps us understand the stated explanation that politics is the "art of the possible: and even better to appreciate the sting in Ambrose Bierce's cynical definition: "politics is a vile exchange of favors."

Perhaps in the wording of the plaintive old ditty "where have all the flowers gone," we should substitute statesmen for posies. Greed for money is indeed the root of all evil just as true as the adage - "These birds will someday come home to roost."

constant storms, either cold rain or snow, and our diet was pork and beans four times a 24-hour day . . . .

"After four weeks of struggle we finally had our raft in the Lower Lake, so we thought that the next day we would be able to reach the head of the River. In the morning the wind was blowing a gale right at us so we made fast our raft and waited for night to come. Looking over my calendar I found that it was Sunday so I suggested to Mr. Austin that we take the boat and go down to Col. Baker's to get our mail. At that time it arrived once a week by horseback and I had not heard a word from home since leaving there. We went via the River and Mill Pond route and arrived at the post office. I immediately asked Baker if I had any mail and without even rising from his chair to look, he said there was none. I instantly took in his monstrous 300 pound pomposity and told him how long we had been without a square meal. Having heard that he served the best meals in the county (which was true because there wasn't anyone else in the area in the business), we wished he would get us up the best meal his house afforded. He gave the order and as it was being prepared I started conversation with him, soon found out that he was a rank copperhead so avoided that subject, but interested him in more general topics. In fact he became so interested that he accepted an invitation to join us at dinner, which did full justice to his reputation, and to a good cigar.

"He was so pleasant with my including his dinner and smoke in the bill that he willingly granted my request to look into the mail matter again — and found a fat envelope, two weeks old, from home. Well, we finally got our logs down through Miller Pond (also called Oseetah) and ready to slip at the dam when the constant exposure to horrible weather and the infernal diet had its cumulative effect so I sought a bed in Blood's Hotel . . . I spend a miserable five days there, high-lighted by a lobelia emetic administered by the kindly landlady. But I survived the ordeal and left for home."

Competition within the ranks of the lumbermen was always ruthless and conducted according to the age-old law of the jungle — either eat or be eaten — as evidenced by C. F. Norton and Capt. James Pierce of Bloomingdale, a smaller operator, in their bitter feud over the control of the strategic Sweeney Carry between the Raquette River and Upper Saranac Lake. Both men claimed the land but Norton outsmarted his less resourceful adversary by enforcing the premises that actual possession was the real clincher in the case. Therefore C. F. stationed Oliver Tromblee on the river end and O.S. Coville, a well-known guide, in the Sweeney-Daniels cabin at the Wawbeek terminus and thereby decisively settled the matter once and for all.

Although the use of flumes was fairly common in the California Sierras, the Oregon Cascades and in the Southern Appalachins, at least one Adirondack lumbering company — J. & J. Rogers of Au Sable Forks — also employed this means of getting logs down the steep slopes of Whiteface Mountain. There is somewhat unsubstantiated evidence that C. F. Norton logged the northern and western ramparts of the same peak in the same manner. Without the use of this device it would have been impossible for horses and teams to negotiate the sharp gradients. According to C. A. Schenck in his classic text *Logging and Lumbering*[1] the flumes resembled mill races made of boards and must be watertight. Sideboards were about 16 feet long and the angle of the V was 110 degrees; the top width was 3 to 4 feet. The square box flume required more water than the V and it failed to have its strongest current in the center. An even constant grade of from 1 to 5 degrees was

[1]Schenck, C. A. — *Logging and Lumbering* or *Forest Utilization*. Darmstadt, Germany — L. C.Wittich. n.d. Schenck was director of the Biltmore Forest School, Biltmore, N.C.

Sweeney-Daniels Cabin, Upper Saranac Lake, Wawbeek End of Carry — Photo Courtesy of Horton Duprey

necessary, also slight curves and large water supply. The main flume sometimes had a number of tributaries which required a crew of men to patrol side as well as main trough.

The longest chutes in the country were at Chico in the Sierra Nevadas — 40 miles and the Great Madeira, also in California — 54 miles, costing $5,000 per mile and with a daily carrying capacity of 400,000 feet of lumber. The Roger's slide, which handled only 4 foot pulp logs, was 7½ miles long.

The lumbering concerns had other headaches besides rivalry from other timber-owners and, although the opposition was seldom as vicious and persistent, they could nevertheless become formidable and costly. A typical situation was epitomized in the following Sangemo (corruption of St. Germaine) Carry confrontation; these letters were published in the *Forest and Stream* magazine, issues of Sept. 17 and 21, 1874:

"A few days ago a squad of men in the employ of C. F. Norton & Co., felled trees and blocked the Sangemo Carry between Lake Clear and the St. Regis Chain of lakes, and also Clear Pond outlet. By doing so they prevented the usual traffic between Paul Smith's and the Saranacs. The motive for this act is not apparent but is supposed to be prompted by pure cussedness. The whole army of Adirondack guides, backed by their sportsmen and hotel keepers have united forces, removed the obstructions and reopened the carries. Now they are waiting for the operation to be repeated. Blood is in their eyes and the excitement is intense."

With the next copy came the reply from O. A. T., who was Oatman A. Tefft, a well-

Log Slide — J. & J. Rogers Co. For Transporting Pulp Logs to the Au Sable River, Essex Co., N.Y. This Water-Trough is seven and one-half miles long. — F.A. Van Sant Photo

Log Drive on the Ausable River, Essex County, N.Y. — F.A. Van Sant Photo

208

known Plattsburgh logger: "In your last issue is an editorial relating to some acts of C.F. Norton & Co. and the subsequent actions of sportsmen, hotelkeepers and guides of the Saranac region. This item, in my opinion, is ill-considered and nearly on the verge of flippancy. I have bought your periodical for some time past and have gained the impression that you do not intentionally go off on a wrong tack. Therefore I venture to ask what legal or moral right the said sportsmen, hotel owners and their guides had to trespass upon the Sangemo Carry or to launch their boats in the outlet of Big Clear Pond? Is not this land and this stream the property of C. F. Norton & Co., upon which they pay taxes to the State and which is indisputably Norton's property? The "sportsmen" et al, I assume, do not claim any shadow of title to the lands and waters from which they are removing the obstructions and therefore have no more right there than they would to enter your office and pitch out the window any piece of furniture which chanced to be in their way.

"But why this controversy between these parties? Norton & Co. are lumbermen and therefore own large tracts of land exposed to the incendiarism of the Arab of the wilderness — the Saranac guide. They have not incurred this ill-will without great provocation, I assure you. What Norton has suffered I do not know but I can give you a few instances of what I personally have experienced in lumbering on Saranac waters. From 1852-1865 inclusive I got sawlogs out of Upper Saranac and was part owner of the northwest third of Township 33. On this tract was a large stand of valuable white pine. A fire, which started on the shore of Lead Pond, destroyed about 15,000 standards (trees) out of that section at a loss to me of at least $5,000. That fire, as I now can prove, was caused by the carelessness of a wealthy "sportsman" (now dead). These men and their appendages — hotel-keepers and guides — have caused me great loss and annoyance. So much so that we were compelled to watch our rafts and booms night and day until our logs were safely in the river.

"Our logging camps were burned down, the roofs were ripped apart for fuel or else were carried away; our dams were ruined and our timberstands were set afire. Moreover, our logs were systematically stolen for all the uses of the neighboring area. I also had occasion to build several boats but not having any suitable lumber just then, I got in touch with a man named Reynolds, who was supposed to have some. I paid him an exorbitant price and when the logs were delivered I found my own mark on some of the pieces! The fellow had coolly stolen exactly the right kind of log when my drive was passing through Miller Pond.

"I firmly believe that up to 1885 there were not a half-dozen boats floating on the Saranac waterways that had not been made from stolen timber! I am also sorry to state that the so-called sportsmen — with a pitifully few exceptions — that I have chanced to encounter during a 15-year period were not deserving of my admiration or even my respect. As a rule they were always ready and willing to back up their guides in any deviltry they wanted to try. I repeat that in my opinion the whole crew — "sportsmen," hotelmen and guides — were then and are now nothing more than interlopers and trespassers. Being squatters and therefore having no permanent interest in the region, nine-tenths of the guides don't own even a foot of land and half of them don't have even a nominal home there. Therefore they are a nuisance and a curse to any country they invade. Furthermore, the fact that they (the guides) are a convenience to your sporting people should not blind you to their faults, or make you willing to assist them in such unlawful enterprises as they seem to be involved in now. You can rest assured that C. F. Norton & Co. have not risked a general conflagration of their property without adequate cause. I know the hotel-keepers and guides of the Saranac section through and through, so I don't honestly believe that *Forest and Stream* has anything in common with them and therefore will not permit the magazine to make itself their mouthpiece or champion."

"Editor's note: Our correspondent has stated to us in a supplementary note that he wrote his article in general terms. (probably in very logical fear of retaliation). He recognizes honorable exceptions among guides and other classes who have come under his displeasure. This matter of trespass and rights involves serious and complicated legal issues which can only be settled by wise adjudication in the future . . . ."

Judging by all criteria the longest, most difficult and dangerous of the three major annual drives was down the North River, as the Hudson is called above North Creek, to the Big Boom at the Big Bend, four miles above Glens Falls. This was reckoned a two-day trip for logs launched at Newcomb — that is if conditions were right and the river was in a favorable mood. This combination, however, seldom matched up so there was usually plenty of action all along the route due to frequent jam spots. There the drivers were constantly on the move patrolling known problem areas such as sharp bends, sandbars, islands and ornery rock formations and ledges, and keeping the logs moving. Other men tailed the drive and swept the strays from the shore.

According to Lyman Beeman, President of Finch Pruyn & Co., "logs generally traveled about two miles an hour with a good stream flow. Usually three-quarters to nine-tenths of the wood went straight through. The balance might be held up a few hours or many months. The time required to pick up wood stranded in the rear of the drive extended from the breakup, usually around April 15th until sometime in June, and we generally employed about 40 men in that operation. Logs still left behind had to wait until the water reached them again, which might require anywhere from one to several years." Too many derelicts could easily make a sizeable dent in an operator's profits or, as it often happened to hard-luck or inexperienced firms, could put that outfit on the proverbial financial skids.

For that reason every effort was made to speed up the progress of the drives as much as possible and particular pains were taken to prevent jams — the bane, pain and often nightmarish headache of all the crews. Rock-filled cribs, riprap and anchored booms were constructed to deflect the on-rushing logs into the main flow and thus head off pile-ups. The mid-stream jams were the most troublesome and had to be handled by crews in jamboats, especially built 14-footers, — but up to 30 feet long on the Saranac.

Three men rode these boats — the bowman, the oarsman and the sternman — and they had to know their business thoroughly if they were to survive. They had to use their heads and feet with split-second precision as they boarded the jackstrawed log, worked their way to the cork or key log, hooked on their peavies, pulled the plug and then scampered nimbly back to their craft, hopped in and rowed away rapidly just before the jam broke suddenly loose with a deafening roar. Occasionally the pile-up had to be dynamited but customarily the men preferred to let brain, brawn and savvy handle the situation.

As Pieter Fosburgh aptly described it in his fine book — *The Natural Thing*:[1] "The Boreas was bad all the way down. The Hudson was bad at Ord Falls, below Newcomb and bad again just above the mouth of the Indian and very bad on the big bend below Blue Ledge, near the Deer Den. Even if the drive got through these spots it could always hang up on the Moulton Bars at Warrensburg.

"Every day was different on the drive. It was easy going down Blackwell's because there the Hudson ran slow and deep and each man used to pick a good log and ride it for two or

[1]Fosburgh, Pieter. *The Natural Thing: The Land and Its Citizens.* N.Y.C. Macmillan 1959.

The big boom at Glens Falls, Warren County, N.Y. — F.A. Van Sant Photo

three miles, smoking his pipe. Sometimes he would run the wood from log to log just to pass the time of day with another driver across the river. But when the drive passed the Cedar and came to the mouth of the Indian there was always a dull roar coming up from below and that meant tough times ahead.

"But the worst stretch of all was the one past the Deer Den. That was where Russ Carpenter smashed up his bateau and disappeared under a boiling mass of logs. Months later some children found him 30 miles downstream when they saw a piece of red cloth sticking up through the gravel near Stony Creek. It was Carpenter's handkerchief, still tied around his neck.

"Among other casualties were McGar, Culver, Bruno, Lewis, Houghton, Dillon and a fellow called 'Frenchie' who would never tell anyone his name."

My friend, the late Leslie Rist of Newcomb, in a well-researched article[1] added many more names to the roll-call of river victims. Among these were Irish, French-Canadians and old-time Yankees such as Asa Bunker; young Frank Fuller of Wells; Will Timball and Dare Devil Dick Siple, both drowned in the Saranac and buried in Plattsburgh; Morgan King on the Lemon Thompson drive of April, 1891; Bill McGeer of Aden Lair, who tried to break up a jam on the Boreas in 1882 and left a widow and six small children destitute; Harry Darling, who had left home without saying where he was going in June 1918 and met a watery death in the Boreas. His obit was the first and last news his mother had of his

[1] *"The Old North River is Boiling Brown"* in John Thurman Historical Society Quarterly, September 1970.

whereabouts.

Also Frank Ovitt, on the 1896 Cedar River drive and Jerry Donahue on May 1, 1902 near the mouth of the Indian. And the double tragedy which took the life of Jim Little, who futilely tried to save a young French-Canadian in the Rock River a mile east of the present Lake Durant. And James Gallagher just below the Duck Hole on the Cold River Drive. And James Kelley, who was blown apart while checking a delayed dynamite blast. The list is very lengthy.

At North River, on May 7, 1961, with Bill Roden as master of ceremonies and Lyman Beeman of Finch-Pryn as principal speaker, a monument was impressively dedicated "In Memory of the River Men and Foresters who made the Hudson River Drive from Forest to Factory 1850-1950."

Recent years have brought many changes to the logging industry. The big stuff stopped moving down the Hudson in 1924 and before that in all the other Adirondack waterways. Four-foot pulp sticks filled the rivers until 1950, the last year for Finch-Pruyn, and that form of transportation gave way completely to the huge trucks which could travel over well-maintained woods roads leading directly to the areas where the logging was being done. Nowadays mechanized monsters, which will eventually employ laser beams to do the actual cutting, make short work of what formerly required untold weeks of human brawn and skill. The long-gone, heedless, wasteful era has given way almost completely to enforced, enlightened forest practices as the companies seek diligently to prolong, protect and perpetuate their otherwise dwindling natural assets.

So those not so good good old days have gone forever and exist only in the memories of the men who were fortunate enough to survive the perils and the inevitable, concomitant muscular miseries caused by endless hours of exposure to all 57 varieties of Adirondack weather and water. But while it lasted — the glamorous, extremely dangerous river-running days were like an irresistible, mighty magnet drawing men, young and old, and daring them to test their strength and courage against the awesome power of the treacherous rapids and thundering logs. Truly one of the most momentous and spectacular periods in Adirondack history and one which has not been and probably never will be adequately recorded. At the very least this is an honest start in that challenging direction.

Chapter 20

The Rip-Roaring, Rum-Running Days

Prohibition, the hopefully great moral experiment, did not suddenly descend upon an unsuspecting nation like a lightning bolt from the heavens because it had in fact been waiting impatiently in the wings for nearly two centuries. Therefore, when the 18th Amendment became the law of the land it, according to Frederick Allen in *Only Yesterday*, was "accepted not willingly but almost absent-mindedly."

Undoubtedly the two most potent factors behind its passage were the well-remembered excesses of the free-wheeling, uninhibited, hard-drinking frontier days and the deep-rooted Puritan guilt complex which had to reconcile an intense inherent love of riotous living with an ever-present sense of nagging misgiving over self-indulgence. And the result was that "the era of clean thinking and clean living" so exultingly proclaimed by the Anti-Saloon League, launched the nation into the most traumatic alcoholic binge in its already bibulous history. It promptly transformed millions of people who previously had been relatively disinterested in hard liquor into rebellious boozers, defiant flask-toters and impromptu homebrew specialists.

"By late 1920," wrote Herbert Asbury in the *Underworld of Chicago*, "women began to invade the speakeasies, young people began to carry flasks and stage whoopie parties — at which the goal was to see who could get plastered first. They also helped their parents operate the family still and saw the grown-ups make drunken passes at each other's wives and husbands...Drinking became romantic and adventurous, the socially correct thing for all up-to-date young folks to do."

A poem of the period described accurately the almost total disregard and disrespect for the newly-enacted law:

> Mother's in the kitchen
> Washing out the jugs,
> Sister's in the pantry
> Botteling (sic) the suds.
> Father's in the cellar
> Mixing up the hops,
> Johnny's on the front porch -
> Watching for the cops!

The Tupper Lake *Herald* offered its own facetious home-brew recipe to prove that the Adirondack region could also produce witty social satire. "Chase a wild frog 13 miles. Toss it and the hops into a slightly-used garbage can. Add 10 gallons of well-aged pickle brine, 2 quarts of high-viscosity shellac, 1 bar of Fels Naphtha soap, 1 level pint of sweet spirits of nitre and a generous dash of iron filings for flavor. Boil 3 weeks then strain through a sock from an I.W.W. (Independent Workers of the World, a Socialist-Communist organization) to keep the concoction from working. Then bottle, take out $10,000 insurance policy and sip slowly while standing over an open grave."

If the 18th Amendment had prohibited only hard liquor, as was wisely urged by the best brains of the time, it is very likely that the subsequent moral and legal disaster could have been avoided because the bulk of the huge bootleg traffic was in beer. While the wealthier element bewailed the oppressive restrictions on the consumption of rye, scotch, bourbon etc., the wage-earners griped because they were being gypped out of their daily pots of brew.

But underlying all the outspoken resentment felt by many intelligent, basically moral but unchurched people was the galling conviction that their constitutional rights and pattern of living had been grossly violated by a group of religious fanatics and bigots.

Max Lerner in his perceptive book, *America as a Civilization,* summed up the situation very convincingly in these words: "Basically America was then and always has been a lawless society and an over-legislated one. We consider crime a problem that we cannot completely control, one which will continue to grow because it represents the eruption of inner, deeper social diseases. To feel mastery over the environment, over things and money and yet to feel baffled by so basic a fact as crime has become a source of intense national frustration and exasperation."

At the outset of the "noble experiment" and to implement it the Prohibition Bureau was authorized to operate as a division of the Treasury Department and rapidly recruited 1512 men the first year. [Maximum manpower was 3,000]. Their budget allocation was a piddling $500,000 and the starting pay scale was $1200-$2300 a year, later raised to $2800. Since there were no civil service selection standards for enlistment, the organization attracted a motley group of mercenaries, political hacks, stooges and near-gangsters who were lured by the prospect of abundant graft opportunities.

According to the newspapers of the day most of the agents, who were sent out into the field with no legal or other training and with few qualifications except ability to handle a gun and act tough, were usually held in deep contempt. The average wet or moderately wet citizen detested him and his function, the bootleggers considered him a dishonest and expensive nuisance and the local police naturally seethed at such Federal intrusion into their bailiwicks. Of course there were some outstanding agents among them but they were greatly outnumbered — especially in the metropolitan areas.

Things were so flagrant in New York City that one department chief decided to clean house in a hurry. Assembling his detachment around a large office table and banging his huge first resoundingly to gain total attention, he gave this ultimatum: "Now hear this! Everybody put both hands on the table. And every S.O.B. with a diamond ring is fired!" After a few seconds of stunned silence he watched half his detail head for the door with no arguments or backward glances!

When you consider that this small force of men, aided when needed by State Police and Border Patrolmen, was expected to cover not only the long, sleazy Canadian frontier but also the Mexican border as well — plus 18,000 miles of Atlantic and Pacific seacoasts — it is a wonder that they did as well as they did. Despite such odds the Prohi Bureau — or rather the efficient incorruptibles on the job — had posted a rather impressive record. During the first ten years they arrested 572,000 suspects (less than two-thirds of whom were convicted), seized 1,600,000 distilleries, stills, worms[1] etc., confiscated a billion gallons of malt liquor, hard cider and mash and had captured 45,000 cars and 1,300 boats.

Counter-balancing this performance were the known killings of 2,000 citizens — mostly hoodlums, rum-runners and their ilk — but also an appalling number of non-criminals as well. One agent casually admitted having dispatched 42 persons with his trusty Thompson sub-machinegun. He explained that whenever anyone he encountered in line of duty made even the slightest move after having been ordered to freeze — he took no chances and zippered him with .45 bullets. Five hundred agents had to be replaced because they lost their lives in the 14-year period of mutual violence and sudden death...

In his provocative essay, "Of Aristocracy," Spinoza aptly analyzed the mood of such an era: "All laws which can be broken without injury to another person are considered but a laughing stock and are so far from bridling (curbing) the desires and lusts of men that, on the contrary, they stimulate them. For we are ever eager for forbidden fruit and desire what is denied."

So much for the admittedly superficial coverage of the background events and learned opinions on the Prohibition Era. By narrowing the scope to concentrate on the State and North Country scene the story takes on added interest because its participants are better known.

Although the New York State Legislature passed the bill providing for the formation of a State Police force in early 1917, it was not until 1921 that Troop B, the famous Black Horse Brigade, was established in Malone, to enforce law and order along the extremely lively Canadian Border. Headed by Capt. C. J. Broadfield the detachment consisted of 56 men, later increased to 96, many of whom had seen action in World War I.

Armed with Colt .45's and Winchester .30-30's these men, operating in pairs, covered from 20-25 miles per day through the rural areas on extended patrols. ["strictly an R.F.D. outfit," one ex-trooper labeled them.] Since the next patrol would come through a week later but not on a regular schedule their presence usually kept in line the local outlaws and wife-beaters. The men maintained contact by postcard or by telephone. Anyone who spotted them reported it to the local telephone operator who, in turn, relayed the info to the Troop B Headquarters in Malone. These patrols were especially effective in Winter when auto traffic was minimal and greatly hampered.

Incidentally, a trooper's starting pay was then $900.00 a year for round-the-clock duty.

Originally assigned 50 horses for transportation purposes, the troopers shortly acquired four Harley-Davidson motorcycles, which were divided equally between Adams and Champlain sub-stations. In 1925 Troop B got its first Fords — a Model T roadster and a coupé for the captain's use but the ever-dependable horses were used right up to 1932, when Prohibition was repealed.

Sgt. Henry Schermerhorn of Malone, who worked the motorcycle detail provided a vivid picture of this unpleasant mission. "It was miserable! We were always cold, always crummy dirty. Our eyes behind the almost useless goggles were always watering, burning and felt as though they were being pulled right out of their sockets. The big regulation Stetson hats looked good but were at times a damned nuisance because the brims would flop up and down and block our vision. But the boys figured out a way to take care of that: we coated the brims with layers of white shellac."

Broadfield's Boys were obviously operating under serious handicaps since their job rapidly shifted from R.F.D. patrols to matching wits with bootleggers while assisting the

---

[1] A spiral tube used in distilling.

Troop B. N.Y. State Police about 1925

Caught With the Goods

Two Members of Troop B-1. Walter Dixon, r. Edward Van Schaick — Frank Noel Photo

Two-Horse Power

Feds. Their quarry would usually hit the mostly dirt roads in 40 horsepower — fast for the time — Cadillacs, Marmons, Stutz Bearcats, Packards, Mercers, and an occasional Lincoln, Locomobile or Peerless plus the more common souped-up Buicks and Dodges. The speed advantage was soon minimized by using confiscated cars in the pursuit capers and by developing an intelligence system which made midnight chases unnecessary. Well-placed informers, many of them Canadians, found it very profitable to alert the G Men and collect their half of the fines.

Another obstacle was the legal stipulation, later lifted, which limited the involvement of the State Police to an auxiliary role even when the rum-runners were caught red-handed with the wet goods. In spite of these problems the Black Horse Troop was credited with the capture of 375 cars and their high-priced cargoes during the first year of their participation.

During the peak years of Prohibition (1923-25) auction sales of captured cars brought $35,000. Legally but ironically, many of the buyers were their former owners who had paid their usually minimal fines, had served their short prison terms and were understandably ready, willing and eager to resume operations. The impounded cars were expensive jobs to begin with and their usefulness had been enhanced by increased cargo capacity, armor plating and the installation of smokescreen gadgetry.

A scrapbook at the Troop B. barracks indicates that the Grey Riders played a conspicuous part in that exciting era of "the great moral experiment." Trooper, later Sgt. Jim Welch, for example, was personally responsible for the seizure of over 200 cars — very few by close pursuit. According to him, "You either got them or you didn't. The odds were definitely against you if you chased them." Most of his successes were attributed to Canadian informants who provided advance info on car identification, probable itineraries etc. Curiously enough many such tip-offs came from competing out-laws who were trying to muscle in on established monopolies.

The fascinating scrapbooks contain many newspaper accounts of trooper action in those frenetic years. One of the most unusual took place early one Summer evening on the Adams-Carthage road. Having been alerted that a big seven-passenger Caddy loaded to the gunwales was headed their way — Gouverneur, the two troopers waited its arrival. Soon it came into sight, moseying along at first but accelerating rapidly when the driver realized his predicament and started to jettison his cargo — not only to destroy evidence but also to litter the road with broken glass to discourage the chase. At this point the troopers started shooting at his tires; one shot found its mark and sent the Caddy careening across the road and crashing into and over a rock-filled deep ditch before bounding into a meadow in a cloud of dirt and gravel. All four wheels were sheered off and the canvas top catapulted another 50 feet farther along.

Before the two law-men arrived the car had caught fire so they rushed to extricate the trapped driver. When they had hauled him to safety they were astounded to discover that he had only one arm! How he had managed to toss out bottles of booze while steering the heavy car on the winding, narrow road at the same time was a matter of considerable mystery and frequent speculation for a long while afterward.

Another hairy incident took place about 1925 at the covered bridge in Hogansburg. Trooper Dave Benjamin and another officer, alerted shortly beforehand, had blocked the road at the south end of the structure. They didn't have long to wait before a heavily-loaded open Buick rounded the bend and headed toward the bridge. Benjamin got out of the trooper car and stationed himself in the middle of the road and, with upraised hand tried to flag down the approaching car, whose driver wasn't about to stop. In fact he

Trooper Henry N. Schermerhorn & Smoky Joe

kept on accelerating and forced the trooper to backtrack rapidly in order to avoid being run down. Realizing that the desperate bootlegger had designs on his life, Benjamin knew that he had to do something — and fast. Instinctively he jumped up with outstretched arms, grabbed an over-head rafter and chinned himself while at the same time tucking his legs under him to prevent their crashing into the windshield. Then, as the Buick passed underneath, he dropped into the back seat, guzzled the guy, over-powered him and yanked on the emergency brake just in time to soften the impact of the collision with the Troop B car.

Still another encounter with a tough hombre occurred when Trooper Henry Schermerhorn and his partner were on horse patrol just outside Schroon Lake. Their adversary was a particularly vicious character and well-known for his dirty tricks. Tipped off that he was headed their direction the officers positioned themselves on the sandy shoulder of a sharp curve. Seeing them there the rum-runner apparently figured that the only good troopers were dead troopers — and tried his damnedest to knock down both men and their horses before departing in a cloud of dust.

A few days later he pulled the same caper and again made the troopers jump for their lives. This time they decided that they had taken all the crap they were going to from that punk — and made arrangements to settle the score but good.

So when the joker came through the next time they were eagerly awaiting him. As usual he came barreling around the bend and was well on his way toward another encore. But this time things didn't work out as before: when the car narrowed the gap to ten feet or so, one of the intended victims heaved a heavy Stilson wrench smack into the non-shatter-proof windshield and almost scalped the astonished driver. Needless to say, that menace to society was removed from circulation for many moons thereafter.

Although the bootleggers understandably dreaded the Lawmen, they were even more fearful of the gangs of predators called hi-jackers. These jackals, some of whom were ex-officers themselves who had been fired or quit voluntarily when they had learned the ropes, had found that it was less dangerous to prey on their own kind than to run the gauntlet from the Canadian border to the downstate cities.

Their usual game plan was to waylay a load of ale or wine, rough up and rob the driver and then take the load to a tavern down the line. The proprietor, nearly always in the market for the wet goods, would settle up and gladly accept their offer to help unload the cargo. By doing so they would find out where the stuff was being stored and, in general, case the joint. Then they would drive away — but later that night they would return, break into the oasis, steal the stuff and shove off for a similar escapade farther down the highway. Obviously, this could be a very profitable business as long as the supply of suckers held out.

Probably the weirdest experience of them all happened to friends of mine, the Bazinets of Saranac Lake, who one beautiful Autumn day drove down to the Witherill Hotel in Plattsburgh, had dinner and started home by a different route. Rounding a bend in the road a short distance north of Keeseville, John's attention was drawn to two objects on the shoulder of the road. As he drew closer he saw a man leaning over the side of his car, jumping up and down like a kangaroo and shouting unintelligibly. Closer inspection showed that the tires on the car, an open Dodge, were all flat — and that the man was handcuffed to the steering wheel.

As my friend walked toward him the fellow yelled, "Get me out of this! Do you hear me? Get me out of this!" and all the while hopping mad.

"How can I help you? I haven't any tools," replied John.

"All right then but stop at the garage in Clintonville and have him come out. Right away! Do you hear me?"

So the Bazinets drove on into the next village, where they found the garageman and relayed the message.

"What did the guy look like?" inquired the mechanic. John described him very accurately apparently because the native burst out laughing, slapped his side and said, "Why that's _____. The damned old coot. They finally caught up with him and it serves him right. Haven't you heard of him?"

"Nope," replied my friend.

"Why, he's the U. S. Marshal but he's also the sneakiest old hi-jacker in this neck of the woods. Boy, this is really rich! Will he be glad to see me comin'! This will fix his wagon for a while."

Occasionally Broadfield's Boys had the opportunity to make a pinch and in the process give the pinched one a friendly break. One blustery Winter day the troopers chased a sleek Wills St. Clair and forced the driver into a ditch between North Hudson and Split Rock Falls. The occupant high-tailed it into the woods to escape arrest but would have been easy to locate because of his tracks in the deep snow. Searching the car Trooper Schermerhorn found the man's heavy jacket and, knowing that the fellow would be mighty cold without it, yelled in his direction, "I'm leaving your jacket for you! We're leaving now so come on out and get it!"

A voice from the shrubbery replied, "O.K. thanks a lot!"

The Troop B boys soon had the snazzy car and its cargo of rye and Scotch back on the road and on its way to Headquarters. The owner undoubtedly had an unenviable hike back to his homebase.

Every section of the Adirondacks had its share of action during those hectic years. One of these incidents featured an early Autumn visit to the Lake Meacham Hotel, when Rob Stevens was manager. He and his wife Ruby were sleeping soundly when a series of loud knocks broke the silence. Dressing himself and going to the door he called out, "Who is it and what do you want?"

"It's me — B.F.! I had to leave my car back on the road and the Law is on my tail. I want someone to drive me home!"

"O.K. Just a minute," called Rob. "I'll have _____ take you over! Come on in while you're waiting."

While the hotel chauffeur was getting ready the rum-runner told his story and ended up by asking Rob. "Do you know what I'm going to do? Well, I'll tell you. Tomorrow morning I'm going to report a stolen car!"

And that's exactly what he did — and within a few days he got his car back minus the booze of course.

According to Schermerhorn most of the operation was basically a battle of wits with the adversaries usually well-known to each other through frequent daytime contacts in local hangouts and restaurants. Nothing much happened until midnight or later so all involved merely whiled away the quiet time. Nor was much guesswork or wasted effort necessary because well-paid informers at the Meridian kept the troopers posted on impending plans to "shoot the load," as the trips were called.

One night S., on motor cycle patrol, was alerted that a dare-devil Frenchman of his acquaintance had just left with a cargo of corded stuff (champagne, cordials, Scotch and rye) costing at least $5,000 but worth $15,000 delivered in N.Y.C.

The trooper mounted his trusty Harley-Davidson, parked at a road junction where he could head off the bootlegger and bided his time. Very soon the big black Cadillac announced its presence by a tell-tale cloud of dust as it rapidly headed his way. When the driver sized up the situation he swung off the Main Drag, veered into the sandy side road very close to the Gray Rider, careened back and forth a few times and then started to goose the accelerator.

As S. jockeyed around to start pursuit he hit a patch of soft sand, lost control and flipped over. As he was righting the cycle, he happened to glance up and surprisingly saw that the Frenchman had slammed on his brakes and was peering backward. Then the driver, apparently satisfied that the trooper was uninjured, sped away in the darkness.

The next afternoon, while S. was resting in his room, there was a knock on the door and in came the same Frenchman who had eluded him the previous night. "How you feel?" he inquired. "Stopped las' night wen you tip over. If you no got up I'd hev gone beck to help you. Ta hell wit de load!"...

In the opinion of nearly all North Country residents the most exciting and talked-about event of the Prohibition Era was the Dutch Schultz trial in July, 1935. The scene of the action was the eminently respectable town of Malone, most of whose residents were not even remotely interested in being subjected to that type of notoriety. Dutch, whose real name was Arthur Flegenheimer, was being tried — not for his numerous bloody crimes but for income tax evasion, a gambit that had successfully put out of circulation Al and Joe Capone and other assorted hoods across the country.

Dutch had become the ruthless overlord of various nefarious New York City businesses including Harlem policy rackets, restaurant and night-club extortion and protection activities, numerous breweries and bootlegging sidelines. Moreover, his reputed record of 139 murders to his discredit, plus those in which he was the contractor — he assigned others to do the job — was very lengthy. Bribed police and public officials enabled him to operate

Schultz and Dixie Davis, his mouthpiece

brazenly and unhampered.

Advised by former U.S. Attorney E. H. Reynolds in March, 1926, Schultz's legal and financial consultants had taken advantage of an apparent tax loophole which made it unnecessary to report illegally-acquired income. Later, when the law was changed and any type of income had to be reported, Dutch shrewdly offered to shell out $100,000 as settlement so he sent his agents down to Washington to dicker directly with the I.R.S. However, the offer was refused because the Department was building a file which showed that he owed far more taxes than that, basing their claim on Dutch's seized black ledger.

But the ironical part of all this — and the angle that his battery of clever lawyers exploited twice — was this very point: Schultz had offered to pay the delinquent taxes but the I.R.S. had turned him down.

This strategy paid off when Schultz, to avoid a hostile jury in New York, got a change of venue which transferred the trial from there to Syracuse. His legal staff hammered away on the old refrain — here he was trying to pay his taxes like any other citizen but the Government wouldn't take his money. He certainly wasn't evading the law so how could there by any reason to convict him? A dead-locked jury — seven to five — set the stage for more months of freedom before another change of venue brought the case to Malone the following July.

Federal Judge Frederick Bryant quite reasonably felt that the chances of getting a conviction were far better in his hometown than in the downstate cities. It also provided a far more pleasant and comfortable haven from city heat and criminal influences.

Dutch and his retinue of lawyers and consultants of various types arrived in Malone about a week before the start of the trial and set up their headquarters in several suites of

222

the Flanagan Hotel, Malone's best. Heading his staff were James M. Noonan and the clever J. Richard (Dixie) Davis, whose task was made more tolerable by the presence of a very well-endowed, red-headed show-girl named Hope Dare, who became the center of attraction and distraction in the crowded courtroom during the trial.

At the suggestion of a well-known North Country politician, George Moore and Bud Main, two of the most capable area lawyers, were retained as local counsel to help head off potentially unfavorable reaction to city-slicker legal tactics.

Of even greater influence on the conduct and outcome of the trial was the presence of Eugene F. McGee, an exceptionally sharp New York attorney who had been the partner of the "Great Mouthpiece" — William Fallon, probably the most successful and unethical legal wizard of his day. Both partners — but almost entirely because of Fallon's shady deals and flagrant flouting of the law — wound up discredited and disbarred. Therefore since McGee was not allowed in the courtroom, he was provided with a hotel suite stocked with enough lawbooks to make many small law-school deans green with envy.

The prosecution was headed by Martin Conboy, a protege of Thomas Dewey, and John Burke, Jr., who arrived with their large coterie of assisting lawyers, auditors and secretaries, etc. — and with stern orders to go all out in order to get a conviction and thereby regain some of the legal lustre which had been diminished by the Dutchman's previous court victories. Also present was John H. McEvers, one of the most prominent lawyers in the Dept. of Justice, Washington, D.C. Conboy set up his headquarters at the Franklin Hotel and rented a cottage at nearby Lake Titus to escape the oppressive heatwave that prevailed all during the trial.

During the period preceding the courtroom encounter some of the more presentable of Dutch's minions tried and seemingly succeeded in convincing — by treating — some of the local citizens — especially the bar-fly element — that their boss was the innocent victim of unjustified persecution and that actually he was a misunderstood, great guy with a heart of 22 carat gold. Money was also left with restaurant and saloon owners with instructions to tell anyone with any degree of importance that his meal or drink was being paid for by Mr. Schultz, who incidentally had heretofore been notorious for his stinginess as well as for his crimes.

Such pre-trial generosity incurred the official displeasure of Judge Bryant and presumably influenced his later decision to revoke the $75,000 bail. Obviously the gangster, faced with a possible maximum penalty of fourteen years in prison plus a $40,000 fine, felt that any effort to create a favorable climate for the pending trial was well worth the expense involved.

While Dutch was still in circulation, riding horseback and attending two baseball games as the box-seat guest of the local legal counselors and Mayor Cardinal, he willingly gave interviews to reporters. One of them was my late good friend Del Forkey, who covered the case thoroughly and well for the Malone *Evening Telegram*. In answer to Del's inquiry if he had ever been in the North Country before Schultz said, "Not this far up but in 1931 I spent about six months, off and on, at Long Lake. I was appointed deputy sheriff there and wore the badge." Very likely his identity was never revealed to the area residents, and probably was a display of hi-jinks and low-grade humor on the part of some Hamilton County politico.

Many Malone people were not only unimpressed but also acutely embarrassed by the wide-spread publicity generated by the shenanigans being pulled by the unsavory visitors. Among these was Rev. John R. Williams, pastor of the First Congregational Church, who commented in his sermon on "the tendency of certain humans to desert spiritual for

223

material gains"; he found it deplorable "that men in high places would fawn over gangsters and that communities would hail them with rejoicing because their arrival meant money."

Reporters from all over the East flocked to Malone for the trial. Hotels, rooming houses, camps, stores of all types, gin-mills (especially), telephone and telegraph companies — all prospered and bore out the paraphrased adage that it's an ill wind indeed that doesn't blow some good to somebody.

According to my friend Bill Herron, a member of George Moore's law firm who attended all sessions of the trial as well as the defense staff meetings afterwards, Dutch cut down on his socializing after his earlier public exposure. His favorite hangout became one end of the long Flanagan bar, where he minded his own business and occasionally bought a drink for some sympathetic toper. Judging by reports his personal booze-carrying capacity was reckoned to be formidable.

Schultz was described as being about 5 feet 7 inches tall, weighed about 170 pounds, was quiet-voiced, low-key and very conservatively dressed — definitely not the traditional killer type. It's hard to reconcile such a description with his reputation as New York State's Public Enemy Number One and a man with a multitude of murders chalked up to his and his henchmen's guns.

Since the trial was of prime national interest and the press coverage was so extensive, every effort was made to empanel a blue ribbon jury. Fred Fiske, commissioner of jurors and president of a local bank, carefully supervised the process so that those selected were just about as representative as Franklin County could produce. Picked to serve were the following: (1) Arthur M. Quinn, (2) Hollis Child, (3) Ralph Westcott, (4) Hugh McMahon — all Malone farmers; (5) L. P. Quinn, Tupper Lake school superintendent; (6) Charles Bruce, Santa Clara storekeeper; (7) Leon Chapin (foreman), North Bangor farmer; (8) John Ellsworth, Ft. Covington farmer; (9) Arthur Riedel, Malone baker; (10) Hugh Maneeley, Malone farmer; (11) Floyd Brown, Owl's Head farmer and (12) Frank Lobdell, Saranac Lake guide. Alternates were Thomas Dewey and Robert Parks, both Malone farmers.

At the very outset of the courtroom clash it was clearly obvious that Judge Bryant was determined to do everything in his power to set up a situation conducive to conviction. In doing so, according to several experienced jurists, he made at least one intentional and unfortunate procedural mistake. In the presence of the jury he directed that the defendant's bail be revoked and that he be confined to jail for the duration of the trial. While these orders were legally permissible they are nevertheless customarily never given until after the jury has been excused. Such action of course made it difficult for the defense staff to confer with their client.

As the trial progressed it followed fairly closely the pattern previously developed in Syracuse. Since the only charge against the Dutchman was alleged income tax evasion, the outcome of the case hinged entirely upon whether or not the defendant had deliberately avoided the payment of taxes on his many sources of income, legal or otherwise. His sinister reputation and gory record were to have no bearing whatsoever on the verdict.

On the sixth day the prosecution lawyers suffered a severe set-back which confused and confounded them. At that time Judge Bryant, at the request of the defense staff, ruled that the famous black ledger containing all the incriminating details of the Schultz organization's operations had been illegally seized and directed that it be returned. The ledger being the core of their case the Government lawyers were stymied and practically futile without it. By that time the Government had called 69 witnesses, the defense 17.

In his summation Conboy told the jury: "No matter how many other juries you may

Headlines in Prosecution's Case

TUESDAY, JULY 23.

Judge Bryant jails Schultz for duration of trial as case opens. Jury of 12 with two alternates is selected in hour and half. Prosecution and defense outline cases.

WEDNESDAY, JULY 24.

Gangster guns echo in court room as New York detectives tell of Joey Noe, ill-fated Schultz partner. Prosecution seeks to link Schultz with gangland activities in Bronx. Twenty witnesses sworn.

THURSDAY, JULY 25.

Judge Bryant jails four former Schultz aides, "Big Bo" Weinburg, Rocco DiLarmi, "Weeping Charlie" Miller and Moe Margolese as material witnesses when Miller displays reluctance to testify. Police wire tappers show Schultz high court and mediator in Bronx gangland through conversations heard over telephones. Speakeasy proprietors tell of buying beer from Schultz syndicate. Sixteen witnesses sworn.

FRIDAY, JULY 26.

"Big Bo" Weinburg comes from jail cell to testify against ex-chief fortified with declaration of constitutional rights and is released from jail. Moe Margolese wins jail release after scant testimony. Bronx bank employes identify checks deposited in numerous Schultz accounts. Fourteen witnesses sworn.

SATURDAY, JULY 27.

Rocco DiLarmi jailed "until willing to purge self of contempt, after refusal to say if he knew Joseph Harmon, conceded by defense to be Dutch Schultz. Miss Margaret Scholl, stenographer at Schultz headquarters, tells of handing Schultz ledger to federal officers following police raid at Schultz office, 215 East 149th Street. New York detectives describe raid. Ten witnesses sworn.

MONDAY, JULY 29.

Court order returns ledger to Schultz on grounds it was illegally seized. New York detectives describe arrest of Schultz June 18, 1931, and slaying of bodyguard, Danny Iamasscia. New York detectives and G-men describe efforts to apprehend Schultz during two years hiding. Nine witnesses sworn.

TUESDAY, JULY 30.

John Saxon, Jr., recalled to stand, quotes from prepared chart to show Schultz accounts listed over $2,000,000 deposits and credits during years 1929, 1930 and 1931. Judge Bryant jails DiLarmi for six months when Schultz satellite again refuses to answer prosecution question. Government rests.

Headlines in Prosecution's Case & Chronology of Movement of Jurors

---

Chronology of Movements
Of Schultz Case Jurors

Wednesday, July 31

4:31 p.m. Jury gets case and begins deliberations.

6:30 p.m. Leaves jury room for supper at Franklin Hotel.

7:15 p.m. Returns and resumes deliberations.

8:00 p.m. Comes to court for instructions saying indictment not clear.

8:13 p.m. Returns to jury room.

Thursday, August 1

12:15 a.m. Jury told to retire to hotel until morning.

9:30 p.m. Arrives at court house and goes to jury room.

10:02 a.m. Called to court room. Judge Bryant gives further instructions of Count 3 of indictment.

10:14 a.m. Resumes deliberations.

12:25 p.m. Left court house for lunch at hotel.

1:50 p.m. Returned to continue deliberations.

---

serve on in the future, you will never sit on a more important case. The verdict will give you as citizens an opportunity to vindicate the law and to say to a defendant of this character: you can't ridicule, flaunt or deride the authority of the United States Government!"

In his closing remarks, which lasted for 80 minutes, Defense Counsel Moore stressed two points: (1) Has it been proved that the defendant had taxable income and (2) has the defendant willfully evaded his tax payments? Noting that said defendant seemed to be a kindly dispositioned man, Moore claimed that the only reason his client was on trial was for violation of Prohibition laws, laws which were no longer in force. He kept reminding the jurors that it was not a racket case, not an assault case but an income tax case and that no prejudice should influence their decision.

After the charge by Judge Bryant the jury was given the case at 4:30 P.M. on July 31. They deliberated for 28 hours and 20 minutes, returning twice to the courtroom for further clarification and information. At 8:55 P.M. Thursday, August 1 they reached their decision and the foreman, Leon Chapin, announced the verdict — not guilty. This came as a definite surprise to everyone, including Schultz, and was greeted by cheers and applause from the throng of spectators, an outburst quickly suppressed by the Judge, who was visibly astonished, disappointed and thoroughly exasperated. In fact he practically "lost his cool." "Your verdict," he declared, "is such that it shakes the confidence of law-abiding citizens in integrity and truth. It will be apparent to all who followed the evidence in this case that you have reached a verdict not on the evidence but on some other reason. You will go home with the satisfaction, if it is indeed a satisfaction, that you have rendered a blow against law enforcement and given aid and encouragement to people who would flout the law. In all probability they will commend you. I cannot!"

Understandably the men who had just been scolded were themselves outraged, humiliated and indignant. They resented the implication that they had been influenced by the pre-trial ballyhoo and showed it in no uncertain manner by rapidly cutting the principal character down to size. When the jubilant Dutchman walked across the courtroom with hand held out to thank the jurors, much to his surprise and chagrin the first man he approached ignored the gesture and shriveled him with this remark: "Mr. Schultz, I wouldn't shake hands with you under any circumstances — especially here!"

There were a few people in town who weren't quite so particular so when Dutch called at Moore's office the two secretaries accepted presents of 5 pound boxes of chocolates. He had already congratulated and thanked both Main and Moore profusely for their victorious legal efforts and promised that he would take care of them very generously. However, except for the retainer fees already paid them, the expectant lawyers never saw a dollar of the sizeable fees he still owed them — let alone handsome bonuses.

As could be expected reactions to the verdict from Federal and State officials were tinged with consternation and disapproval. Attorney-General Cummings called it "a terrible miscarriage of justice," while the N.Y.S. Tax Commissioner expressed "amazement."

Speaking for his fellow jurors, foreman Chapin gave this explanation: "I am sure that no man on the jury approves of racketeering or anyone connected with it. In fact the jury considers Schultz to be a public enemy. But the fact that he was a racketeer and in the beer business could have no bearing on the case. We felt that the Government did not prove its case. The whole discussion centered around whether or not he was guilty of willfully evading tax payments. We were instructed to follow the evidence and that's what we did. Pre-trial influence had no bearing whatsoever on the verdict, which was 9 to 3 for

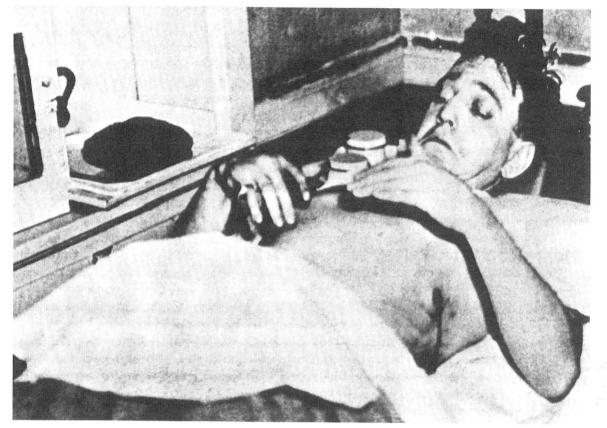

The Dying Dutchman

acquittal. "An easy acquittal", Schultz boasted afterward.

However, the end of the line was rapidly nearing for the 33 year old mobster. During his absence upper-echelon thugs such as Albert Anastasia, Lucky Luciano and Louis (Lepke) Buchalter had opportunely moved in on many of his enterprises and decided to eliminate him as a ruthless and unnecessary rival.[1] Less than three months after his return to his restless bailiwick Schultz and three bodyguards were relaxing in the back-room of the Palace Chop House and Tavern in downtown Newark, N. J. Schultz left his compatriots to answer the call of nature shortly before Charlie (The Bug) Workman and one of his business associates arrived on an important mission. On their way there one of the assassins casually opened the toilet door and cut down the occupant with a single rusty .45 slug [a variation was use of garlic-coated shells to expedite gangrene] Simultaneously, the second exterminator zippered the Dutchman's protectors before they could unlimber their own arsenal. On their way out they discovered that they had already got their man.

Although gravely wounded Dutch hung on well into the next day. While receiving the last rites of the Catholic Church, he delivered a lengthy, delirious and cryptic soliloquy which featured such moralistic maunderings as these: "Mother is the best bet and don't let Satan draw you too fast.... A boy has never wept nor dashed a thousand kim." [?]...

Although Malone, because of its nearness — less than 10 miles — to the Canadian border, was anything but a monotonous town during Prohibition, Saranac Lake was also downright lively indeed. Trudeau San was well populated with many well-heeled, thirsty

---

[1] It was the considered opinion of the Big Six (Murder, Inc.) that Schultz had to go because he had openly announced that he was going to kill Thomas Dewey, smartest prosecutor in the business. The Boss Hoods felt that Dutch's threat constituted very poor public relations.

patients; the wealthy camp-owners on the nearby lakes and guests at the posh resorts of Saranac Inn, Paul Smith's and Loon Lake provided a ready and eager market for the ever-obliging area wet goods purveyors. The village was then at the height of its prosperity and attracted a goodly share of the notorious as well as the noted visitors and residents — undesirables as well as desirables.

Mike D'Ambrisi, a local barber, recalled vividly a convivial gathering of 15 or 16 such worthies in the backroom of his father's shop on Broadway a few years ago before Repeal. Playing cards, lapping up the best of booze and discussing business in general while waiting for car repairs and travel orders, the men, mostly local characters, started bragging about their exploits and newly-acquired wealth. Since some were somewhat skeptical of others' claims, they proceeded to back up their words by producing the long green as proof. The show-down revealed wads of bills and checks ranging from a relatively piddling $6,000 to the high man's approximately $50,000.

About that time one of the most enterprising area rum-runners heard that Hotel St. Regis was on the market. Thinking that it would be an ideal investment he walked into the place, told Morgan, the owner, that he wanted to buy it at the rumored price. To prove that he was serious he reached into the pocket of his overalls and pulled out a roll of bills that would choke the proverbial mule — $100,000 in not-so-cold cash. The slightly amazed owner did a fast double take and then refused the offer for reasons of his own.

One of the most amusing episodes took place one wintry night when a Saranac Lake extra-legal firewater-supplier got word that he would be raided in a half-hour, just time enough to move the contraband to another location. By moving fast he and a helper loaded up two cars with Scotch and rye and transported it to the double garage of a friend on Dorsey Street. Once there they covered all openings and started hoisting some of the cases up through the rear window and onto sleds, over which horseblankets and several sticks of wood were placed.

A local youth, who had a long Flexible Flyer fitted with a four-foot rack, was hired to assist in the evacuation chore and quickly piled seven or eight carefully-packed corrugated cases aboard. Then he started hauling the load up Sumner Place hill. Half-way up he heard a voice at his shoulder ask, "Need some help, sonny. Looks like a pretty heavy load!"

"No-o-o, I can make it O.K." said the lad, shaking in his boots as he turned and saw Constable Matt Jones loom up beside him. "Thanks just the sa-s-am-me!"

The obliging and much-liked officer nevertheless took hold of the rope and together they tugged the sled to the top of the hill and down to Broadway, where the trembling boy thanked the policeman again and continued on his way to his destination farther down the street.

In the meantime the two men back at the garage had also started hauling away a sled-load and from farther down the street anxiously watched the action, fully expecting that at any moment the roof would cave in on him and them. However, all concerned were greatly relieved to get a first-hand report from their young friend, who legged it back as fast as he could after disposing of the tell-tale evidence.

The bootleg business in the Saranac Lake area was so brisk in the mid-1920's that it drew in mobsters from Buffalo to Brooklyn who resorted to tough tactics in order to squeeze out or gain control over the traffic. Some of the local guild wisely decided to kowtow to the strangers but a few rugged independents defied them and paid the usual penalty. One family in particular lost both husband and wife in retaliation for alleged excessive watering of their still's high-octane alcohol combined with their detailed and potentially dangerous knowledge of their rivals' operations. The man never returned home after a short trip to a

Legs Diamond and Dan Prior, his lawyer

neighborhood store and the wife was apparently murdered in a manner to simulate suicide.

While Malone derived a degree of unwelcome — to many — publicity, Saranac Lake also had its exposure to gangsterdom in the occasional presence of Jack (Legs) Diamond, who earned his nickname by his ability to outrun cops back in his native Brooklyn. Thief, kidnapper, bootlegger, hi-jacker, extortioner, dope dealer and murderer he got his sadistic kicks from toasting the tootsies of his hog-tied victims. During his periodic shoot-outs with the Law and his other enemies he collected so much lead that he became known as the clay pigeon.

Although his main hangout was in the ultra-respectable Catskill village of Tannersville, from which he supervised the illicit liquor commerce from Albany to N.Y.C., one of his busiest distilleries, ostensibly a paint factory, was in Yonkers. There, an elaborate system of firehoses and electric control panels led from the plant through the city's sewer system and connected with a truck depot on the banks of the Hudson.

During this period Diamond's brother came down with T.B. and went to Saranac Lake to cure at Lynch's Cottage on upper Riverside Drive. Legs made several trips north to see him but, since his reputation was so unpleasant, the welcome sign was never displayed for his benefit. Moreover, since he was very high on the list of the most wanted criminals he was constantly under surveillance. Therefore his visits were generally nocturnal but on at least one occasion, according to Charlie Green, local grocer, he showed up in full daylight.

The observant Scotsman recalled that Legs was togged out in a well-tailored grey suit and jaunty blue polka dot bowtie. Accompanying him was a sleek, well-coiffed, attractive but frozen-faced blonde wearing an obviously expensive white fur coat. Just outside the door of the shop were two formidable characters on guard to make sure their boss was given proper treatment and protection. While they were standing there the local police-chief came along, glanced in their direction and, suddenly realizing their mission — discreetly crossed the road.

Even though his homebase was near Kingston, Legs often sought entertainment in the Rainbo Room of Albany's Hotel Kenmore, which featured all the big-name bands of the day — Cab Callaway, Ben Bernie, Tommy Dorsey, Hal Kemp et al. Usually with him was Kiki Roberts, ex-Ziegfield showgirl, and always present were several burly bodyguards. Since it was then considered downright fashionable to be on first name terms with underworld denizens, Legs always got a royal reception from management and guests alike. The bandleaders and vocalists were eager to play requests for his favorite ballad — "Happy Days and Lonely Nights."

In February, 1931 Diamond was tried in Troy on the charge of allegedly torturing by fire a rival Green County bootlegger. And this time the evidence was so strong that even the resourceful Dan Prior was unable to get him off the hook so Thomas Dewey, Assistant U.S. Attorney, thereby scored a legal victory that had eluded many other eager prosecutors over the years. But while free on bail pending his appeal Legs saved the State of New York considerable money by becoming the surprised recipient of three soft-nosed .38 caliber bullets fired at close range in his Dove Street, Albany, rooming-house. Those in the know claimed that he was the target of Schultz mob retribution.

While the visits of two gangsters can hardly be considered to be Adirondack highlights, they nevertheless made a considerable impact on the usually relatively uneventful life pattern of the region and provided ample opportunities for gossip sessions and animated conversations.....

By 1932 Americans realized that the great moral experiment had been an even greater moral disaster so F.D.R. was able to defeat incumbent Herbert Hoover very handily at the polls. With the national nightmare then over, other more crucial social problems such as the Great Depression and its massive unemployment agonies could get the top billing they urgently demanded.

And so the hectic, rip-roaring, rum-running years became part of Adirondack history leaving behind a fascinating residue of fortunes and misfortunes, adventures and misadventures, memories and legends.

Chapter 21

Paul Smith and His Yarns

As you check out the background of Adirondack personalities, it is rather amazing that so many of them came from Vermont. This is especially true of the very successful hotel-keepers such as the Stevens Brothers and Henry Allen of Lake Placid, Ferd and Mary Chase of the Loon Lake House and of course Apollos — shortened to Paul — Smith, unquestionably the most famous of them all. Stuart Holbrook in his classic *Yankee Exodus*, delved deeply into the brain drain from the doughty little Green Mountain State and analyzed the reasons why so many of its finest young people, confronted by the obviously limited prospects for a reasonably good life, reluctantly left home for greener pastures elsewhere. As one cynical individual aptly expressed it: "Although money admittedly isn't everything, it's a hell of a lot better than the next best thing." That salty observation recalls another equally pragmatic barb — "Those who had any git up and go got up and went." Whatever the reason the result was that Vermont — and the rest of New England and even upstate New York as well — has been incalculably handicapped by the departure of its most precious natural resource — its children.

Born in Milton, Vermont in 1825, the son of Philip Smith, a lumberman, Paul's first real job was on one of Peter Comstock's canal boats that carried grain and farm produce to New York and a return cargo of merchandise and foodstuff which they sold at the communities along the Vermont shore of Lake Champlain.

A died-in-the-wool hunter and trapper Smith headed as often as possible for the Loon Lake (Franklin County) region, where he made his headquarters at John Merrill's place. His skill as a guide and hunter, plus his affable personality, made him very popular so he finally decided to settle down in that area and start a resort of his own. In 1848 he rented Prentiss (Paint) Lovering's small stagecoach inn for three years before he built his place, Hunter's Home in 1852. This was located only a mile away on the North Branch of the Saranac River. Then he brought his father and mother over from Vermont to help him run the place. This sharp real estate deal — 211 acres at $1.50 an acre — was the first of many such acquisitions which eventually totaled nearly 40,000 acres, including ten lakes and numerous streams and 5,000 acres along the Saranac River.

Hunter's Home, which consisted of only one large living room and kitchen section and 8 or 10 thinly partitioned sleeping cubicles, was well patronized from the start by prominent Boston and New York City doctors and lawyers, but it was strictly a man's resort and there were no accommodations for women. Board was $1.50 per day; the guide got $2.00 for his services. Since there were no game protection laws in those days, most of the

Paul Smith's, St. Regis Lake — Stoddard Photo

Paul Smith's, St. Regis Lake — Later Photo

food came from the area woods and waters.

One of Paul's choicest and most scenic hunting grounds was Lower St. Regis Lake, a place which also intrigued Dr. Hezekiah Loomis of N.Y.C., who suggested that Paul build there and offered to advance the money to do so. Using all his own money — $350.00 — Smith bought 50 acres of the best land available and using Loomis' $13,000 he built a 17 room hotel, to which he kept adding every year thereafter.

During the Civil War period Paul had a houseful of wealthy young draft-dodgers who legally hired substitutes to do their fighting for them but who didn't care to face the embarrassment engendered thereby. By 1865 he had not only paid off the mortgage but had salted away $50,000 more besides.

From that time on he had it made. Guests flocked to the place in constantly increasing numbers and some of the most famous bought property from Paul so that they could build their own palatial "camps." One transaction, a sale of five acres to the Garrett family of Baltimore, netted him a cool $20,000 — which exactly matched the sum he had paid for 13,000 acres in the deal in which he outsmarted the smart Smith M. Weed of Plattsburgh. Within the next few years the old smoothie had sold building sites on Upper St. Regis Lake, Spitfire and Osgood Pond to Anson Phelps-Stokes, Frederick W. Vanderbilt, Whitelaw Reid and William McAlpin and about 100 other notables. The only big fish that slipped through his acquisitive fingers [he was land-poor at the time] was the chance to buy the 40,000 acres — at $1.50 per acre — around Brandon which was later picked up by William G. Rockefeller.

Much of his money came from lumbering. He had his own trees, his own sawmills which turned out lumber, shingles, window frames, doors and blinds. He also had his own stores and warehouses from which he sold supplies and camp furnishings. He founded an electric power and light company which supplied light and power not only to his own buildings but also to Saranac Lake and Lake Placid. To this he added a telephone company and generating plants at Piercefield, Franklin and Union Falls. Other investments were the Fouquet House in Plattsburgh, where he spent many winters before his California trips became his regular winter routine; the famous old Franklin Falls Hotel and the Mirror Lake *House* at Lake Placid. Obviously, if anyone ever was an expert at diversification, it was Paul Smith.

It may very well be an oversimplification but the main explanation for his success was Lydia Martin Smith's ability to cook good meals and Paul's prowess as a story-teller. Add to these attributes his refusal to kowtow to anyone regardless of his position and pedigree. Very likely the novelty of being treated like a man instead of like a bank-account was just what millionaires liked and needed.

Paul Smith's wit, like his proverbial Vermont shrewdness, was inherited from his almost equally sharp father. Nobody ever accused him of being an intellectual — his wife took care of that rarified department. Actually he looked upon book-learning with undis-guised contempt. One of his stock expressions and, incidentally, one used frequently by practical, mentally uncluttered people then and now — and for many valid reasons — was: "there's no fool like an educated (pronounced edjicated) fool." The backwoods prince felt strongly and correctly that you were born either with or without a legacy of keen-mindedness, that you profit by experience or you don't and are forced to fumble your way through life. To him and his numerous pragmatic kind, books and formal education were frills, distractions and handicaps — and he certainly exemplified his theories impressively. Although his own training was very sketchy and basic, he nevertheless proved on many occasions that he was more than a match for all the pompous, polysyllabic pedants and pundits who still unfortunately infest the halls and groves of academe and — perhaps even more regrettably — far too many of our nation's pulpits. Small wonder Oom Paul was unimpressed by those personages who were long on theory but short on practical experience.[1]

According to Dr. E. L. Trudeau, who spent several seasons and one winter with Smith and therefore knew and liked him well: "He had a keen, incisive sense of humor and was a jovial host, abounding in jokes and stories which he told at the expense of guides and sportsmen alike."

Paul proved to be a shrewd judge of women too. He never failed to give his wife full credit and praise for her great part in their many successes; they were married in 1859. A graduate of Emma Willard School in Troy, Lydia was a very intelligent business woman; she kept the accounts, wrote the contracts, did most of the buying, hiring and firing and kept the huge caravansary neat and comfortable in spite of the lack of central heating and the benison of running hot water.

The couple had three children — all boys — Henry, who died at the age of 29; Paul Jr., who died in 1927 and Phelps, who virtually took over the management of the complex of holdings after his father died, aged 87, on Dec. 15, 1912, in the Montreal Royal Victoria Hospital, from complications following a kidney operation. Phelps died in 1937. Mrs. Smith died in December 1891, less than a year after the death of Henry, her first-born son. Geraldine Collins, retired librarian at Paul Smith's College, had access to much of her correspondence and concluded that Mrs. Smith may very well have "grieved herself to death" over her great loss.

Phelps Smith's will stipulated that the estate, which was appraised at over two million dollars, should be used to endow a college specializing in forestry and hotel management, in memory of his father. The terms of the will and its exclusionary clauses aroused the ire and antagonism of a reputed twenty-two relatives who fought a long but losing legal battle to invalidate it. Lawyer's fees were also adjudged exorbitant and the concerned attorneys reluctantly settled for about a third of their original claims. But the Paul Smith's College of Arts and Science finally did open in 1947 and has since gained a well-deserved prominence among the ranks of the private, co-educational junior colleges.

While definitely snide in tone and mildly censorious the following article, which appeared on Jan. 29, 1937 in the Pleasantville *Press* and the *Vintnor News*, nevertheless reflects the calculated opinions of an editor who was thoroughly familiar with Paul Smith and his eventful career and could back up his premises with chapter and verse.

The Emancipation of Paul Smith

"The soul of Paul Smith, who started life as a loping Lake Champlain packet-boatman and Adirondack Mountain Guide, who could match language with any New York water-fronter and shoot a rifle accurately from either shoulder, is to inhabit a "College of Arts and Sciences," under the terms of the last will and testament of Phelps Smith, Paul's last surviving descendant, who has just passed on. Paul, who died 25 years ago, at the age of 87, was a gangling woodsman when Lydia Martin married him and pulled him from "The guides' side-hall" to the front as a hotel-keeper.

"Their hotel on Lower St. Regis Lake is said to have been more sought by prominent and wealthy New Yorkers during the draft-dodging days of the Civil War than anybody cared to admit. From Paul Smith's it was just a short distance to Canada.

[1] The brilliant Disraeli devastatingly categorized the breed as being afflicted with a "constipation of ideas but a diarrhea of words."

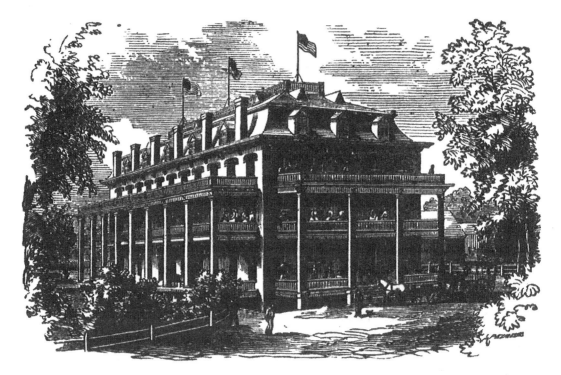

Fouquet House, Plattsburgh, owned by Paul Smith

Mirror Lake House, Lake Placid, Paul Smith, Vice-President   Stoddard Photo

Composite: upper left Paul Smith, Sr.; upper right Lydia Smith; lower left Phelps Smith; lower right Paul Smith, Jr.

"From information taken from a timber-looker's [cruiser's] land appraisal books, Paul saw where he could make a fortune by purchasing a great section of forests and lakes upon which the owner had defaulted in mortgage payments to the Mutual Life Insurance Company of New York, and from that sale developed the Paul Smith's preserve of 30,000 plus acres in which he sold water "camp" sites to distinguished men and women in social and financial circles of New York and Newport and at a price per site about equal to what he paid for the whole tract.

"A hotel at Blue Mountain Lake [The Prospect House] was the first in the world to install electric lights and Paul, not to be outdone, placed a dam in the St. Regis River, flooded the docks of the 'campers' or drew the water down so low that the docks became useless as boat-landings, as the demand upon his small hydro-electric plant varied with the goings and comings of his summer boarders. From the Keese's Mill plant he launched out to buy waterfalls and power sites throughout the region and flooded State-owned lands to engage in the hydro-electric development of power and lighting current and to contest with irate consumers who protested against the rate demanded and collected per kilowatt.

"After the death of old Paul, the youngest son — Paul Jr. weakened and sold his 48% of the vast holdings to the operators of a series of inter-locked electric companies, whose berths these past 10 years have been about as comfortable as the bed of a rocky mountain stream. Phelps Smith, lone survivor, bachelor and man of his own mind has carried on with 52% control. It was the indiscretions of Paul, Jr., his love of New York highlife, his unfavored marriage, his digressions into silver mining and other side money-making ventures and misadventures that swung the control of the Paul Smith properties to brother Phelps and thus made him "the richest man Franklin County has ever known."

"It is the final disposition of the fortune founded by Lydia Martin Smith and Paul Smith, under the terms of the will of Phelps Smith, that the endowment of a "College of Arts and Sciences" is to be built on a 5,000 acre reserve and subsidized to the extent of a couple million dollars, which climaxes the Smith family story.

"The queer part of it is that no one ever heard Paul Smith, Sr., complain about any lack of education. He could read a timber-estimator's book with no difficulty; he could bargain with the owner of a local power plant with the facility of a Gould or a Harriman; he could figure profits on merchandise and supplies he sold along with the camp sites. That Paul dropped his d's and his g's while entertaining his summer boarders detracted not a whit from his popularity. If anything these betrayals only added to his fame.

"There are no descendants of Paul and Lydia Smith but she had brothers and sisters and they had children of whom only two were recognized in bequests. These cousins of Phelps will receive a total of $1,500 a year for as long as they live.

"Could it be that the soul of the old pioneer will feel a little out of place when it comes to inhabit a "College of Arts and Sciences?"

According to Alfred L. Donaldson, premier Adirondack historian, who knew Paul Smith well and admired him greatly, he belonged in the same league with Mark Twain, whose story-telling manner was very similar. "He could put a champagne dryness into his voice, use the drawl, the pause, the facial grimace and the swift descriptive gesture with consummate skill and unpremeditated art. For years his stories were the verbal currency of the woods. They passed from mouth to mouth and men could cadge a drink by merely repeating the latest quip from the St. Regis jester."

There's a moss-grown adage to the effect that truth is not only stranger than fiction but twice as interesting. This was certainly applicable to many of Paul's apt remarks and anecdotes. One of the best and most characteristic situations arose during the early era at the rambling hotel and before the advent of the bellboys. A fussy guest had apparently spent several minutes yanking what he supposed was a bell pull. Finally and in a state of angry frustration he strode downstairs to vent his feelings to the manager, whom he found ensconced in a big chair on the front piazza (porch). He couldn't have picked a more inappropriate time because Paul, surrounded by a large group of intent listeners, was smack dab in the climax phase of one of his choicest yarns and, although considerably annoyed by his ranting guest, managed to hide his displeasure.

"What was it you wanted?" he quietly inquired.

"I want some water!" answered the exasperated one. Paul immediately sauntered into the hotel and returned with a pitcher, which he handed to the fractious man. Then Paul pointed emphatically to some fairly distant object. "There's the pump," he casually explained. "Go and help yourself and take all you want. There's plenty of water here for everybody." So said he returned to his wicker throne and resumed his fractured story. This was a typical instance and one that epitomized the place. No discourtesy intended — just simple, direct operating procedure. The guests either liked or lumped it: you either bitched and left in a twelve-cylinder huff or, after you had partly recovered from the somewhat disconcerting — even humiliating — shock you smiled, laughed and stayed — which most of them did. Often, enchanted by the wholesome and open charm exuded by the place and its colorful proprietor they and their friends would come back year after year for a seasonal dose of the same delightful woodsy therapy.

Uncle Paul always had some urgent business which required his prompt personal attention just about church time every Sunday but finally got trapped into promising the rector of St. John's-in-the-Wilderness that he would go if Mrs. Smith did, banking on the strong likelihood that she would legitimately be too busy to go so Paul, true to his word and finding that he couldn't weasel out, went to the service and gave the following report of his unusual experience:

"I got all mixed up: I got up when I should have stayed down and sat still when I should have stood up. Bye and bye I saw Dr. Trudeau coming down the aisle with a platter full of five and ten-dollar bills. I felt around in my pockets and couldn't find anything bigger than a torn dollar bill. When I put it tenderly on the plate the Doc leaned down and whispered 'Paul, that will return to you ten-fold.'

"Well now, I thought that was pretty good business but didn't pay too much attention to it. A little while afterwards, however, I was walking down one of the halls when I heard voices in one of the rooms. Inside there were four fellers playing poker. They invited me to take a hand so I did — and won $13.00. Then I hunted up Trudeau. "Doc," I said, "I heard what you whispered to me in church about the 10-1 business but you had it a mite wrong. You said I'd get my money back ten-fold but I want you to know that I just won $13.00 in a poker game."

Another classic Smith anecdote also had a religious overtone: "I once lent $40.00 to a blacksmith who did a little preaching on the side. He was poor and couldn't pay me, but I was a good waiter and finally got my money back. Several years after I made the loan some of the wealthy people boarding with me asked if we could have a Sunday service. I told 'em course we could and asked 'em — how they'd like to have a blacksmith-preacher conduct the meeting. Oh, wouldn't they be dee-lighted. So I got the blacksmith and he held forth. The people liked his sermon and as it was easy to see that he was poor they passed the hat and all chipped in liberally, some even dropping ten-dollar bills in.

"When it was all over I tipped the preacher the wink that I wanted to see him in

St. John's in the Wilderness — Stoddard Photo

another room. When he got there I said, 'Now you can pay me that $40.00.'

'Sure thing.' said he, for he was honest enough. 'But hadn't we better go off somewhere in the woods because it'll look funny if anyone sees me forking out money to you?'

"He was right of course so we headed for the tall timber, he with a pocketful of expectations. We sat down on a fallen tree to sort out the forty from the wad of crumpled bills.

"However, we didn't realize that some of the men had followed us to see if the preacher and I were planning to hold a special meetin' out there in the woods. They saw him pass the money to me and of course thought it was a divvy deal. Well now, I tell you they weren't bashful about speaking of the matter. It cost me several times that $40.00 before all the men had finished 'smiling' over the affair."

Paul could also handle dialects pretty well as indicated by this dilly: "Angus McTavish, who use to work here, was no feelin' just weel so he hied heemself to a doctor and described his complaint.

'What do you drink?' asked the medic.

'Whiskey.'

'How much?'

'Maybe buttle a day.'

'Smoke?'

'Yus.'

'How much?'

'Two ounces a day.'

'Well, here's my advice: give up drinking and smoking altogether!'

"Andy picked up his cap and in three steps was at the office door.

'Andy,' called out the M.D., 'you didn't pay me for my advice!'

'Ah dinna owe ye nuthin bekuz ahm no a-takin it!' snapped Andy as he slammed the door behind him."

Another example of Paul Smith's business acumen is shown by his handling of the sale of a certain camp-site on a picturesque point in Upper St. Regis lake, for which he felt that he could get about $3,000. He visited around until he found a likely customer. After the usual preliminaries the summer resident inquired about the price tag and Paul told him to work it out with the boys. In the meantime he saw them first and briefed them on the prospective buyer.

When the wealthy prospect did contact Paul Jr. and Phelps, they quoted him a figure of $10,000. Still reeling from the shock he went directly to the father and blurted out: "Say, Paul, what do you think Phelps wants for that lot we were talking about the other day?"

"Don't know," replied Paul.

"Well — I'll have you know that they want $10,000!"

"Too much, much too much!" exclaimed the wily one. "Why they're robbers! Now I'll tell you what we can do. I'll sell you that piece of land for $6,000 and take my chances."

"Sold!" chortled the wealthy one.

Still another revelation of Uncle Paul's ability to manipulate people took place one busy day at the height of the season. A new arrival was remarking about the deplorably crowded condition of another hotel where he had recently stayed over-night. He claimed that there were four guests assigned to his room and that he was informed that he either had to put up with it or else sleep in the parlor, which was already occupied by 18 or 20 others.

"Why, that's nothing!" Paul assured him, "you should have come up here before there were so many hotels. Things were really crowded then. Why, I remember oncet a fella came to the desk and squawked about the size of his bill — said it was far too much for what little service he was gettin'. You know, we really had people sleeping everywhere. The place was so packed that my son Phelps and my clerk Jack Harding used to have a race every night to see who would get to sleep on the last couch. Then, I asked the complainer where he had been sleeping.

'On the billiard table.'

"Why," said I, "don't you know that we get $2.00 an hour for that table? It's the only one in the mountains. Believe you me — that shut him up but fast!"

The story-pump being well primed now, Paul squeezed out another somewhat similar but rather more pathetic incident: "This time it was an ordinarily patient and accommodating New Yorker who, after three hectic nights, apparently couldn't put up with his particular predicament another night so he looked me up and came flat out with a minor ultimatum.

'Paul,' he declared, 'you'll just have to find me another place to sleep!'

"Where in thunder are you sleeping now?" I asked.

'Well,' began the feller, 'it's this way. I've been sleeping on a sick man but he's much better now and won't stand for it much longer!'"

During his waning years "Uncle Paul" spent his August afternoons talking with friends on the big, lake-facing front veranda and cautioning would-be woodmen about the dangers that lurk in the forest — especially from the horrible haw-yaw, the sinister-swamp-sogger and the vicious man-devouring side-hill sweeper.

One day Fred Penfield commented on the fact that P. S. had been postmaster for a remarkably long time. "How come," he asked, "that you keep right on holding the job through every change of administration?" "Well, Mr. Penfield, I'll tell you exactly how it

Guide House at Paul Smith's — Stoddard Photo

Afternoon Tea, Paul Smith's

241

happens," he drawled. "There ain't no administration that can change any quicker than what I can!"

Paul Smith Jr., told Editor Goldthwaite of the *Adirondack Daily Enterprise* the concluding story in this anthology of yarns, a story that his father told many times. It happened about 1888 on the Beaver River. At the time Dr. Seward Webb was just getting ready to build the Adirondack & St. Lawrence R.R. and invited several of his best friends to spend a Sunday at the Kildare Club. Frederick Vanderbilt, who later put up the Japanese camp on Upper St. Regis, was also in the party. P.S. went in Webb's boat with Fitz Halleck as guide. There were five or six guideboats in all, including one carrying C. M. Eaton, who later built the swanky Ampersand Hotel on Lower Saranac. His guide was a cross-eyed fellow, a former bartender at the Berkeley House in Saranac Lake. They spent the night at the Club and next day went down to Little Rapids on the Beaver, where Webb had about 12 engineers, who had been there about three weeks and had run out of meat.

About 3 p.m. the owner of the small hotel where they had dinner drove in his cows from their pasture. Among the cattle was a very big bull.

Webb looked him over and asked, "What will you take for that bull?"

"About $45.00," answered the owner.

"I'll take him!" announced Webb.

The boats were parked about two miles above the Rapids so Webb asked the seller to drive the animal to the carry. When they got there Webb said, "We'll kill the bull here, load him into the boats and take him up with us."

A Killdare Club guide had done a lot of butchering and the cross-eyed guy had a rifle.

"I saw a big stump nearby," as Paul told it, "and warned Webb to climb it because it was hard to tell what might happen next. Webb declared that he'd join me — and did."

One of the other men then took hold of the rope and the cross-eyed individual prepared to do his job. Hesitatingly he drew what he considered to be a bead on his massive target.

"Now hold on thar!" shouted the ropeholder.

"What's the matter?" asked the rifleman, getting set again.

"Do you always shoot where you look?"

"Of course I do!"

"Well, then I refuse to hold this rope!" Thereupon he dropped the tether and took to his heels. As the intended target hadn't moved, the crossed-optics hombre took steady aim at the bull's head -- and shot him in the stomach! Now I tell you, you never saw a sicker-looking bull in your life but by standing directly over him and at point-blank range the man finally got in a shot to the head that finished the obliging critter"....

As is so often the case, by far the best stories have a solid factual basis and are therefore much more believable and memorable than those which are spawned by great imaginative effort. Told with due attention to effective delivery techniques and personal flourishes, such as those practiced by Mart and Harvey Moody, Henry van Hoevenberg, Ferd Chase and other such gifted and garrulous people — with Paul Smith up there very near the top of the tall story totem pole. These mountain Munchausens richly deserve their own special niches in any Adirondack Hall of Fame.

Sharing the billing and the credit should be the authors who first gave the story-tellers their fame — purple prose purveyors such as Charles F. Hoffman, Alfred B. Street, Joel T. Headley, S.H. Hammond, Jeptha R. Simms, Adirondack Murray, Seneca Ray Stoddard, Irving Batcheller, Alfred L. Donaldson and Harvey L. Dunham — for his superb *French Louie*. These were the truly gifted ones who made the greatest contribution to Adirondack literary lore.

Too bad they broke the mold and don't make them like that any more.

My good friend Bill Petty recently summed up the situation very aptly and succinctly when he remarked, "Yup, the color has sure gone from the Adirondacks!" And by that he didn't mean that the Autumn foliage season had gone by for another year. Too bad indeed!

Martin's, Lower Saranac Lake — Stoddard Photo

Martin's, Ready to Shove Off — Stoddard Photo [Stereoscopic View]

Chapter 22

The Moody Guides and Their Ear-Benders

Jacob Moody, the first permanent settler in the Saranac region, having arrived there in 1819, was the father and grandfather of a numerous and deservedly prominent Adirondack family. Five of his sons lived to become famous hunters, trappers and guides who had far more than just a local reputation since their names occur frequently in many of the early Adirondack travelogs. Although Smith and Daniel were undoubtedly competent and interesting men, their brothers Harvey, Cort (Cortez) — and especially Mart — attracted the most publicity.

The first really big literary break for the newsworthy clan came in the late 1850's when Alfred B. Street, the New York State Librarian and a group of his friends started from Baker's, near Lower Saranac Lake, on a leisurely hunting and fishing trip through the Saranacs, up the Raquette to Long Lake, then back down the river to Tupper Lake and, after several side-trips to the picturesque smaller ponds, back to their starting point and homeward via Whiteface Mountain.

All through the fascinating book, entitled *Woods and Waters*, Harvey, the oldest Moody, was not only the boss guide but also the featured raconteur. The author gave Harvey front stage center every evening before the campfire and his reservoir of exciting experiences and creative talent never ceased to produce top-drawer entertainment for the whole party. Harvey was by common consent the best area authority on Indian lore and his stories of Old Sabele and other Redmen are just about the best and earliest sources available. Interestingly enough, although Mart, along with Cort and Harvey's sons — Phineas and William — was also in the party, he contributed relatively little from the vast repertoire of yarns for which he later was celebrated. Very likely at this stage of the game he was content to watch his garrulous brother in action and thus learn matter and manner from an acknowledged expert.

But here's Street's visual reaction to his head guide: "He was dressed in the sober colors I found it his custom to wear; thus blending himself with the natural hues of his haunts, so as not to startle his game — the hues of the oozy shore, where he set his mink-trap; of the bark of the runway trees, where he lurked for his deer; the log at the pool where he stealthily approached to lure the trout; the sand-banks and gravel-beds of the stream where he prowled for the otter and the dawn and evening grays of the shallows where he tried to waylay the fisher and the muskrat." [Slightly purplish prose but nevertheless good]

And here's a sample of Harvey's enthusiastic patter. In answer to Renning's inquiry

---

[1] Street, Alfred B. *Woods and Waters* or The Saranac and Racket (sic) N.Y. M. Doolady, 1860.

Jacob Moody, Earliest Saranac Lake Resident

about the sporting potential of Racket Falls, Harvey expounded thus: "Fust best! You can't git no better place then Racket Falls and all above and then all the way down to Tupper's Lake. Well, now, as fur fishin' you won't hev much till you git to Palmer's Brook — then there's the Falls — then Cold Brook — then Cold River. As fer thet Cold River, you may bleeve there's trout there, and some on 'em full grown too. As fur huntin', the deer's around up about those slews. It's real inkstand there with 'em. There's Stony Slew and Loon Slew and Moose Slew," counting on his fingers, "below the Falls, and Moose Creek above. Ef there ain't the places fur night huntin' then there ain't none; and ef you could git only two or three of them big bucks I've seed at Moose Slew alone, you might hold up your head like a schoolmarm. It's all sorts of a nice place, I_____."

Harvey's story of old Sabele is a grade A bonafide Adirondack classic: "Sabele was an old Injin. I knowed 'im well. When I fust knowed 'im he was shantyin' where old Leo is campin' now, jest above Racket Pond. He was as good a shot at a deer, and could ketch as big a lot o'trout ez the next man, and he wan't no man's fool at trappin'. He wuz an orful old critter, though. When he got mad... was as smart, active a man for his years ez I've most ever seen an' ez a ginral thing wuz purty good-natured. But when he got rum aboard, look out! Why he'd kick an' dance about, and keep his tommyhawk a-goin' and sssss-sing, he would sing like a dozen bagpipes "Hah, hah, slammerawhang, hooh,' he'd go. 'hah hah wah-hay.... Well, he useta tell me some o' the terr'blest long yarns about what he did when he wuz a young man in Canady in the last war. He fit fur us he said and he musta bin round some, 'cordin' to his tell. 'Sabele,' he usta say, 'put on der war *paint* — all red on one side de face an black on toder — den he dance de war *dance*, an' hit de war *post* all down to

246

no-*ting*, an' den he took de war-trail; thet is he went out on a gin'ral spree agin the British, a tomahawkin' an' a sculpin — there's a blue jee agin! What a squawkin' sarpent 'tis — the wust way!

"He wuz livin with his tribe on the 'Tawy (Ottawa) River, and fell in love with a white gal — what a tattin' that plaguey woodpecker keeps up! But as I wuz sayin 'bout Old Sabele. This white gal wuz the darter of an old trapper thet lived nigh the tribe. Now as Old Sanko would hev it there wuz two things agin Sabele an' the gal: one wuz that it wuz agin the law o' the tribe fur to marry enny but Injins, an tother wuz the old chief of the tribe wanted Sabele to marry his own darter an' as he wuz a bright, smart, actyve chap an' a great warryor (as the Injins calls their fightin' charackters), the old chief — let's see, what wuz his name? — Well, I fergit it; but no matter, he forbid the match. But thet didn't make not a mite o'diff'rence with their feelins — thet is Sabele and the gal — they had sech a orful sight o'love aboard. So the old chief, ez you may s'pose, didn't like it at all.

"But afore he did ennything, he had a talk with Sabele. Old S. has telled men this ere talk more'n twenty times. When he got very drunk he useta tell it, I tell yer, with all the hifilutins.

"Well, the old chief, s'ze to Sabele, s'ze 'Wing o' the clouds,' s'ze, 'Eagle o the sun!' The old — lemme see — wuz it oak? I disremember, but 'twas some old tree or tother — the old whatever 'twas — cedar, white pine or maple fur all I know is now — the idee wuz — a tott'rin'like — an'll soon — the idee wuz — fall down — that is — the p'int on't wuz — thet the old chief might soon die off en then the Eagle — if so be he behaved 'imself — would be head o' the tribe. 'But,' s'ze, 'listen,' s'ze, 'the Eagle,' s'ze, 'when he — kinder tries, you know, to fly right agin a blast o'wind — w-e-l-l — a harricane like — thet's the idee — he's — the idee wuz — throwed back catwallopus right agin the rock, where — ez a body may say — he breaks all the bones in his carcass!...

"When the old chief heerd o' the love scrape — I hed a bit then but I guess 'twas only a minnie — he hed quite a jaw with Sabele, a 'smoothin' on 'im at fust by callin' him an Eagle en so on, which I don't think, fur myself, wuz enny great shakes 'us a name. I don't think half ez much o' an' eagle ez a fish-hawk — one's honest an t'other ain't!! I can't give yer all the speech, but the long an' the short uv it wuz that it didn't do no good, an' so the old chief wuz detarmined on suthin else. So — aha, how de do, sir!" (jerking up a big trout, breaking its neck on the boat's edge and casting it to the bottom), "so one day Sabele went — these deerflies bite most as bad ez mitchets this mornin' — he went to see his gal, an' found the old trapper dyin' — hold 'im well up, Mr. Smith! taut line — not too taut though or he'll break away! — jest so thet he'll feel the bit. Give 'im line now! That's a two-pounder!

"But ez I wuz a sayin' there wuz the old trapper dyin' and the gal dead, and the trapper telled Sabele thet the old chief an' another fightin charackter 'ad come to the shanty an 'ad tommyhawked an' sculped 'm both. Now, wa'nt Sabele mad? Wa'nt he though? I tell yer he could a chawed up a wolf-trap 'cordin' to his tell! His heart wuz a bustin' too — massy alive — I b'lieve I've got the great grand'ther uv all the trout in this ere part o' the country on my hook! sizz — whizz — don't ye wish yer could git off? — but yer can't, yer know. There, yer hed to give up, didn't yer — though yer ain't so big ez I thought yer was!" Then he hoisted in an immense trout, broke its neck and tossed him down among the others.

"Well, when Sabele found he couldn't let inter the old chief he sez to 'im, s'ze — I can't give it to yer ez the old feller used ter, 'tickelly when he's drunk (which wuz, 'twixt you an' me, nigh about all the time) for he'd go high up, I tell yer, like a crow in a gutter — but the idee wuz you — that is, ef you, as a body may say, was dreffle mad, and wanted to tell a man he wuz a — I dunno ez as I know 'zactly how to say it — but if you thought he wuz a great villyan, an' scoundrel, an' rascal, and mean feller, you'd say, wouldn't ye? and mebby not say it scripter fashion nuther — well this was the idee on't. Sabele said to the old chief, "You con-demned old villyan! I've found yer out! You've killed the gal! — Them wan't the words but thet wuz the idee, the p'int on't.

"'S'posen I did!' said the old sarpent, 'thet's my business!'

"Well it's my business too," sez old Sabele — he wuz young Sabele then though — 'tisn't the rael words but the idee — 'an' I'm a-going to let daylight thru yer dod-darned old pictur-frame!' With that he rips out his knife agin' but they held him back tight agin by his coat-tails -no-not coat-tails, fur Injins don't wear none a bit more'n a frog — but they held him back enny way 'So, s'ze — they is Sabeles'ze — 'yer want me to marry yer darter! now, go to the' — that is Sabele s'ze — the idee wuz — go to t'other place with yer darter an I'll go to Texas — thet is there wa'nt no Texas but thet wuz the idee — an' with thet he turns on his heels an' off he goes. At first he felt so bad he thought he'd kill himself. But then decided thet this love business is no killin' matter.

"Now, he'd heered tell o'this wilderness region so he came down here to git a living' an the fust I knowed uv him he wuz ashantyin' on Long Island in the lake here. He used to hunt and trap an fish there an' then he went to Injin Park at the outlet. An' then further down to where I telled yer — where old Leo is now. Finally at least he — that is Sabele — got to be old and ragged an' went back to Canady an' found' all the tribe gone west; en then he cum back an' wuz dreffle lonesome, and got the rheumatiz an' couldn't trap much, nur hunt, nur fish, fur thet matter, an' didn't git no money an' couldn't git no rum caze he hadn't no fur, nur no venison, nur no trout, nur no nothin' ta git rum with, and nobody 'ud give 'im enny an' the older I grow the more I see thet nobody don't give much to nobdy ennyway — an' so when he foun' he couldn't git no rum he made up his mind he wouldn't live no longer, an got in his canoe an' went singin' his death song, as he called it. I heerd Sabele one time, when he wuzn't as drunk as common! oh, how he did d-r-o-n-e and draw-l-l it out, hah-hah-je-me-seddy-hah-hah-massy on us! Hah-hah-'lasses candy, an then he'd give the warhoop. Well, ez I wuz sayin', he went floatin' down the Racket, an' finally at last he went whipperty fling over — there's a duck, a copperhead [Mallard] I'll fetch him." Throwing down his rod the bird fell with Harvey's bullet directly through the green polish on his head.

"Where did he go over, Harvey?"

"He went over Pussyville [Piercefield] Falls, an' ennybody that wants to go over them, may go an' be darned. 'Twon't be me, this year at any rate!"

Although this ending was possible — and what isn't for that matter ? — it was nevertheless highly improbable. Not very much is known about Sabael (or Sabele) Benedict and very little of that can be thoroughly substantiated. Ted Aber and the late Stella King have documented most of the available information in their hefty *History of Hamilton County*. Originally a Penobscot Indian he was born on that Maine river about 1747. He later joined the Abenakis, a Canadian tribe. When 12 he was present at the Battle of Quebec when Wolfe and Montcalm both were killed and the French rule came to an end. The youngster was helping his father to supply the British invaders with provisions.

During the Revolutionary War the Abenakis aided the British but the unsympathetic Sabael promptly left that tribe and headed for the mid-Adirondack wilderness where he was credited with the discovery of Indian Lake, then a chain of three small ponds. A relatively short but powerful man, his most distinguishing feature was a nose permanently flattened by the kick of a horse. According to Rev. John Todd, Sabael's worldly goods

248

consisted of a few deerskins, a pot and a frying pan. Both the old buck and his equally legendary son, Lewis Elijah (who guided the Henderson party to the iron dam at Tahawus in 1826) were much addicted to alcohol. Old Sabael told Dr. Todd that he found the rich Keeseville iron deposit but had sold it to a white man for a bushel of corn and a dollar.

. Like his friends and relatives, the Sabattises, Old Sabael hunted, fished and trapped over much of the Adirondacks and had outpost camps in many sections so it is quite logical that Harvey Moody would have encountered him often.

What actually did happen to the old Indian will probably never be known. There are three options open; — (1) that he was murdered by a French-Canadian lumberjack named Sav'ree [no doubt a corruption of Savarie] for the money he had acquired by a recent fur sale, (2) that he had been killed by his own son, a rather far-fetched story and (3) that, aged about 110, he had disappeared while on a long trip starting from 13th Lake, where he was last seen. His body was never located. Figure it out for yourself.

As readily seen Harvey excelled in the long drawn-out, frequently interrupted but nevertheless suspenseful type of narrative which required a considerable degree of acting ability and effective use of the dramatic pause. This is also the type of story that requires not only imaginative power but a fly-paper memory as well. Moreover, it is the category of tall story or ear-bender that can be expanded, subjected to flash-back treatment, chopped up into installments and, like Scheherazade's Thousand and One Nights technical mastery, served up as countless campfire fodder. Harvey had an endless array of these and apparently parlayed them into many encores as the favored and favorite guide-spellbinder of his era.

Mart, his younger brother, preferred the shorter variety of yarns; many of which show a definite familiarity with the preposterous but nevertheless amusing whoppers made popular by the noted or notorious Baron Munchausen.

Just what was the secret of the better-than-average tall tales dispensed by the more extroverted and flamboyant of the Adirondack guides? Their stock of stories of course consisted mostly of the tried and true numbers that found easy and welcome circulation even in those days of slow communication. The tale-tellers would then add their own personal, topical treatments to disguise the source and make their product sound original. Very few incidentally, were of the latrinal type but were more like those purveyed by Will Rogers, Mark Twain or Bill Nye. Their stories were basically believable but unlike those gifted artists, theirs were seldom subtle — as you'll readily notice when reading Mart's ter-radiddling efforts.

Born in Saranac Lake in 1833, Mart married Minerva M. Read of Bloomingdale in 1861. In 1868, feeling that he wanted more lebensraum (elbow room), he moved to Tupper Lake, which was anything but crowded in those days, as well as nowadays. There, on Big Tupper he built The Tupper Lake House, a small place that he soon outgrew and then put up a considerably larger resort — The Mount Morris House — in 1879. When this one burned he rebuilt it in 1889 and changed its name to Redside Camp, after the small brook which flows into the lake nearby.

In 1893 it was purchased by Jabez Alexander, who operated it for more than fifty years and then turned it over to Percy, his son, who tore most of it down in 1946 and then resumed business as the Waukesha Cabins. Incidentally this is the same Alexander family that built the Alexander House (later changed to the Algonquin) on Lower Saranac Lake in 1884.

All of the Moody boys guided most of the most distinguished visitors that ever came to the Adirondacks but Mart's clients were unquestionably the most prominent. Besides Street

Mart Moody, 1833-1910 — Stoddard Photo

Moody's Mt. Morris House, Tupper Lake — Stoddard Photo

250

and J. T. Headley, whom he guided while still in his early twenties, he was also among those hired in 1848 to convoy Gov. Horatio Seymour, accompanied by Lady Amelia Murray, supposedly the first female to traverse the Adirondacks. He lived for a while with swash-buckling Ned Buntline ("Col." Edward Zane Carroll Judson) at Eagle Nest in the Eckford Chain. Other credits were his acquaintance with Gerritt Smith, the wealthy Abolitionist and patron of John Brown, whose body Mart helped lower into a lonely North Elba grave on Dec. 8, 1859. Besides being the favorite guide of Presidents Chester A. Arthur and Grover Cleveland, he worked for the Emerson party at the Philosophers' Camp, for Adirondack Murray, Wallace, Stoddard, Ely, Colvin et al.

About 1887 Cleveland and Alton B. Parker, N.Y.S. Supreme Court judge and later on Theodore Roosevelt's opponent for the presidency in 1904, stopped off at Moody's on their way through from the Saranacs to the Fulton Chain. What was intended to be an over-night stop was stretched to a three-day stay, due mainly to the visitors' delight with Uncle Mart's tall stories and congenial entertainment. Cleveland later showed his appreciation by making Moody's hotel a fourth class post office and Mart the postmaster.

Prior to his departure the President also invited Mart to visit him in Washington and Mart accepted. Upon his return he was of course asked by excited and curious neighbors to supply details of his trip. One woman asked, "Mart, what was Mrs. Cleveland like?"

"Well, you see, it was a Monday," Mart replied, "and Mrs. C. was busy washing so I didn't see her." Typical but not in the same league with his hunting and fishing stories.

One story was about the time when Mart and his friend Hi were out on the lake shooting ducks. It was one of those halcyonic days when you could see way into the depths of sky and water. Suddenly a flock went winging past and for about the only time in his life Mart lost his cool and dropped his powder-horn overboard. Hi, an excellent swimmer, offered to retrieve the horn and Mart obligingly gave his consent — and down plunged Hi. After a long wait and still no sign of his accommodating friend, Mart peered impatiently into the crystal-clear water. "And what did I see?" Mart would ask at that point in the story. "I see that ornery cuss sittin' down there on the bottom of the lake a-pourin' powder out of my horn and inter his'n." They tell the same story in Vermont with Ethan Allen as the principal character.

Once Mart actually missed a fairly easy shot at a sizeable deer. Completely disgusted he strode over to the nearest hardwood tree and proceeded to wrap his gun around the trunk, thus twisting the barrel into a sloppy letter S. Then he strolled on until he suddenly saw an impressive buck browsing at the foot of a small mountain. Forgetting about his disabled gun Mart let go with a fast shot.

Then Mart would stop for a few seconds until someone would eventually ask, "What happened then, Mart? Didja miss him?"

"Well, yes," he would admit, "I missed the buck but I didn't do so bad after all. You see, the shot out of that twisted barrel went three times around the mountain and killed two bears and a woodchuck. I mention the woodchuck to keep the story accurate."

Adirondack luck and split-second timing combined one day when Mart was in his guideboat busily chopping away at a big tree that blocked his line of sight toward a well-traveled runway leading to the lakeshore. "You know," he would say, "after all my careful plannin' the danged tree didn't fall as I expected; in fact it dropped right across the bow of the boat, flippin' me and my dog out and turnin' the boat end for end in the air. While I was still floatin' in the sky I see the good old boat land right side up in the water. So I give myself an extra flip and the next thing I know I landed square on my center seat, slick's a mink. Kinda shook me up of course so I started a-rowin' fer home. When I got about half-way there, I heered the dog a-barkin' — you know I'd clean fergot about him. He sounded as though he wuz up in the sky. I looked up and sure enuff there I saw a little speck up there about the size of a fly. It come closer'n closer and kep gettin' bigger 'n bigger until I see, b'Jeepers, that it was my old dog. I thought quick, sculled the oars a little — and what dya-know, that dog landed smack dab in the seat he allus rides on!..."

"The fact is, boys, that in these mountains you have to think fast and even then it may not do you any good. There was that day on Ampersand Mountain when a couple bears chased me. I run up a ravine that wuz jes' wide enuff for one bear; thought I'd fight 'em one at a time. Jes'as I wuz ready to turn 'round and take care ovem, I see another bear comin' at me from the other end of the gully. Yep, you sure do hev to think fast in the mountains!"

Here Mart would knock the ashes out of his pipe and pretend to head for the door. Someone would be sure to call out: "Hey, Mart! You haven't finished that story! What did you do then?" Mart would pause with his hand on the doorknob. "Do?" he would exclaim, "I didn't do a dumb thing... the bears et me!"

About that time in the session he would turn to his wife and say, "Now wa'nt that so, Minervy? Wa'nt that so?" And without stopping or even looking up from her work, she would reply: "Why, yes, Mart....Now what was that you were saying?"

One day in February Mart was out hunting deer. Pussyfooting around a steep and narrow ledge he lost his footing and fell into a huge snowdrift. "Now how was I supposed to get out?" he would ask. "Well, I'll tell you that I wondered and thought and then thought and wondered some more. Finally I made up my mind — I walked the three miles home, got a shovel an' dug myself out. How's that fer bein' frustrated?"

Another of Uncle Mart's whoppers had to do with his capture of a live deer. "We had plenty of meat," he said, "so I didn't feel bad when I came upon a young buck one Fall afternoon — and I didn't hev a gun along. The deer was astandin' jes' under a ledge thet I was on and never noticed me atall. The longer I looked at him the more I wanted him for future meat becuz he was so young and fat.

"So I made up my mind, made a leap off'n the ledge and landed astraddlin' his back. 'Fore he got over his 'sprize, I grabbed holt of his horns and headed him toward my barn. He took off lickety-split through the woods with me rough-ridin him like all gitout.

"When we got in sight of the farm, I yelled to one of the boys to open up the barn door. He got there jes' as we galloped into the barnyard so I steered 'im right through the door. He fetched up, still runnin' strong, smack against the back wall and the shock sorta stunned us both.

"We kep' 'im till we needed more meat an' then I knocked im on the head. Mighty good eatin' too!"

One day one of his village friends asked Mart what he thought was the best bait to use to catch pickerel through the ice. "Well, now, thet's a funny thing," said Mart. "I wuz out jes' yesterday and didn't hev no luck fer hours. It wuz perty cold so the holes kep' afreezin' over. Oncet I bent over to stir up the scum to keep them open. I hed on a red tie that hung outa my vest. The end of it touched the water and no more'n it touched when a six-pound pickerel comes rushin' up and jumps clean outa the hole after that tie. I gives him a rap with the side-a my hand and knocks him outen the ice. Then, sir, I took off my tie and dangled it over the openin'. You know, those dog-goned fish kept arisin' fer it an every time one jumped clean I booted him over to one side. They kep' ajumpin and I kep' on a-kickin' and in jes' one hour I kicked me out six bushels of them pickerel."...

"Boys, I'm only tellin' the truth." declared Mart. The uproar that followed Warren Slater's account of the strange death of a deer that died of fright after a sport had shot at it

252

subsided immediately when Mart spoke out.[1]

"I jined the church." he continued and a home-sick expression came into his eyes. The incredulity of Slater's story died out quickly. All faces became grave and serious but the gravest of all was Moody's. "Seven years ago I jined the Methodist Church and since then I've been tellin' only the truth. Now there wuz a time when I could tell as big a lie as the next feller but I ain't as spry ez I once was. My imagination ain't what it useta be.

"But I've seen some strange things in my day. Yessir, I once tracked a deer round'n round a mountain but couldn't ketch up with it. Finally I got desprit. I swung my gun aginst a tree and bent the barrel. Then I jedged the distance 'n pulled the trigger. You won't b'lieve it but that bullet cut off all four leggs of that dab-blamed deer. Remarkable incident that, how things managed to be jedged so beats me."

"Yes and I've seen it rain so hard down at our place that you would think a cloud had busted but to us it would be nuthin' more'n a shower. Minerva wanted me to get up the other night 'n move nother rain barrel. An' it actually rained so hard through the bunghole thet the water couldn't git out tha two ends!

"Funny? If you think that wuz funny let me tell you about our old cat. Minervie'n I had a cat once thet beat all the other cats you ever heard of. We both loved her an' made a great pet outa her. Bimeby she begun to have fits. We put up with everythin' cuz we loved her until she begun to hev those awful spells. We'd bin thinkin' 'bout killin' her but those fits settled it. Minervie 'n I discussed the various ways uv killin' cats. We wanted to make sure uv the job but yet we wanted to do it in the humanest way possible. We decided thet I should cut her head off 'n throw it into the Lake, but Minervie wouldn't help so I hedta do it all alone.

"I put the pieces in the boat 'n rowed downta the foot of the Lake. There I dropped in the head. Next I rowed up to Bog River Falls where I threw in the body all weighted down with stones. When I got home I told my wife what I'd done. Told her I thought it wuz a good job 'n she agreed. But what do you s'spose happened?.... Along 'bout mornin I heerd a noise at the door. Sounded jes' like that old cat wantin' to come in. Minervie thought it wuz a mite spooky but nevertheless I opened the door...An' thar she wuz — our old pet cat — carryin' her head in mouth!!"

These are only a fair sampling of the scope of "Uncle Mart's" tale-telling prowess. Between the two — Harvey and Mart — the mountain Munchausens — there's more than enough material to fill a good-sized book, which would be very representative of the infinite variety and variations of campfire entertainment which made such night funfare memorable for many appreciative sportsmen who, in other surroundings, would be rather difficult to amuse....

Cortez Fernandez Moody — Cort for short — was born in 1822, the first recorded birth within the present-day village limits of Saranac Lake. The foreign connection was nil and apparently was inconsiderately bestowed upon him as a tribute to the celebrated conquistador who pillaged Mexico. Although he was every bit as good a guide as his brothers, he did not have their flair and flamboyance and so was overshadowed by them.

The Saranac Lakes were Cort's favorite stamping grounds; his main bailiwick for years was on Deer Island, opposite the present Wawbeek Hotel on the Upper Lake. In 1850 he decided that he would push even farther into the wilderness, so he bought the cabin and "improvements" at the foot of Lake Simond, near the Moody bridge, from the legendary Elijah (Lige) Simond, originally from Elizabethtown, a pioneer settler, hunter and trapper

---

[1] From this point on through the cat story the material came from an article by Kenneth Goldthwaite entitled "A Few Minutes with Uncle Mart Moody," which appeared in *Forest Leaves*, Autumn 1904.

Cort [Cortez] Moody, 1822-1902

who ranged over the entire northern and central Adirondacks before making the Tupper area his headquarters in the early 1840's. Later on Cort sold his place to George McBride, whose son Jim became a well-known Tupper Lake engineer and surveyor.

In the Autumn 1904 issue of *Forest Leaves*, published at Sanitarium Gabriels, there is a droll description of Cort plus a short anecdote about him. This was written by F.D.K. (probably Frederick Kilburn) of Albany:

"Cort Moody was about six feet six, had deep-set eyes, long black hair hanging through a hole in the top of an old slouch hat. Bushy eyebrows, more than a suspicion of tobacco at each corner of his mouth and deaf as the proverbial fencepost; picturesque in appearance and prolific in innocent profanity.

A priest guided by Cort remonstrated with him over his cursing, telling him not only of the vileness of the habit but also its wickedness. Cort sat looking the padre squarely in the eyes but not hearing a word of what was being said. Then, when the good father had finished, Cort exclaimed, 'Why, I killed a _____ _____ bigger one then that in Square Pond!' Cort apparently thought that the priest had been telling a deer story."

In the files of the Tupper Lake *Free Press* for Jan. 2-9, 1914 there's another story about Cort that's well worth repeating: "In response to a newspaper ad placed by C. M. Daniels, who wanted live otters to stock his fur farm at Sabattis, Cort got busy and caught one only to find that he had tangled with a buzz saw. He managed to cram the formidable animal into his packbasket — and then put his coat over it and sat on it while the angry otter clawed frantically at the obstruction. He finally was able to put sticks and bits of board across the mouth of the basket and bound them on with his trapchains. The otter earned him $100.00 delivered but Moody's coat, pants and packbasket were just about ruined."

Cort died in Saranac Lake in 1902 leaving five sons, several of whom became well-known guides and woodsrunners....

254

Mart and Minerva Moody — Courtesy of Alberta Moody and Carol Dening

Forest and Stream, the most popular sporting periodical of the last century, carried an interesting though unsigned account in its Aug. 24, 1880 issue about Mart Moody's Mt. Morris House on Big Tupper.

"At length we turned into Tupper's Lake and pulled across to Moody's. It was getting quite dark as we reached the landing and secured the boats. After a long trip it's always pleasant to reach a house again and see new faces. Balsam boughs are all very well but a good bed seems doubly soft after a few weeks on them. Indeed many parties, instead of camping out, plan their trips so as to spend every night in one of the well-spaced half-way houses.

"The room we entered was a cheerful one. There was a brisk fire in the stove because even August nights in the mountains can be very cold. Eight or nine men were in the room — some sitting near the fire, some leaning against the wall. One fairly tall, wiry man stood behind a bench pouring liquors. He was Mart Moody. There were piles of duffle on the floor; guns, fishing tackle and clothing hung on the walls.

"Supper was soon ready so we all filed into the dining room. All were hungry so the attack began without ceremony. Plate after plate of steaming venison was emptied, the trout vanished and the corncake melted away. Then came griddlecakes and maple syrup. A dark girl with sharp features and straight black hair brought them.

'Look,' whispered the Professor, 'a red Indian girl! There can be no doubt about it. That's the Huron nose though the brow is more of the Mohawk tribe!'

'That,' broke in Hank, 'why that's old Moody's daughter [since the Moodys were childless, she was probably either a relative or a neighbor's girl].

"She hopped around with the speed of several Indians and now stood beside Sig.

"'Tea or coffee?' she asked with the rapidity of a book agent.

"'Well, if that last was coffee I'll take tea...

255

"After supper host Moody entertained in the Bar-room. The other party there numbered eight: four sportsmen — a clergyman, a lawyer, a merchant and a fat one who was nothing in particular but very fat indeed and jolly — and their guides.

"'I say, Moody,' said the lardy one in a high squeaky voice, "I say — how long did it take you to build this place?'

"Whereupon Moody related how he had cut the logs and shaved them down with a draw-knife and how he had made all the shingles. He said that it wasn't done yet and our party found on going to bed that this was quite true because the walls had been lathed but not plastered and the rooms consequently looked into each other.

"When Moody had finished his narrative the lawyer pronounced the structure a 'successful case;' the clergyman declared that it was a 'noble work and founded on a rock' — which was literally true. The Professor went into a lengthy eulogy on the patience, skill and fidelity of the hardy backwoodsmen...

"That night our party slept soundly and the Professor dreamt of Indian girls. The next a.m. our party decided to stay over another day. At noon the alert Prof. discovered that boats were heading across the Lake. The field glasses were manned and bright-colored dresses and fluttering veils were reported. All hands were immediately on the qui vive. The boats landed and three maidens in bloomers stepped lively out. Guides came up bringing shawls, umbrellas, wraps etc. and the solemn gentleman bringing up the rear was quite overlooked...Dinner was delightful.

"The young ladies soon proved that they were not the type of 'fashionable' who affect a poor appetite at table but gobble in private. A rivalry started as to which one could eat the most trout. Miss Frances and Miss Frederika Smith were both outdone by Miss Josephine, who pronounced the meal delightful and declared that she had never enjoyed a dinner at Saratoga as much.

"The Professor was charmed and when he wrote home that P.M. he stated that they had met a pleasant party at Moody's — Mr. Smith and Frank, Fred and Joe.

"Later that afternoon our party arranged a shooting match for the entertainment of the ladies. Hank bore away the honors and was lionized by Miss Frank but her Endymion behaved toward this Diana much like the original. In fact he declared emphatically that he 'never could go for one of those frizzled city gals!'

"Sig then showed Miss Fred the power of his rifle. 'Do you see that dead pine across the lake?' he asked. 'I think I could send a bullet even that far.'

"'Oh la, how nice! Why I should think that it would strain your rifle to shoot so far!'

"'Oh shade of Nimrod! But what do such women know about guns?' So he went over to talk with Miss Joe.

"'Oh, Mr. P.,' she exuded. 'I'm so sorry you didn't win your match but I'll tell you a secret. The first time I saw you I thought you were a guide! You're just the image of a dear guide we had on the St. Regis from Paul Smith's you know — been to Paul Smith's? Lovely place! It reminds me of a hotel on Lake Luzerne. And the scenery is so like Switzerland, don't you think? Pa is beckoning but don't go away! I'll be back directly. Ta ta!'

"Sig did not wait for her return but called Wren and they went off in search of something. In an hour they were back. Sig drew the Prof. into their room and closed the door.

"'A mud turtle! What in - - -?'

"'Hush,' whispered S. as he produced a can of pitch and four walnut shells. The gooey stuff was applied to the turtle's feet, which were then stuck fast into the shells. Moody's boy, an apprentice, was an accomplice and he lit the light in the room occupied by the Misses Smith; he placed the sluggish creature under the bed and on its back.

256

"Shortly afterward the unsuspecting females retired for the night and all in the same room.

"After an interval which seemed several hours to the party listening expectantly across the hall, the light was put out. While the light was on the turtle stayed perfectly still but after the room had been dark about 15 minutes, it managed to right itself and began to crawl. Since the floor was bare the walnut shells struck it with blows that could be heard plainly. Whack! Whack! Whack! followed by a series of hair-raising screams. Louder whacks and louder screams — then three wraiths in white calling for Papa bolted into the entry hall. Papa, also in white, appeared in jigtime brandishing a pistol. Moody and his frau rushed out with a light. 'What's the matter?' he called out.

"'Horrors! A panther — or a bear — or something — is under our bed! O-o-oh!'

"Moody hurried off for his rifle and all of us now appeared, armed to the teeth. The room was quickly surrounded. The strange noises continued. A light was focused on the spot from where the sounds proceeded and the brute was brought forth. Moody emerged holding the miscreant by one foot while a comical expression played across his face. . .

"The ladies were late for breakfast the next morning and our group got off to an early start.

"Oh, Moody! Wherever they go they will remember you and your good cheer. Often, amid the dust and turmoil of the city, they will see, at times, before them that quiet cabin

Shooting Match at Moody's — Stoddard Photo

257

on Tupper's Lake. And when its timbers are decayed and its owner long since passed away, tradition will perpetuate the fame of both."

Before closing out his career Mart, besides being postmaster, also served Tupper Lake well as justice of the peace, assessor, highway commissioner and pathmaster. Following a paralytic stroke complicated by grippe, he died on May 26, 1910, the last of Jacob's sons to pass away.

The same Kilburn previously mentioned made some well-considered comparisons between the colorful past and the more prosaic present. Besides eulogizing men such as the Moodys who helped make the era memorable, he also commented favorably and accurately on the changing nature of the Adirondack scene.

In F.D.K.'s words: "Guides had more to do in those days than now. A fine, quaint lot of fellows, they were usually splendid physical specimens, intelligent and witty, thorough woodsmen, good cooks and tireless workers. Although they have changed least of all, the charm of their calling is gone. In those days everyone going into the woods needed a guide. Few sports stopped longer at hotels than necessary to fit out for camp. Men came in woolen shirts, belted pants, strong shoes and slouch hats; women in natty bloomers and all or nearly all for recreation. Summer cottages were unknown. The tent or bark leanto was good enough, and filled every want. Nowadays, hunting and fishing are not so good. Stray bullets from guns that shoot at every living thing make the former sport more dangerous for men than deer, and the sharky pickerel has all but spoiled the latter. The changes which sportsmen most deplore I believe are all for the best. Thousands are now enjoying the benefits of the pure air of this great pleasure-ground where formerly only hundreds enjoyed its charm. Good people are paving the way to this health-giving country for those whose circumstances would otherwise force them to die for want of a breath of pure air." [Obviously a tribute to Dr. Trudeau and the health industry he developed.]

Undoubtedly, there were other guides who were every bit as colorful and capable as the Moodys, Phelps, Dunning, Sabattis, Cheney and "Honest John" Plumley but, fortunately for us, as well as for those cited, even though they emerge from the printed pages considerably larger than life, they nevertheless add much lustre and excitement to Adirondack annals.

Even though their perpetuators — writers like Street, Warner, Lanman, Mather, Chittenden, Hoffman, Murray and photographer Stoddard — deserve their full share of credit, they nonetheless needed unusual material in order to turn out exceptional books. A happy combination and a great literary legacy.

Chapter 23

The All-Day Piddley Bird

Fred Mather in *Forest and Stream,* Aug. 11, 1882

"What bird is that which just now sang that singular combination of six syllables and drew them down in a wearied cadence?" I asked.

The guide rested on his oars, listened until I nodded when the song began again and then said. "That's a little wood sparrow, something like a field sparrow. We now call it the all-day piddley bird. Some say it's changed its song within the last 10 years."

"Now that's a queer name for a bird. What does it mean?"

"Well, the story goes that the bird used to have a lively note instead of dragging it out as he does now. But since so many tourists and no-account idle fellows have taken to loafing in the woods all day doing nothing — in fact just piddling with wildflowers or pretending to fish — that the bird has taken to scoffing at and scolding them. Just listen to him and hear him say: 'All-day piddley, piddley, piddley' with rising inflection on the second syllable and then falling in jerks." And he was right.

My guide was a very observant, intelligent man and like all of his class had strong opinions of the people he met and took care of, for the woods is the ideal place to study character or lack of it. There all the conventional trammels are laid aside and the true nature of the person stands revealed. He obviously looked upon the dawdlers with little respect or admiration although he was too tactful to say so.

However, his comments gave me plenty to think about and here are some of my reflections:

Here are plenty of young men who have every advantage, plenty of time and money with which to do something useful for themselves and mankind, but they are apparently contented to have a guide row them aimlessly around the lakes without any objective in mind — or if they have one they do nothing when they get there. They are merely "killing time" and the fleeting time of youth at that. Alas, this is the poorest and least profitable of all occupations. A little boating, a little lying under the trees, a dinner, a little feeble gossip or flirtation and the day is done. A few weeks of such days and the season's over, so the young man has "done the Adirondacks." Yes, but he knows nothing about them beyond the names of lakes, hotels, guides and carries. He knows nothing about the geology, botany, zoology, the character of the timber or the depths of the lakes. He goes to the Adirondacks because it is the fashion and he's bored with it all.

I contrasted his visit with my few weeks leave of absence to gather fish specimens.

Lunch at Half-Way House

Modern Invasion of the Woods

From N.Y. State Forest,
Fish and Game Reports for 1902-03

An Up to Date Portage

Every day I learned something and every day was delightful... One young fellow of whom the bird sang told me one day that he had "exhausted" the Adirondacks. He killed three deer last season and no end of trout this year, but actually had cared very little for it. "Really, you know, there's nothing to be seen in the woods!"

Then I thought of Sir Charles Coldstream and mentally said, "Used up; you've found that the world has nothing new for you at twenty-five. And as we went our separate ways the little bird sang "All-day-piddley-piddley-piddley."

Having lectured him in my mind I looked around to see if there was any chance of its doing him any good, but a field glass showed him flat on his back with a novel and the wise bird singing its sorrowful dirge above him. I hope he will read this because it might help him become a useful man instead of the butt of ridicule for guides and birds.

Chapter 24

An Indian Legend

Stewart Edward White in
Forest Leaves. Sanatorium Gabriels — Spring, 1905

The Indians say that when Kitch 'Manitou had created men he was dissatisfied and so brought women into being. At once love-making began and then, as now, the couples sought solitude for their exchanges of vows, their sighings to the moon and their claspings of hands. Marriages ensued. The situation remained unchanged. Life was one long, perpetual honeymoon. I suppose the novelty was fresh and the sexes had not yet realized they would not part as abruptly as they had been brought together.

The villages became deserted while the woods and bushes were populous with wedded and unwedded lovers. Kitch 'Manitou looked down on the proceedings with disapproval. All this was most romantic, intimate and beautiful no doubt but, in the meantime, mi-daw-min, the corn; mi-no-men, the rice; grew rank and uncultivated while bis-iw, the lynx; swingwaage, the wolverine and me-en-gam, the wolf committed unchecked depredations among the weaker forest creatures.

The business of life was being sadly neglected so Kitch 'Manitou took counsel with himself and created saw-gi-may, the mosquito to whom he gave as dwelling the woods and bushes. That took all the romance out of the situation. As my narrator grimly expressed it "Him go back, go to work!"

Chapter 25

Incidental Intelligence

And then there's the story of the stranger up in the Adirondack wilds a century and a half ago who remarked to his guide: "All the Indians around here are Algonquin and Iroquois I understand."

"All but a few," replied the guide. "There is, however, the Hellarwe tribe."

"Hellarwe?" puzzled the other man, "Never heard of them."

"It's a nomadic tribe," the guide explained. "On the move constantly. Never stop more than a day or two at any one spot. And each time they get ready to move on, the chief climbs the highest hill around, or maybe the tallest tree, and he shades his eyes and peers out over the country-side in every direction. Then he calls down to the rest of the tribe: 'Anybody down there know where the Hellarwe?'"

262

Chapter 26

A Long-Overdue Tribute To My Parents

Since my father, George Joseph DeSormo, died in 1912, when I was only five years old, my recollections of him are understandably sketchy. From conversations with several of his brothers I learned that their parents had migrated from Hull, Ontario in the late 1890's and settled in Watertown. Apparently my grandfather, whom I saw only twice, was a carpenter by trade; my grandmother, a robust, grey-haired, strong-willed person, was born in France but had been adopted when quite young by an English family named Thomas who later moved to Canada.

Incidentally, the original spelling of my surname was des Ormeaux. The first of the family to bring that name to the New World was the 22 year-old Adam Daulac or Dollard, Sieur des Ormeaux, a minor nobleman who had held a military command in France. Traditionally, he had been involved in some affair which made him eager to atone for by some noteworthy exploit.

This he accomplished by leading a band of 16 young Montrealers, later joined by 40 Huron warriors and four Christian Algonquins, up the swollen (late April) St. Lawrence and ascending the formidable Ottawa River to the treacherous Long Sault Rapids at Carillon.

There, in a crude palisaded fort they prepared to waylay a band of 200 Iroquois who had been on an extended raid into Huron country. Then, after a series of futile assaults, the attackers sent for 500 of their brethren who had rendezvoused at the mouth of the Richelieu. The combined forces kept up the round-the-clock siege for eight days before the utterly exhausted defenders were overrun and annihilated.

However, their mission was accomplished because the Iroquois, having been soundly mauled by only 21 defenders behind a picket fence, logically decided that they had little chance against the well-manned stone parapets of Montreal, Three Rivers and Quebec. It meant salvation for the colonies, according to Francis Parkman, who devoted 10 glowing pages of his epic work — "The Old Regime in Canada" — to this Canadian Thermopylae.

Three statues — at Carillon, in Montreal's Lafontaine Park and its Old City — commemorate the heroic episode and stir the pulses of the many des Ormeaux in Canada and elsewhere who are aware of their heritage.

Although I have not personally researched the genealogical background, Dr. Watson Harwood did so and reported that there was a connection — not direct because Dollard died garçon, a bachelor, but other members of the same family reputedly came over from France at a later date and settled near Hull . . .

George J. DeSormo (1880-1912)   *Ida Kennedy DeSormo (1879-1959)*

My parents met in Ogdensburg, where they worked at the State Hospital — she as a nurse and he as attendant. They married and moved to Canton, where my father was employed as a carpenter and cabinetmaker. About 1908 he decided to go into business for himself so he took over a general store in Hermon. My mother managed the business so that he could handle the other details such as buying and slaughtering beef and delivering meat and staples to the scattered mining hamlets in St. Lawrence County.

Among my recollections is sitting beside him on the seat of a horsedrawn van as it bounced over the stony backwoods roads. Not much conversation, I recall, but what there was was very pleasant to an impressionable youngster. Moreover, I remember that his customers were always delighted to see him and that he was apparently a good listener as well as talker.

Another vivid memory was generated by the arrival of a band of gypsies who encamped just outside the village in a riverside meadow. Somehow I heard about them and wandered out to investigate. The gaudily-dressed men and women fascinated me so I made my way closer to the brightly painted wagons. The women made a big fuss over me so I was thoroughly enjoying myself when my father suddenly showed up and with fire in his eyes, grabbed me by the ear and marched me back home.

Still other capers come to mind: learning honesty by having to return and apologize for a stolen orange lifted from a grocer's outdoor display counter; being given verbal and physical comeuppance for cadging coins from the customers in Mix's bar, just down the street from our store; wriggling out of the rope-tether attached to the porch railing and streaking gleefully au naturel down Main Street; and testing out a new pair of rubber boots by sitting smack dab in the deepest part of a large mudhole.

While these juvenile feats were altogether pleasant for hyperkinetic me, they nevertheless caused endless worry and concern for both my busy parents — especially my quick-tempered, hard-working father who didn't exactly appreciate such distractions and excursions.

There were other such memorable escapades and resounding applications of the razor strop but I certainly deserved such periodic and predictable retributions.

Dad was well on his way to becoming prosperous when, while butchering a cow he became infected by tubercle bacillus. After an unsuccessful effort to recover at Wanakena he went to cure at St. Mary's-of-the-Woods (since torn down) on Ampersand Avenue in Saranac Lake, where I saw him for the last time in early January, 1912.

Although I never had the opportunity to really know him, I still can recall many incidents which convince me that he was quite a man.

My Mother (1889-1959)

Ida Kennedy DeSormo, my mother, came from a line of strong-minded and strong-backed Scotch-Irish farmers who had settled near Roxham, Quebec, just across the Border from Champlain, N.Y. Her parents moved to Burke, N.Y. sometime in the 1870's, where they lived in a small home on a hill overlooking the Little Trout River, not far from McKenzie's gristmill.

She got her nursing training in Ogdensburg, where she met and married my father. Of the six children one — a boy — died in infancy; a girl died at the age of 8.

Like most of the people with her background my mother had great physical, mental and moral strength — as did her own mother, who was more inclined to be emotional and who was a loving but relatively stern individual, who lived with us all through my boyhood.

I can still dredge up remembered details of that sad train-ride from De Kalb Junction to Malone, where we changed cars and went to Saranac Lake to see my tubercular father. Although we kids were too young to realize what was going on, we could sense that it was a very trying ordeal for my mother.

After Father's death the family moved to Fort Covington Street, Malone, where we lived for several years with my grandmother before Mother bought a house closeby.

At that time Mother was village and Metropolitan Life Insurance Company nurse and started a long career of dedicated service that continued until she was 70. During many of those years she made her rounds on foot but later on she bought her own car in order to save time. Although other public employees were supplied with transportation and a gas allowance, the village fathers never saw fit to provide either for her. Typically though she never complained to the designated authorities and after one refused request stoically went her own way. Quite characteristic.

She certainly was a financial genius because she got incredible mileage out of her $100.00 monthly salary.

However, when compulsory retirement time arrived and the village dignitaries belatedly announced that they were going to give her a well-earned testimonial banquet, she calmly replied that she wanted no part of it — which shook the brass considerably, no doubt.

As far as she was concerned her true testimonial was the deep affection displayed by the many families whose children she had helped Doc Finney bring into the world and whose needs she met to the utmost of her ability.

Even today I occasionally see women's faces light up when they hear my name. "Are you Ida DeSormo's son? You know she was the finest woman I have ever known. Why, if it hadn't been for her — — !"

In retrospect I can confidently say that I was indeed fortunate in my choice of parents.

"We never sleep."